WAR AND TAXES

Also of interest from the Urban Institute Press:

Taxing Capital Income,
    edited by Henry J. Aaron, Leonard E. Burman,
    and C. Eugene Steuerle

Contemporary U.S. Tax Policy, second edition,
    by C. Eugene Steuerle

Local Tax Policy, second edition,
    by David Brunori

Tax Justice: The Ongoing Debate,
    edited by Joseph J. Thorndike and
    Dennis J. Ventry Jr.

WAR AND TAXES

Steven A. Bank   Kirk J. Stark   Joseph J. Thorndike

THE URBAN INSTITUTE PRESS
Washington, D.C.

THE URBAN INSTITUTE PRESS
2100 M Street, N.W.
Washington, D.C. 20037

Library of Congress Cataloging-in-Publication Data

Bank, Steven A., 1969-
 War and taxes / Steven A. Bank, Kirk J. Stark, Joseph J. Thorndike.
   p. cm.
 Includes bibliographical references and index.
 ISBN 978-0-87766-740-7
 1. Taxation—United States—History. 2. Fiscal policy—United
States—History. 3. War—Economic aspects—United States—History. I.
Stark, Kirk J. II. Thorndike, Joseph J. III. Title.
 HJ2381.B35 2008
 336.200973—dc22

                          2008016827

Printed in the United States of America

11 10 09 08   1 2 3 4 5

THE URBAN INSTITUTE is a nonprofit, nonpartisan policy research and educational organization established in Washington, D.C., in 1968. Its staff investigates the social, economic, and governance problems confronting the nation and evaluates the public and private means to alleviate them. The Institute disseminates its research findings through publications, its web site, the media, seminars, and forums.

Through work that ranges from broad conceptual studies to administrative and technical assistance, Institute researchers contribute to the stock of knowledge available to guide decisionmaking in the public interest.

Conclusions or opinions expressed in Institute publications are those of the authors and do not necessarily reflect the views of officers or trustees of the Institute, advisory groups, or any organizations that provide financial support to the Institute.

Contents

Acknowledgments

We are indebted to the many friends, colleagues, and institutions who helped us write this book. Joel Slemrod, Dennis Ventry, and Ajay Mehrotra deserve special thanks: each provided thoughtful advice and cogent criticism at crucial junctures in the development of this project. Elliot Brownlee, Robin Einhorn, and Mark Leff also offered insight and encouragement. We are grateful for the comments received during faculty workshops at the University of California, Los Angeles; McGill University; and Ohio State University. Still more help came from critics and audience members at the 2006 Critical Tax Theory Conference, the 2006 Policy History Conference, and the 2005 Annual Meeting of the National Tax Association. Two anonymous referees made our lives a bit harder and our book much better—special thanks for their careful reading of the manuscript. Thanks also to the editors and staff of the Urban Institute Press, who patiently guided the publication process from beginning to end. Several people at Tax Analysts, especially Chris Bergin and David Brunori, provided vital advice, encouragement, and support. The UCLA Academic Senate's Council on Research and the UCLA School of Law provided research funding.

Introduction

In the early summer of 1967, veteran Washington journalist Peter Lisagor met with a senior Republican senator to discuss the deteriorating situation in Vietnam. The war had divided the country, triggering massive antiwar demonstrations in several major cities, and the senator agreed to talk only on condition of anonymity. But the topic of discussion was not troop levels or moral arguments over the U.S. presence in Indochina. Rather, the senator wanted to talk about something more mundane: taxes. As Lisagor later explained in a *Los Angeles Times* article, "Absence of Sacrifice at Home Spurs Guilt Feeling over War," the GOP senator considered taxes a question of conscience. "I went to the beach with my son and his children a few weeks ago," the senator explained, "and there we were, enjoying ourselves as if we didn't have a care in the world. We had no sense of a war, no sense of sacrifice. Yet this war is already bigger than Korea. I'll go for a tax increase now."[1]

A generation later, the senator's question of conscience has resurfaced in public debate. On March 19, 2003, the Bush administration launched Operation Iraqi Freedom, a military campaign to overthrow dictator Saddam Hussein. Administration officials defended the action as part of a broader "war on terror," including Operation Enduring Freedom in Afghanistan, which began shortly after the al Qaeda attacks of September 11, 2001. From that point forward, the United States has been actively waging a costly overseas military operation. Within six years, the Department of Defense had confirmed a total of 4,018 U.S. fatalities in Iraq and Afghanistan. And according to estimates from the Congressional Budget Office, by 2007, the budgetary cost of operations in the two countries exceeded $500 billion.[2]

Yet despite the country's great loss of blood and treasure, there is little sense of sacrifice on the homefront. Indeed, in its first six years, the Bush administration has requested, and Congress has approved, a series of major tax cuts.[3] Lawmakers have lowered and flattened rates for the individual income tax, initiated a repeal of the estate tax, eased the burden on capital gains and corporate dividends, reduced the so-called marriage penalty, and enacted a slew of new deductions, credits, and other special-interest provisions.[4] When combined with a steady increase in military, domestic, and entitlement spending, these cuts have turned a projected $5.6 trillion surplus over the 10-year budget window into a $2.7 trillion deficit.[5]

This contrast—between an active war effort on one hand and substantial tax cuts on the other—has no precedent in American history. Beginning with the War of 1812, special taxes have supported every major military conflict in our nation's history. Moreover, many levies have outlasted the wars they financed. Politicians like to talk about their plans for revamping the country's tax system, but important tax reform usually happens when it must, not when it should. War has been the most important catalyst for long-term, structural change in the nation's fiscal system. Indeed, the history of America's tax system can be written largely as a history of America's wars.

Enactment of the Bush tax cuts has called into question the once-axiomatic relationship between war and taxes. The historical incongruity of Congress reducing taxes while increasing spending on the war in Iraq has provided fodder to administration critics who, like the anonymous Senator calling for increased taxes to pay for the war in Vietnam, have wondered publicly if the country has betrayed its tradition of wartime fiscal sacrifice. As one pundit declared in a typical statement, "in his determination to cut taxes even while waging war in Iraq, President Bush is bucking history."[6] Yet another bemoaned, "since 9/11, our government has asked no sacrifice of civilians other than longer waits at airplane security. We've even been rewarded with a prize that past generations would have found as jaw-dropping as space travel: a wartime dividend in the form of tax cuts."[7]

Underlying these comments is an inescapable fact: the United States has a strong tradition of wartime fiscal sacrifice, and the Bush tax cuts mark an abrupt departure from that tradition. As we hope to illustrate, however, America's history of wartime taxation is not quite the heroic tale that many Bush critics seem to imply. Although taxes have typically gone up during times of war, the claim that "we have always accepted heavier burdens as the price those at home pay to support those under fire on the front" misses much of the complexity of American history.[8] Indeed, as a nation, our commitment to wartime fiscal sacrifice has always been uneasy—and more than a little ambiguous. In some wars, political leaders have asked Americans to accept new taxes as the price of freedom and security. But in others, they have tried to delay, deny, and obscure the trade-off between guns and butter. And even when Americans have embraced the call for sacrifice, their elected representatives have often made room for self-indulgence, easing burdens for some constituents while raising them for others.

Exaggerating the American tradition of wartime fiscal sacrifice is understandable but unfortunate. History is most usable, at least for politicians, when it can be recast as a morality play. But it is most valuable, at least for the rest of us, when it honestly probes the inconvenient truths of human nature and political struggle. In our search for the historical context of current debates, we should be careful not to compare today's policies to some cardboard cutout version of an imagined past.

* * *

This book explores the long history of American taxation during times of war. As political scientist David Mayhew recently observed, since its founding in 1789, the United States "has conducted hot wars for some 38 years, occupied the South militarily for a decade, waged the Cold War for several decades, and staged countless smaller actions against Indian tribes or foreign powers."[9] The cost of these activities has been immense, with important and lasting consequences for the tax system, the economy, and the nation's political structure. By focusing on tax legislation, we hope to identify some of these consequences. But we are not interested in simply recounting statutory details. Rather, we hope to illuminate the politics of war taxation, with a special focus on the influence of arguments concerning "shared sacrifice" in shaping wartime tax policy. Moreover, we aim to shed light on a less examined aspect of this history by offering a detailed account of wartime *opposition* to increased taxes.

Historically, two features of wartime politics have prompted tax reform. The first is sheer necessity. There is simply no other government activity that requires as much revenue as fighting a war. Success on the battlefield requires economic resources, and taxation is the best means of marshalling those resources. While explicit taxes are not the only means of extracting resources from a nation and its people, practical limits on nontax forms of war financing (e.g., borrowing, seigniorage, conscription, expropriation) generally push tax changes onto the legislative agenda. Second, wars often create a new political atmosphere—one characterized by feelings of solidarity and shared sacrifice. Wars may foster a feeling of "civic engagement" or a "public mood" as citizens "rally 'round the flag." Whatever term is used, war creates new political opportunities when it comes to tax policy. Taxes are never popular, but they are never more popular than during wars.[10] In combination, these two features of wartime politics—fiscal necessity and political opportunity—set the stage for sweeping and durable tax reform.

The most compelling example of wartime fiscal sacrifice comes from World War II. In the months following the Japanese attack on Pearl Harbor, fiscal necessity and political opportunity converged to produce dramatic changes in the nation's tax system.[11] Though authorized by the Sixteenth Amendment in 1913 and established by statute shortly thereafter, the income tax has its modern roots in the Revenue Act of 1942. That legislation, enacted less than a year after the official U.S. entry into the war, subjected millions of new taxpayers to the income tax, converting what had long been a "class tax" to a full-fledged "mass tax."[12] More than just raising revenue for the war, the Revenue Act of 1942 gave rise to a whole new taxpaying culture. The federal government launched an all-out campaign to market the new tax changes, including Disney-produced animated shorts featuring Donald Duck touting the importance of "taxes to beat the Axis!" The campaign was a success. Asked in February 1944 whether they considered the amount of income tax they paid to be "fair," a stunning *90 percent* of Americans answered yes.[13]

The experience of World War II, so important to the image Americans have of themselves and their place in the world, has no doubt also shaped our intuitions about the American tradition of wartime fiscal sacrifice. Yet in many ways, World War II is an outlier on the continuum of war tax politics. Taking a wider historical view, beginning with the nation's founding and continuing through the present day, we observe greater heterogeneity in the country's willingness to accept heavier burdens of taxation during times of war. While the World War II example has parallels in certain other conflicts—most notably World War I and the Korean War—the country's political instincts have often pushed in the opposite direction, prompting Americans and their elected leaders to resist the burdens of heavy wartime taxation.

Indeed, resistance and reluctance are recurring themes in the history of American wartime taxation. In the War of 1812, for example, congressional Republicans repeatedly balked at imposing new taxes to fund "Mr. Madison's War," with nearly disastrous consequences for the nation's fiscal health. Their reluctance stemmed from a widespread conviction that the war would be quick and relatively painless. It also reflected no small amount of fear that new taxes might be politically disastrous for anyone who supported them. Either way, at this early stage in U.S. history, the evidence hardly supports our cherished image of selfless Americans rushing to shoulder their wartime fiscal burdens.

In the Civil War, politicians again resisted the need for fiscal sacrifice—at least initially. Eager to minimize internal opposition to the war, leaders of both the Union and the Confederacy predicted a short—and relatively cheap—conflict. Eschewing heavy taxes, they relied on other, less onerous forms of war finance, including loans. But as evidence of tangible sacrifice grew—through the loss of life, liberty, and property—that strategy faltered. The demand for fiscal sacrifice grew ever stronger, with lawmakers seeking to finance the war with taxes that spread the burden equitably among the populace. Notably, this call for shared sacrifice accompanied the creation of a military draft, with political leaders linking the conscription of able-bodied men with the conscription of national wealth.

The war in Vietnam reveals a similar experience. As with the War of 1812 and the Civil War, political leaders initially hoped to avoid new war taxes. The immediate political calculus was, of course, different; Lyndon Johnson refused to ask Congress for higher taxes to fight the war because he feared doing so might endanger his cherished "Great Society" programs, especially among conservative Democrats who controlled the two congressional tax-writing committees. When he eventually did submit a surtax proposal, it was held up for almost a year because Johnson refused to agree to congressional demands for corresponding cuts in domestic spending. Again, the historical experience departs significantly from the popular notion of a country eager to put its fiscal muscle behind its military might.

By highlighting this alternative tradition of wartime finance—a tradition marked by reluctance and resistance, as well as willing sacrifice—we do not mean to minimize the burdens that previous generations agreed to bear. The United States does, indeed, have a tradition of wartime fiscal sacrifice. But this tradition has been more complex—and more hotly contested—than might seem convenient for modern critics of the war in Iraq. America's wartime leaders, and its presidents in particular, have often been reluctant to demand much fiscal sacrifice from their fellow citizens, at least initially. Unwilling to risk domestic achievements, or fearful of eroding support for an unpopular war, they have shrunk from the tough decisions that wars invariably demand. Eventually, however, they all accepted the hard realities. Whether ardent tribunes of fiscal sacrifice (like Franklin Roosevelt) or reluctant champions of fiscal responsibility (like Lyndon Johnson), they all accepted the need for some sort of homefront sacrifice, as both an economic and moral necessity.

* * *

This book seeks to convey the rich, and sometimes problematic, history of wartime taxation in the United States. Organized into six chapters, it describes tax policy during the nation's major wars in chronological order. A brief note about coverage will help clarify certain decisions and assumptions made in structuring the book. First, we have chosen to focus on some wars while excluding others. We have omitted, for instance, any extended treatment of the Mexican-American War and the Spanish-American War. While both meet the most obvious, formal definition of a war—having been declared by Congress—they were quickly eclipsed by larger conflicts with more enduring effects on the nation's revenue system. By contrast, we have included several of the nation's many undeclared conflicts, including those in Korea, Vietnam, and the Middle East. Undeclared wars have become the rule rather than the exception since the end of World War II, yet their effects on the nation and its tax system have been indisputable. While somewhat arbitrary, our choice of wars reflects an attempt to use major historical episodes to shed light on the nation's current situation in Iraq.

We have also made important assumptions about what constitutes a "tax." The definition may seem obvious, but it's not. Many wartime practices, especially conscription, might reasonably be treated as a form of taxation. What difference is there, one might ask, between forcing citizens to fight in war and requiring the payment of taxes to finance a voluntary army? Similar questions arise with regard to the commandeering of industry and other wartime regulations of the economy. While not taxes in the common sense of the term, these devices still represent a means by which governments marshal economic resources. But tempting as it may be to include in our discussion every coercive device for enlisting scarce resources, we want to keep our analysis within certain manageable limits. Our principal focus is on explicit taxes—or, more precisely, on wartime amendments to the nation's internal revenue laws.

Even with the more restricted focus, however, complications abound. Consider the question of whether the United States has ever "cut taxes" during a war. What if lawmakers cut taxes for some people while raising them for others? What if one *type* of tax goes up while another goes down? And what if taxes are increased during a time of war, but spending hikes outstrip the new flow of revenue, leading to higher budget deficits? These situations might be classed as tax cuts, after a fashion, but they might also be cast as tax increases. It depends on who is talking. We offer no single definition or methodological answer to the question of what constitutes a tax cut. Rather, we have focused on the complexities and historically rooted meanings of such "fiscal language."[14] We have, in other words, let our subjects define the terms. If political leaders in a particular era called something a tax cut, then so do we. If they called it a tax hike, then we follow suit. And if they *argued* about what to call it, then we examine the argument. Indeed, such arguments lie near the heart of our fiscal tradition, illuminating the meaning and contours of homefront sacrifice.

Finally, while all fiscal language is subject to interpretation, "sacrifice" is perhaps the most malleable and important term for wartime tax debates. Politicians have never agreed on what it means to sacrifice through the tax system. Consider modern debates over taxes to pay for the "war on terror." While numerous commentators have criticized President Bush for failing to demand any sort of fiscal sacrifice, others—including Bush himself—have insisted that Americans have already sacrificed by paying "a lot in taxes." Indeed, during one interview, the president responded to a question about "shared sacrifice" by noting that Americans "sacrifice peace of mind when they see the terrible images of violence on TV every night."[15] Although we use the term throughout the book, we have deliberately avoided assigning it any particular definition, choosing to let historical actors speak for themselves when invoking—or refusing to invoke—principles of shared sacrifice.

* * *

As we finish writing this book in early 2008, we cannot ignore its most obvious contemporary context: is the war in Iraq somehow different from all the wars—and taxes—that preceded it?

Despite the huge expense and the lingering nature of the conflict, Congress and the president have refused to ask the American public for fiscal sacrifice in the form of higher wartime taxes. Indeed, they have reduced the overall tax burden multiple times. We may simply still be in the early stages of the pattern exhibited in the Civil War and Vietnam, mired in the initial reluctance to call for public sacrifice. If so, then fiscal policies may change as we tally the war's other forms of sacrifice—lost lives, de facto conscription in the form of extended tours of duty among the regular military and the National Guard, higher gas prices, or even new terrorist attacks.

Or maybe we, as a nation, have decided to shift the fiscal sacrifice to future generations. In past wars, borrowing has been justified as a device to spread the fiscal burden forward in time. Perhaps Americans have embraced this unsung element of our wartime fiscal tradition, expecting our children and grandchildren to foot a larger share of price we pay for security. If so, however, we will have also *changed* this tradition, not only asking future generations for more fiscal sacrifice, but explicitly reducing the fiscal burden on ourselves.

NOTES

1. Peter Lisagor, "Absence of Sacrifice at Home Spurs Guilt Feeling over War," *Los Angeles Times,* July 9, 1967, J3.

2. On fatalities, see U.S. Department of Defense, Operation Iraqi Freedom (OIF) U.S. Casualty Status and Operation Enduring Freedom (OEF) U.S. Casualty Status (http://www.defenselink.mil/news/casualty.pdf). On war costs, see the statement of Robert A. Sunshine, assistant director of the Congressional Budget Office, before the House Committee on the Budget, 18 January 2007, 1.

3. See the Economic Growth and Tax Reconciliation Relief Act of 2001, the Jobs and Growth Tax Relief Reconciliation Act of 2003, the Working Families Tax Relief Act of 2004, the Tax Increase Prevention and Reconciliation Act of 2005, and the Small Business and Work Opportunity Tax Act of 2007, which was enacted as part of the U.S. Troop Readiness, Veterans' Care, Katrina Recovery, and Iraq Accountability Appropriations

Act of 2007. This does not include tax relief for disaster-affected areas, even though the tax reductions enacted benefited more than just those affected by the disasters. (See the Gulf Opportunity Zone and Katrina Emergency Tax Relief Act of 2005.)

4. For an overview and description of these most significant changes, see David L. Brumbaugh, "Major Issues in the 109th Congress" (Washington, DC: Congressional Research Service, 2005).

5. Alan J. Auerbach, William G. Gale, and Peter Orszag, "New Estimates of the Budget Outlook: Plus Ça Change, Plus C'est la Même Chose," *Tax Notes,* April 17, 2006, 349.

6. David E. Rosenbaum, "Tax Cuts and War Have Seldom Mixed," *New York Times,* March 9, 2003, N17.

7. Frank Rich, "Supporting Our Troops over a Cliff," *New York Times,* June 4, 2006.

8. Ronald Brownstein, "Bush Breaks with 140 Years of History in Plan for Wartime Tax Cut," *Los Angeles Times,* January 13, 2003.

9. David R. Mayhew, "Wars and American Politics," *Perspectives on Politics* (September 2005), 473.

10. On wartime sacrifice, see Mark H. Leff, "The Politics of Sacrifice on the American Home Front in World War II," *Journal of American History* (1991). On civic engagement, see Mayhew, "Wars and American Politics," 475 (citing Theda Skocpol and Robert Putnam). On the relative popularity of wartime taxes, see Naomi Feldman and Joel Slemrod, *War and Taxation: When Does Patriotism Overcome the Free-Rider Problem* (unpublished manuscript).

11. During World War II, federal spending on national defense averaged 76.4 percent of total outlays, absorbing 37.8 percent of gross domestic product in the final years of the war.

12. Carolyn C. Jones, "Class Tax to Mass Tax: The Role of Propaganda in the Expansion of the Income Tax during World War II," *Buffalo Law Review* 37 (1989): 685.

13. See American Enterprise Institute, "Public Opinion on Taxes," AEI Studies in Public Opinion.

14. Daniel Shaviro, *Taxes, Spending, and the U.S. Government's March toward Bankruptcy* (Cambridge: Cambridge University Press, 2006), 3–14 (discussing concept of "fiscal language").

15. The News Hour with Jim Lehrer, January 16, 2007 (http://www.pbs.org/newshour/bb/white_house/jan-june07/bush_01-16.html?mii=1).

1

The American Revolution and the War of 1812

"A nation cannot long exist without revenues. Destitute of this essential support, it must resign its independence and sink into the degraded condition of a province."

—*The Federalist Papers,* No. 12

Americans have a reputation for hating taxes, not least among themselves. We remember the War for Independence as a tax protest, replete with images of the Boston Tea Party and cries of "No taxation without representation." People in every country run for cover at the sight of a tax collector, but tax resistance in the American style has been driven by a powerful and persistent strain of antistatism. We hate paying taxes, just like everyone else. But we also hate the intrusions of big government, including—and especially—the power to tax.[1]

There is more than a little truth to this civic mythology, which makes it all the more striking that taxes have been so important to the nation's political development. The power to tax has long been the engine of American state building, shaping the evolution of the federal government from its origins to the present. War has been the catalyst for this process, paving the way for statist innovation in the midst of an antistatist political culture. In the crucial years of American state formation—stretching from the Revolution through the War of 1812—advocates of a robust federal state forged a powerful connection, both rhetorical and ideological, between national security and fiscal capacity. The success of this argument—made manifest in the Constitution and given its first trial by fire in the War of 1812—established the fiscal infrastructure for the next two hundred years of American political development.

Taxes and National Security in the New Nation

During the Revolution, the Continental Congress refused to consider any sort of national revenue system. As colonists, Americans had enjoyed a light tax burden, and neither the states nor the national government possessed a robust fiscal bureaucracy. Moreover, the revolution's roots in a tax protest—or more precisely, in a protest over the authority to levy a tax, not over the tax itself—led most political leaders to shun any suggestion of a centralized revenue authority.[2] As a result, leaders of the Continental Congress assumed from the start that the war would be financed by other, nontax means, including foreign and domestic loans, impressment of necessary matériel, and paper money—lots and lots of paper money.

The dependence on paper money, known as currency finance, was not unreasonable. Many colonies had used the technique to support government spending in times of war and peace. Indeed, as a method of war finance, it enjoyed broad support and acceptance, having been widely employed to help pay the colonies' expenses during the Seven Years' War. When badly employed, currency finance could, and did, lead to ruinous inflation; the New England colonies had a particularly poor experience with fiat money. But the theory of currency finance—and quite often its reality—required that new paper money be reabsorbed quickly through taxation. By withdrawing the new money from circulation promptly, government officials could ensure that inflation would remain under control.[3]

In 1775, Congress created a continental currency, thereby endowing itself with an independent means of war finance. And lawmakers employed this power with abandon. Over the course of the Revolution, lawmakers issued $226 million in paper money, roughly six times as much as the various colonies had issued during the Seven Years' War. Against this inflationary onslaught, the continental currency retained its value for about a year, but it soon began to depreciate badly. By 1781, it had collapsed completely, the states having refused to reabsorb the money through taxation (and Congress lacking authority under the Articles of Confederation to levy any sort of tax).[4]

Meanwhile, Congress turned to domestic and foreign loans to help pay for the war. Initially, domestic borrowing showed promise, but a failure to stay current with interest payments condemned the various loan certificates issued throughout the war to speedy depreciation. Still, Congress continued to issue loan instruments, including some offered to soldiers in lieu of pay. By 1783, Congress had run up some $27 million in debt, and by 1786, efforts to float further loans met with stony silence from investors.[5]

Efforts to secure foreign loans were more successful. Initially, Congress received more than $2 million from France and smaller amounts from Spain and private Dutch lenders. After 1781, when Philadelphia financier Robert Morris accepted the post of superintendent of finance and managed to restore a modicum of order to the government's financial arrangements, French and Dutch lenders provided another $8.8 million. But by 1785, Congress had defaulted on the interest payments to the French (it had never made any payments to the Spanish in the first place). Lawmakers continued to service the Dutch debt only by using new loans to pay the interest on old ones.[6]

Finally, Congress turned to matériel impressment and mass expropriation as a means of financing the Revolution. "The Continental Army took from the people what the people would not offer to sell," observed historian Max Edling. In return, the army offered a "supply certificate," a receipt of sorts that carried a low probability of subsequent compensation—a desperate measure, to be sure, but one in keeping with the fiscal impotence of the Continental Congress.[7]

The Crisis of Confederation

The Articles of Confederation had condemned Congress to this penurious existence. Adopted by Congress in 1777 and fully ratified by the states in 1781, this founding charter of the national government provided Congress with no independent source of revenue. Instead, the national government was expected to requisition money from the states, with each state contributing "in proportion to the value of all land" within its borders (including buildings and improvements). Lawmakers in each state could then raise the requested funds in any manner they preferred.

The delegation of tax collection to the states was reasonable. The fledgling national government lacked the administrative capacity to enact, assess, and collect its own taxes. Every state, by contrast, had a workable revenue structure, although northern states tended to have more modern, sophisticated systems than their southern counterparts.

The apportionment requirement, however, was manifestly implausible. As historian Robin Einhorn pointed out, no southern state had ever tried to assess real estate values, and many northern states had avoided this laborious task for decades. Even if the states had possessed the necessary administrative capacity, they could never have mustered any cross-state uniformity in valuations.

So why require property-based apportionment in the first place? According to Einhorn, the provision was designed to sidestep divisive arguments over slavery. By linking revenue quotas to real estate values—rather than population, the most obvious alternative—national leaders avoided a sectional confrontation over how to count slaves for apportionment purposes. Fearful of disrupting the delicate politics of cross-sectional confederation, lawmakers embraced a revenue system—however dysfunctional—that promised to avoid the controversy.[8]

The fiscal regime enshrined in the Articles condemned Congress to the role of a groveling supplicant. Through the Revolution, Congress issued requisitions, asking the states for more and more money, while receiving precious little. The urgency of such requests only increased after the end of hostilities in 1783, as foreign creditors stepped up their demand for repayment.[9]

The states were not entirely unwilling to collect taxes on behalf of the national government. Rather, as historian Roger H. Brown has shown, they were *unable* to extract much revenue from their own citizens, whether for Congress or themselves. In the years just after the Revolution, state lawmakers had heeded the advice of political and financial elites, imposing heavy taxes on their unwary populations in the name of sound finance. But long accustomed to a light tax burden, taxpayers balked at the new levies. And in a pattern that would repeat itself throughout the states, lawmakers retreated from fiscal austerity, reducing taxes in the face of popular unrest and occasional violence. As a result, the states' capacity to extract revenue was highly attenuated.[10]

The cash-strapped states were disinclined to share their meager revenue with Congress. Between 1781 and 1786, they provided 37 percent of the total amount requested. And whatever enthusiasm the states *could* muster was pretty much exhausted by 1787, when payments to the federal treasury dropped to almost nothing. Repeated exhortation by national leaders had a negligible effect on compliance. In the six months between October 1786 and March 1787, the federal Treasury received just $663.[11]

Lacking adequate funds, Congress was unable to maintain a reasonable military force. The nation's pathetically small, post-Revolution army dwindled to just 625 men, leaving the new nation dangerously vulnerable. Just as important, the tiny military establishment weakened the country's diplomatic hand. National security worries loomed large in these years, as other powers probed the new government for weakness. Great Britain, for instance, refused to abandon nine forts along the U.S.–Canadian border despite treaty commitments to hand them over after the Revolution. Spain closed the Mississippi River to U.S. merchant traffic, while also maintaining a series of forts in regions claimed by the United States. The Barbary pirates preyed on U.S. shipping, capturing vessels and holding crews hostage. And on the nation's western frontier, white settlers and Indians skirmished over territory.[12]

But in every case, the tiny American military hampered efforts to secure trade, security, and sovereign rights. Many in Congress were eager to increase the size of the army, but lacking funds from the states, they were forced to watch helplessly as other nations flouted American rights. Britain and Spain continued their territorial intransigence, the Barbary states continued their depredations on American commercial vessels, and settlers and Indians continued their bloody skirmishing on the western frontier.[13]

Congress twice sought authority from the states to levy a special 5 percent tax on imports, the funds to be earmarked exclusively for debt repayment. If it had passed, the impost would not have been apportioned but would have applied equally to imported goods in every state. This arrangement would have allowed Congress a reliable source of revenue while again sidestepping any apportionment debate that might raise the divisive issue of slavery.[14] But both times, the impost failed to win unanimous approval, a requirement under the unwieldy Articles. Major commercial states were particularly unwilling to accept a duty on imports, since they derived much of their own revenue from that source. By the latter half of the 1780s, the federal government's financial problems— and the military and diplomatic threats that flowed from them—had prompted interest among political and economic leaders for thorough political reform. While the nation's problems were not yet critical, they underscored the fundamental weakness of the nation's decentralized power structure, especially in financial matters. Left unchecked, these problems would threaten the success and security of the still-loosely united states.[15]

The Constitution

In 1786, nationalist political leaders—including George Washington, Robert Morris, James Madison, Benjamin Franklin, John Jay, Alexander Hamilton, and John Adams—stepped up agitation for political reform. In September, Madison organized a commercial conference in Annapolis, Maryland, to discuss trade issues, with each state invited to send delegates. While no specific recommendations emerged from the sparsely attended conference (only five states sent representatives), the Annapolis Convention did produce a call for another gathering, this time in Philadelphia. While declining to specify exactly what the representatives at this new convention should do, the Annapolis delegates suggested that they might "devise such further provisions as shall appear to them necessary to render the constitution of the Federal Government adequate to the exigencies of the Union."[16]

When they gathered in the summer of 1787, delegates to the Philadelphia convention quickly agreed on the need to remake the national government, rather than simply reform or enhance it. In particular, they moved to endow the new federal government with a broad and flexible power to tax, convinced that taxing authority was essential to a functioning national state. The proposed Constitution granted Congress exclusive authority to impose tariffs and coin money. Perhaps even more important, at least in terms of the nation's long-term political development, the charter gave Congress the right to impose excise taxes and other internal levies. In the spirited ratification debate that ensued, advocates of the Constitution stressed the need for such robust fiscal powers. "A nation cannot long exist without revenues," declared Alexander Hamilton in one of the most famous passages from the *Federalist Papers*. "Destitute of this essential support, it must resign its independence, and sink into the degraded condition of a province." While insisting that the federal government should be empowered to impose internal taxes, both direct and indirect, Hamilton and his allies (the Federalists) assured their wary readers that tariff duties would be the mainstay of federal finance. Internal levies were best suited to emergencies, they explained, especially war finance.

The Federalists underscored the connection between national security and a robust power to tax. If the federal government were to be charged with guarding the nation's security, then it must be granted a broad authority to collect revenue. "As the duties of superintending the national defense and of securing the public peace against foreign or domestic violence involve a provision for casualties and dangers to which no possible limits can be assigned," observed Hamilton in *The Federalist No. 31,* "the power of making that provision ought to know no other bounds than the exigencies of the nation and the resources of the community." Revenue was the "essential engine" for any government charged with security. Consequently, "the power of procuring that article in its full extent must necessarily be comprehended in that of providing for those exigencies."[17]

Faced with suggestions that the federal government be confined exclusively to tariff duties, the Federalists again invoked the specter of dysfunctional war finance. Lacking the power to levy internal taxes, the central government would necessarily divert tariff revenue to national defense. But since that tariff revenue was usually earmarked for servicing the public debt, the diversion would imperil the nation's credit at the worst possible moment. "It is not easy to see how a step of this kind could be avoided," Hamilton declared in *The Federalist No. 30,* "and if it should be taken, it is evident that it would prove the destruction of public credit at the very moment that it was becoming essential to the public safety."[18]

The Federalists won the day, on taxes, national security, and various other grounds. When leaders of the new federal government gathered in New York in 1789, they assumed control of a broad and powerful taxing authority. In one of his first acts as president, George Washington signed into law the Tariff of 1789, imposing a range of duties on imported goods that yielded more than $1 million annually. Notably, these duties were not the sort of flat-rate impost proposed (and rejected) under the Articles. Members of Congress simply couldn't resist the opportunity to dole out favors through the revenue system. By setting high rates for some items and low rates for others, lawmakers took their first tentative steps down the road of economic planning. Revenue debates would never be the same again.[19]

In 1790, lawmakers agreed to raise tariff duties further as part of the financial plan put forth by Alexander Hamilton, now serving as Treasury secretary. The next year, again at Hamilton's behest, they raised tariffs on manufactured goods higher still, while reducing duties on raw materials that might be useful to a rapidly industrializing nation. Even after these several increases, however, the tariff duties remained generally low, yielding ample revenue without unduly restricting trade. Between 1789 and 1815, tariffs provided roughly 90 percent of total revenue.[20]

Hamilton's tax program also included a less popular element: excise taxes. In 1791, Congress levied a tax on distilled spirits, prompting an outcry that soon shaded into rebellion. Burdened by the heavy cost of overland transportation, farmers on the frontier (then located around western Pennsylvania) had taken to making whiskey, converting their bulky grain into a product with a better weight-to-value ratio. The new federal tax upset this calculation, and many farmers resolved not to pay it. By 1794, opposition had grown brazen and vociferous, with angry whiskey farmers and their neighbors challenging the legitimacy of federal authorities. President Washington called up state militiamen to quash the insurrection, firmly establishing the reach of federal power.[21]

The Whiskey Rebellion underscored the vital but complex relationship between taxation and national security. During the Constitutional debate, Federalist champions of the charter had insisted that the power to levy internal taxes was vital to national defense. Now, when that same taxing power prompted a domestic rebellion, the Federalists used the nation's security apparatus (in this case, the president's authority to compel state forces under the Militia Act of 1792) to assert and enforce the legitimacy of its fiscal authority.

Having established the federal government's fiscal powers, the Federalists chose to avoid most internal levies for the rest of the 1790s. To be sure, they imposed a few on selected items of personal consumption, including carriages, snuff, and sugar. They also taxed auction sales, certain legal transactions, and bonds. And perhaps most striking, they levied a direct property tax in 1798 to help fund a naval buildup. As the Constitution required, lawmakers apportioned this direct tax among the states on the basis of population, with each state assigned a revenue target. The tax applied to many forms of real and personal property, including houses, land, and slaves, and it even included a progressive feature: states were required to tax expensive houses at higher rates than cheap ones. But through it all, tariffs provided most federal revenue. Internal taxes of every sort were considered a supplement to this tariff regime.[22]

Despite their relatively narrow scope, however, the Federalists' internal taxes were unpopular. "The time will come," warned a member of Congress in 1790, "when the poor man will not be able to wash his shirt without paying a tax."[23] In the presidential election of 1800, Thomas Jefferson vowed to roll back all internal taxes, and after defeating John Adams in the latter's bid for reelection, Jefferson made good on his promise. But even in defeat, the Federalists could look with some satisfaction on their fiscal accomplishments. Jefferson and his Republican allies may have repealed the nation's internal taxes, but the Federalists had still established the government's *right* to impose them. That right would prove crucial in the years ahead, as the nation faced its first major test of wartime fiscal capacity.

The War of 1812

Since the end of the Revolution, Great Britain and the United States had remained at loggerheads, bickering over a range of trade and territorial issues. In 1812, the two nations came to blows in what many called the Second War for Independence. The United States survived this conflict but did not win it. After a decade of Republican stewardship—marked by low taxes and frugal spending—the nation was ill-prepared for war. Reductions in military spending had left the army and navy weak, hardly ready to face one of the world's preeminent military powers. Perhaps worse, the Republican predilection for low taxes proved hard to shake, even in the face of a national emergency. Lawmakers came late to the realization that internal taxes were a wartime necessity.

The American Revolution formally ended in 1783 with the Treaty of Paris, but for years afterward, the fledgling United States continued to joust with Great Britain over a range of trade and territory disputes. These arguments divided not just the two nations, but American political leaders as well. Members of the Democratic-Republican party, which grew up around Thomas Jefferson in the 1790s, considered Britain a serious and continuing threat to U.S. interests. Federalists, by contrast, were more worried about the strategic and ideological danger posed by France, which was engulfed in its own Revolution and locked in a long-running military struggle with Britain.

While Federalists held the reigns of power in the 1790s, they introduced a wide-ranging program of financial and military preparedness. Indeed, much of Hamilton's economic program—assumption of $75 million in state debts, creation of new taxing devices (including both internal and external levies), establishment of a national bank—was developed with national security concerns keenly in mind. Federalists used the revenue flowing from tariff duties and internal taxes to help finance a larger army and navy. Between 1789 and 1801, the army grew from 840 men to 5,400. The navy, almost nonexistent at the start of the 1790s, grew to include

13 frigates and six ships-of-the-line over the same period. Federalists also invested some $1 million in coastal fortifications.[24]

For all their faith in war preparedness, however, Federalists were committed to the notion of neutrality. When war broke out between Britain and France in 1793, President Washington insisted that the United States not take sides. Some members of the fledgling Democratic-Republican party argued that the United States was still bound by treaties with France signed during the Revolution. But Washington successfully made the case for neutrality; even his ardently pro-French Secretary of State, Thomas Jefferson, accepted the argument.

But then, in 1794, Washington dispatched John Jay to London. The president charged Jay, then serving as chief justice of the Supreme Court, with defusing the growing tension between the United States and Great Britain. Jay obliged, hammering out a pact that resolved numerous territorial and trade disputes between the two nations. In doing so, Jay paved the way for years of prosperity, as American merchants built a lucrative transatlantic trade with Britain. But Jay's Treaty, which passed the Senate only after rancorous debate, proved explosive. Democratic-Republicans insisted that closer ties with Britain would undermine the young United States and corrupt its nascent republican institutions. Federalists, by contrast, embraced the pact as a step toward peace and security. This division helped establish the contours of the emergent party system, providing unity and coherence to both factions.[25]

Jay's Treaty also fractured relations with the French, who considered it a betrayal of the alliance forged during the American Revolution. France severed relations with the United States and began harassing American merchant ships. In this undeclared quasi war, lasting from 1798 to 1801, the two nations jousted continually on the high seas. Indeed, this naval conflict with the French helped prompt the direct tax of 1798, which Federalists designed to help pay for their rearmament program. The success of this preparedness campaign—both financial and military—was soon apparent, as U.S. naval victories prompted the French to retreat from their hostile stance.[26]

Between 1801 and 1803, France and Britain took a break from their long-running war. But when hostilities resumed, the United States was again thrust into the middle. This was a lucrative position to occupy; the profits from the neutral trade were enormous, and many American merchants grew rich from the war. But neutral trade was dangerous, too. The British established a tight naval blockade of Napoleon's major European ports, severely restricting trade between France and neutral nations like the United States. France retaliated by banning all trade with the British Empire, even by neutral nations. And in response, the British imposed the Orders in Council, effectively prohibiting neutral trade with France and its dominions. British ships began harassing American ships trading with the West Indies, and routinely violated U.S. territorial waters in search of war contraband.[27]

British interference with American trade was deeply unpopular. Making matters worse, the British stepped up their practice of impressment, boarding American vessels in search of British deserters who were then forced back into the Royal Navy. The practice was bad enough in itself, but it also involved mistakes. Some 6,000 American citizens were impressed between 1803 and 1812, and while procedures existed for correcting such errors, it was a slow and cumbersome process.[28]

A Republican War

As Jefferson and his political allies tried to navigate a course through the treacherous waters of European warfare, they sought to force both combatants to respect America's neutral rights. Economic warfare was Jefferson's chosen weapon, especially because it came cheap, at least on the spending side of the budget. Through a range of trade restrictions—collectively known as the restrictive system—Jefferson and his successor, James Madison, tried to coerce respect from both Britain and France. These restrictions had ample precedent. In the years leading up the Revolution, Americans had used a variety of non-importation and non-exportation measures to protest British trade and tax policies. In the 1790s, leaders of the Democratic-Republican party had urged Congress to once again use trade restrictions to coerce respect from London. Federalists were skeptical of the efficacy of such measures, and they successfully blocked them throughout their years of political ascendancy. But among Jeffersonians, the utility of trade restrictions remained an article of faith.[29]

In an effort to defend neutral trading rights, Jefferson induced Congress to pass a non-importation act in 1806 barring certain British imports. The following year, lawmakers approved the Embargo Act of 1807, prohibiting *all* exports from the United States to *any* nation and effectively confining U.S. ships to port. The measure proved an abject and painful failure; many American merchants flouted the embargo, and neither the British nor the French showed any inclination to relax their hostile stance toward neutral shipping. Two years later, Congress revised the embargo in the Non-Intercourse Act of 1809, which scaled back trade restrictions to focus solely on Britain and France. But this ban, too, proved ineffective and unenforceable. Finally, in 1810, Congress passed Macon's Bill no. 2, which lifted all trade restrictions. But lawmakers still hoped to encourage better behavior from Britain and France; the law allowed the president to reinstate trade restrictions against *either* Britain or France whenever the other combatant agreed to stop harassing American merchants. In 1811, Congress returned to a focus on Britain, prohibiting all British imports.[30]

The restrictive system notwithstanding, violations of American neutral rights continued, and resentment toward Great Britain (whose naval preeminence and frequent violations of neutral rights made them much more unpopular than the French) continued to grow. Notably, however, resentment did *not* grow in New England, home to most of the nation's merchant shippers. Trading with combatants was dangerous but highly profitable, and most merchants were eager to avoid military conflict of any sort. Prowar agitation remained relatively strong throughout the western and southern United States, and political leaders from both regions took the lead in urging a military response. But agitation from these War Hawks met with strong opposition among New Englanders.

The War Hawks hailed from Jefferson's Democratic-Republican party, although not all their party colleagues shared their militant attitude toward Great Britain. But the election of 1810 gave the War Hawks new power in the House of Representatives, with one of their leaders, Henry Clay of Kentucky, installed as Speaker and another, John C. Calhoun of South Carolina, taking a leading role in the march to war. The War Hawks offered a variety of arguments for standing firm against Britain. First, they insisted that protecting American neutral rights—including the right to trade and the right to be free of impressment—was imperative. Backing down would imperil not simply the nation's prosperity but its political viability. If the United States and its republican experiment were to survive, the nation must stand firm against foreign encroachment of its sovereign rights. In addition, the War Hawks saw political advantage in a successful confrontation with Britain. A war could unify the sometimes-fractious Republican party and consign the Federalists to permanent defeat. And finally, some war supporters even cast eager eyes on British Canada, suggesting that victory in the north would secure the nation's border.[31]

On June 18, 1812, such arguments carried the day, and the United States declared war on Great Britain. Almost immediately, things went poorly for the Americans. Along the nation's northern frontier, a series of forays into Canada met with disaster, and forces in Detroit and Chicago surrendered by mid-August. Naval battles went better, with several key U.S. victories in 1812; the frigate *United States* captured the British *Macedonian,* and the *Constitution* destroyed the British *Java.* But the British easily maintained a strong blockade of American ports, all but halting U.S. commercial activity.

Things went from bad to worse, and 1814 proved a disastrous year for the American cause. The British captured Washington, D.C., in August, forcing the president and Congress to flee and setting the torch to the White House. The military outlook was bleak, and many Americans began to questions whether the war could be won.

And then the money ran out.

Principles of Republican Finance

Albert Gallatin, a confidant of Jefferson and one of the leading lights of the Republican party, was born in Switzerland in 1761. Arriving in the United States in 1780, he eventually settled in western Pennsylvania and became an active figure in local politics. Elected to the Senate in 1793, he was an ardent critic of the Federalists—so ardent that they engineered his immediate removal from office, pointing out that he had failed to satisfy the Constitution's nine-year residency requirement for senators. Gallatin returned to national politics in 1795 when he was elected to the House of Representatives. He arrived in the House with a pair of quintessentially Republican values: an aversion to public debt and a resistance to most forms of internal taxation.

Indeed, while serving in Congress, Gallatin established himself as a leading critic of Federalist economic policy, including Alexander Hamilton's program of debt finance and internal taxation. In fact, while living in Pennsylvania after his ouster from the Senate, he had been a leading figure in the Whiskey Rebellion, opposing violence by his neighbors but spearheading resistance to federal liquor taxation. When he returned to Congress—after narrowly escaping prosecution for his role in the rebellion—Gallatin resumed his attacks on debt, internal taxes, and Federalist finance. By the end of the decade, he was widely viewed, along with Thomas Jefferson and James Madison, as a founder of the anti-Federalist political faction known as the Democratic-Republican party.[32]

Gallatin loathed public debt as a symptom of fiscal irresponsibility and spendthrift self-indulgence. He also resented its tendency to advance the fortunes of the creditor class, usually at the expense of borrowers. He accepted the importance of repaying the nation's lingering debt from the Revolutionary War. But he viscerally opposed Hamilton's effort to transform this debt into a financial blessing and the engine of economic growth. To Gallatin's way of thinking, the debt was something to eliminate, as swiftly and completely as possible.[33]

When it came to taxes, Gallatin was more flexible than many of his Republican colleagues. He recognized that adequate revenue was necessary if the government were to free itself from debt. And like most political leaders of his generation, Gallatin believed that tariffs should provide the bulk of this revenue. But to the extent that internal taxes were sometimes necessary—in war, for instance, or to pay for extraordinary but unavoidable expenditures—then direct property taxes were the least objectionable. Even as he defended direct taxes (including the Federalist levy of 1798), however, Gallatin stressed that internal taxes should be temporary. Defensible when used to fund extraordinary needs, he argued, they should not be tolerated as a continuing tool of federal finance.[34]

After his election in 1800, Jefferson appointed Gallatin to be the nation's fourth Secretary of the Treasury. Once ensconced in his office, Gallatin moved quickly to roll back many of the Federalists' signature economic policies. He harbored doubts, however, about the wisdom of repealing internal taxes. Ideologically, he was as eager as any Republican to see them go. "If this administration shall not reduce taxes, they will never be reduced," he wrote to Jefferson. Only by repealing taxes could the power and ambition of the federal state be kept in check. But a healthy dose of pragmatism tempered such thoughts. Taxes should be cut or eliminated "provided there is no real necessity for them," he stated. And given the uncertain state of federal finance, Gallatin was unwilling to declare that tax revenues were, in fact, unnecessary.[35]

Eventually, Gallatin acceded to Jefferson's demand that internal taxes must go, for both ideological and political reasons. Having campaigned against the Federalist tax system, Republicans could hardly now embrace it. To help pay for the resulting revenue loss, Gallatin vigorously pursued the Republican line on retrenchment, slashing expenditures across the board. In fact, the government initially ran a surplus under Gallatin's supervision, and he used the extra money to pay down the federal debt.[36]

Gallatin's reservations about internal tax repeal were well founded. In the short run, internal taxes may have been dispensable. But by eliminating this element of federal taxation, Republicans placed the government in a dangerous and ultimately untenable position. Wholly dependent on tariff duties for necessary revenue, the nation was ill-prepared for war. Any foreign conflict would almost certainly disrupt the flow of tariff revenue, leaving the government in dire financial straits. And while Gallatin and many of his Republican colleagues believed that internal taxes could be revived in the event of such an emergency, they underestimated the difficulty—both political and practical—of imposing, assessing, and collecting new taxes in short order. Their error would soon be all too obvious.[37]

Gallatin's Plan for War Finance

In 1807, as tensions with Great Britain continued to escalate, Gallatin offered Congress his thoughts on war finance. His opinions were, in many respects, utterly conventional, reflecting broader European thought on the question of war finance. The extraordinary expenses of fighting a war should be paid for with loans, he maintained, while taxes should be used to pay for normal, nonwar expenses, as well as interest payments on past and current borrowing. Gallatin was confident that the country could borrow the funds necessary for a war with Britain (which he initially estimated at $10 million) without resorting to heavy taxation. But he did suggest a range of revenue options to cover regular expenditures and debt service in the event of war, especially since hostilities would likely interrupt revenue from the tariff. Internal taxes on consumption might be necessary, he told Congress, at least as a temporary measure. And Americans could be expected to embrace their patriotic fiscal duty. "Indirect taxes, however ineligible, will doubtless be cheerfully paid as *war taxes,* if necessary," he wrote. A direct property tax, along the lines of the 1798 Federalist levy, might also be helpful, despite the inequities that plagued its assessment, administration, and collection.[38]

Congress did not respond to Gallatin's speculation about war finance, but many Republican leaders were deeply suspicious of his call, however oblique, for internal taxes. After all, these same internal taxes had helped shatter the Federalists in the late 1790s. But as time passed, the financial outlook deteriorated, and talk of taxation continued to mount, at least around the Treasury. Jefferson's trade embargo was wreaking havoc on the nation's economy. Exports fell from $108.3 million in 1807 to $22.4 million in 1808, while imports dropped from $138.5 million to $57.0 million over the same period. Tariff revenue fell in tandem, dropping from $17.1 million in 1808 to just $7.8 million in 1809. And all the while, expenses were soaring; normal expenditures (excluding debt service) rose from $4.9 million to $6.4 million over the same period.[39]

Still, Gallatin held out hope that tariff duties could provide adequate revenue. "No internal taxes, either direct or indirect, are, therefore, contemplated, even in the case of hostilities carried against the two great belligerent Powers," he assured lawmakers in 1808.[40] By 1809, however, his confidence had begun to wane. He warned lawmakers that if tariff revenue fell faster than anticipated, then internal taxes might be unavoidable.[41] In 1811, with the prospect of war increasing, he again suggested that Congress might consider "a proper selection of moderate internal taxes" should tariff revenue not suffice to meet normal expenses and debt service requirements.[42] In a letter to Ezekiel Bacon, chairman of the House Ways and Means Committee, Gallatin was more specific, suggesting $3 million in direct property taxes and $2 million in excise taxes, should the nation find itself at war. Gallatin was at pains to minimize the burden of these new taxes:

> With respect to internal taxes, the whole amount to be raised is so moderate, when compared either with the population and wealth of the United States, or with the burthens laid on European nations by their governments, that no doubt exists of the ability or will of the People to pay, without any real inconvenience, and with cheerfulness, the proposed *war taxes.*[43]

Gallatin recommended that new federal excises be levied on goods already taxed by the states, thereby minimizing political and administrative difficulties. In any case, he continued, failure to move swiftly on the full set of revenue recommendations would imperil the nation's long-term prosperity. If Congress failed to pay for normal expenses and debt service with tax revenue—instead relying on still more loans to cover these nonwar expenses—then the nation would ultimately be consigned to a vicious spiral of growing debt and soaring tax increases that would long outlast the war.[44]

Gallatin's proposal proved explosive among Republicans, who were loath to abandon their long-standing opposition to internal taxation of any sort. Many party faithful warned that it was political suicide to consider reinstating the hated excise duties of the Federalist era. One lawmaker accused Gallatin of "treading in the muddy footsteps of his official [Federalist] predecessors," and some Republicans even accused "The Rat in the Treasury" of trying to sabotage the war, sapping the nation's resolve with his draconian recommendations.[45]

The tax debate eroded Republican unity, but soon even the War Hawks had to acknowledge fiscal reality. In March 1812, they took up Gallatin's plan, and both houses approved a bill authorizing the Madison administration to borrow $11 million. They also agreed to double tariff duties. But provisional tax legislation—which merely put Congress on record as *intending* to levy certain war taxes should they prove necessary—met with a howl of protest in the House. One Federalist even wondered whether "the war [would] float the taxes, or the taxes sink the war." Eventually, however, lawmakers approved the revenue measures, including a range of new internal taxes slated to take effect once war was declared, including levies on stills, bank notes, and carriages. But, as later became apparent, announcing the *intention* to tax was a far cry from actually *enacting* a tax. The hard work of war finance remained undone as lawmakers pushed the tough decisions further into the future.[46]

Three months later, after formally declaring war, Congress again took up the question of war finance. The $11 million loan authorized in March had been a disappointment, raising only $6.5 million from investors unimpressed by the interest offered to subscribers. Lawmakers approved additional borrowing of $5 million, this time using short-term Treasury notes. They also doubled customs duties and other taxes on international trade (including a surcharge for goods imported in foreign ships). But legislators once again declined to impose new internal taxes, still worried about the political implications of such a move.[47]

New England representatives complained that an overdependence on import duties forced their constituents—who consumed more imported goods than residents of other states—to shoulder a disproportionate share of the war's cost. And since New Englanders were not fans of the war in the first place, asking them to bear a disproportionate share of its cost seemed perverse. Federalists also complained that the entire Republican financial program was unsound, pointing to the failure of the March loan and the dependence on Treasury notes. "The public credit must be supported," insisted one Federalist critic, "or you put at hazard the best interests of the country—you hazard, indeed, the very existence of the government." But Republican leadership refused to consider new taxes.[48]

As the war progressed, bad luck on the battlefield did little to encourage fiscal responsibility in Congress. An initial blush of patriotic fervor—evident outside New England if not within it—faded quickly, making tax hikes even more politically difficult for Republicans. In January 1813, Gallatin projected annual expenditures of $36 million and just $17 million in revenue from existing taxes. He cast doubt on the prospects of using loans to close the gap, especially given the dismal record of government borrowing to that point. The situation was dire indeed. "We have hardly money enough to last till the end of the month," Gallatin told Madison. Congress approved another $16 million loan but adjourned on March 3 without acting on the administration's tax recommendations.[49]

Congress returned in May for the express purpose of sorting out the tax situation. "This can be best done," President Madison declared, "by a well digested system of internal revenue." Gallatin, however, was not present to make the case for his tax proposals, having been dispatched in mid-March as part of a diplomatic mission to Russia (which had offered to mediate a peace treaty between the United States and Britain). Republicans in Congress—long suspicious of Gallatin's sympathies and hostile to his proposals for internal taxation—accused the absent Treasury chief of treachery. "It is freely imputed to him that he fled to avoid the odium of the system of taxation . . . which he himself asserted necessary," observed one Republican senator.[50]

Acting Treasury Secretary William Jones forwarded tax recommendations to Congress in early June, but Republican leaders continued to dither on the critical finance issue. "The authors of the war," observed one Federalist critic, "approach the subject with *fear & trembling.*" Republican lawmakers displayed a general eagerness to spare their constituents from as much pain as possible. "Every one is for taxing every body, except himself and his Constituents," noted one observer. Republicans and Federalists argued with each other—and within their respective caucuses—to ensure that any new taxes would spare their particular regions and constituencies. There was hardly a rush for fiscal sacrifice.[51]

But Republicans surprised their critics, and perhaps themselves, by voting to approve a broad tax program, projected to raise $5.5 million in new revenue. The plan included a direct tax on land, as well as excise levies on retailers, stills, auction sales, sugar, bank notes, and carriages. The land tax was to last for just one year, but the rest of the levies were to remain intact until the year after the end of hostilities. None of the taxes, however, would take effect until the end of 1813.[52]

The direct tax was expected to raise $3 million. An earlier attempt at direct taxation in 1798 had been sobering, with federal officials impressed by the complexities of assessment and collection. This time, lawmakers invited states to assume responsibility for the taxes of their citizens and pay the necessary sum directly to the federal treasury. Seven states took the option, but the rest declined for fear of having to raise their own taxes to help foot the bill. The Rhode Island assembly also pointed out that assumption would give the federal government an easy way out, relieving "the General Government from the odium of collecting a tax which their own mad policy has brought upon the country."[53]

The Republican experiment with fiscal responsibility—never very energetic in the first place—managed to ease the economic crisis only briefly. In January 1814, acting Treasury Secretary Jones projected a dramatic shortfall in the nation's finances, with $45.4 million in expenses and just $16 million in revenue. New taxes were imperative, he said, if only to keep the nation current on its debt service. But Congress would only agree to float a new loan of $25 million and authorize the issuance of $10 million in additional Treasury notes. Federalists complained that Republicans were courting financial disaster, using new loans to pay the interest on old debts. But the Republican antipathy to internal taxation proved stronger than such criticism.[54]

In September 1814, Treasury Secretary George Campbell warned Congress that new taxes would be necessary to cover anticipated shortfalls for the remainder of the year, which he estimated at $23.3 million. Notably, Campbell declined to recommend any specific course of action, merely encouraging Congress to address the issue directly. Campbell's successor, Alexander Dallas, was even bleaker in his assessment, projecting a $12.3 million shortfall for 1814 and calling for a round of new taxes. In January 1815, Dallas released another report, projecting 1815 expenses of $56 million and revenue of just $15.1 million— less than the $15.5 million necessary to service the existing federal debt. Absent new taxes, the nation would have abandoned widely accepted notions of sound finance. Already, the government was having trouble finding investors for its loan offerings. Dallas outlined a range of possible tax changes and even floated the notion of an income tax—still a fiscal novelty in the United States, although it had been used in Great Britain since 1799—but he remained pessimistic about the prospects for keeping the government afloat.[55]

Dallas's report surprised even many of his Republican colleagues, who somehow had managed to ignore the severity of the financial crisis despite repeated warnings from the Treasury department. Upon hearing from Dallas, one Republican lawmaker asked a Federalist colleague, largely in jest, if the Federalists would be willing to take back control of the government. "No, sir," he replied, "not unless you will give it to *us* as we gave it to *you*."[56]

Confronted with this looming disaster, Republicans finally agreed to impose a broad array of new taxes in 1815. Congress approved a new direct tax of $6 million, twice the amount expected from the similar levy enacted in 1813. They also imposed a new whiskey tax, returning this controversial levy of the Federalist era to the nation's revenue system. This was just the beginning. The revenue laws passed in 1814 imposed or raised taxes on numerous goods, including carriages, hats, umbrellas, paper, beer, tobacco, leather, and jewelry. Several excise taxes were clearly aimed at the rich, including levies on gold and silver watches, as well as expensive furniture. Lawmakers did not, however, embrace Dallas's suggestion of an income tax.[57]

Opposition to this tax program was significant but not overwhelming. Southern and western representatives complained that it overburdened their constituents, and from his retirement, Jefferson registered his firm opposition. But most Republicans had finally recognized that such tax measures were an unpleasant necessity. And Federalists, for their part, were more than a little smug: "You must pay for the whistle you have purchased," observed Thomas P. Grosvenor of New York.[58]

The 1814 tax increases were the last before fighting came to a halt. In December of that year, diplomats for the United States and Great Britain hammered out a peace treaty in Ghent, Belgium. Word of the pact did not reach the United States, however, in time to halt the last great battle of the war in New Orleans. General Andrew Jackson handily defeated his British opponents in their attack on the city, giving the United States a moral victory, of sorts, obscuring for many contemporaries the country's undistinguished military performance during the early years of the war.

Conclusion

The war taxes of 1812–15 were followed by an additional increase in the direct property tax in 1816. But agitation to roll back the war tax regime began almost immediately after the end of hostilities. Several levies disappeared in 1816, and the remainder were repealed in 1817. The United States soon resumed its normal peacetime dependence on tariff duties as the principal source of federal revenue. The War of 1812, unlike subsequent wars, would leave no lasting mark on the federal tax system.

Still, the fiscal history of the War of 1812 remains important. As the first major test of federal tax capacity in the face of national emergency, it revealed both strength and weakness. The steely resolve necessary to enact painful war taxes was slow in coming. Republican leaders in Congress delayed fiscal pain well beyond the dictates of prudence, and the nation's credit suffered accordingly. In the early years of the war, lawmakers authorized numerous loans, only to find a cool reception among investors. The nation's finances approached a truly perilous state in the early part of 1813, and lawmakers only agreed to raise taxes when fiscal realities forced their collective hand.

This political and economic failure has long been obvious to historians. "The principal reason why the treasury broke down during the war of 1812," remarked finance scholar Albert Bolles in 1891, "was because Congress, in the beginning, dared not go deep enough into the pockets of the people."[59] In part, this reluctance stemmed from a deep-seated Republican aversion to internal taxation, mixed with a healthy dose of political expedience. But it also reflected the divisive nature of the war, as well as its tepid support in many parts of the country. Even prowar Republicans were lukewarm in their preparation for the fight. "The advocates of the war appeared to support the conflict more with their heads than their hearts," observed the war's leading historian, Donald R. Hickey, "and more with their hearts than their purses."[60]

But the fiscal history of the War of 1812 was not an abject failure. When Congress finally screwed up its courage, lawmakers enacted a wide range of internal taxes. The revenue from these levies paid for more than 40 percent of the war's total cost.[61] In the latter years of the conflict, internal revenue even outstripped tariff duties as a source of funds. Indeed, internal taxes salvaged the nation's credit in the nick of time, demonstrating the resilience of the fiscal infrastructure created in the Republic's early years. The power to tax—which Federalists so earnestly sought and Republicans so unwillingly employed—proved adequate to the task of war finance.

2
The Civil War

"Let colossal wealth, protected, meet the full share of burdens, which are lighter in this country than in any other civilized country in time of war."

—Representative J. B. Grinnell

I f the War of 1812 left no lasting mark on the nation's revenue system, the same cannot be said of the conflict that followed a half-century later. The Civil War transformed American federal taxation, replacing the nation's first revenue regime with a new, more modern—and far more robust—successor. Long dependent on tariff duties for nearly all its revenue, the federal government emerged from the Civil War with a broad array of internal taxes, including the nation's first income tax. And while many of these wartime levies did not survive Reconstruction, they nonetheless established the sinews of our modern fiscal state.

The Civil War tax regime resulted from the interplay of exigency and politics. Fighting the war put extraordinary demands on a cash-strapped Union government and a still-nascent Confederate treasury. In the North and South, the war disrupted traditional sources of governmental support, including the tariff and debt finance. In both Washington, D.C., and Richmond, policymakers understood that some sort of tax reform was imperative, if only to pay the most pressing bills of both belligerent states.

But the wartime fiscal watershed was not solely the product of economic necessity: it also reflected political and moral imperatives. The conflict demanded extraordinary sacrifice from citizens of both the North and South. More than half a million soldiers paid with their lives, and millions more shouldered the heavy implicit tax conscription imposed. Meanwhile, farmers and business owners, especially in the

South, struggled in the face of wholesale government expropriation of goods, products, and services. Together, conscription and expropriation fueled a demand for progressive tax reform, as lawmakers in Washington and Richmond cast about for ways to balance the scales of sacrifice.

Economic and political imperatives prompted large-scale experimentation in public finance. Most notably, the Union imposed an income tax in 1862, with the Confederacy following suit a year later. Both levies included a graduated rate structure designed to shift the fiscal sacrifice up the income scale. But neither represented an effort to place the burden of war taxation solely on the rich; each was part of a larger fiscal regime that included less progressive revenue tools, including taxes on consumption. Policymakers in the North and South were determined to spread the cost of the war throughout their respective economies and across their populations.

This is not to say that there was unanimous or immediate agreement that painful fiscal sacrifice was necessary. Both the Union and Confederacy initially resisted calls to dig deep for the war effort, with many sanguine observers predicting a short and relatively inexpensive conflict. Optimism was particularly appealing in the Confederacy, where a fear of centralized state power made direct taxation unpalatable. The Confederate government paid for much of the war with unsupported Treasury notes, prompting disastrous inflation. While the Union more quickly realized the gravity of the fiscal situation, manufacturers actively opposed new tax burdens throughout the war. Moreover, even the Union eased its commitment to fiscal sacrifice when the crisis began to abate. Self-denial is seldom an easy sell in the political arena, and its durability—even in the midst of war—is never something to take for granted.

Antebellum Period

During the first half of the 19th century, tariffs supplied the overwhelming majority of federal revenues. There was disagreement about how tariffs were used, though, often following sectional lines. In the North, manufacturers sought heavy, protectionist tariffs to help shield them from foreign competition. By contrast, rural planters in the South preferred a less burdensome tariff regime, with tariffs limited to items not produced domestically. Since Southern farmers were net exporters to Europe, they insisted that protective tariffs only raised the price of goods they purchased from northern manufacturers without increasing the price they could obtain for their agricultural products sold abroad. South Carolina even threatened to secede over the "Black Tariff," or "Act of Abominations," enacted in 1828, which imposed rates of almost 50 percent on some goods. In a compromise Henry Clay negotiated in 1833 after the Tariff Act of 1832 aroused similar reactions, tariff rates were scheduled to decline significantly over the next decade, although a downswing in the economy halted many of the rate cuts scheduled to take effect in 1842.[1]

In 1846, tariff rates resumed their downward trajectory, just as the United States began its war with Mexico. To modern observers, these tariff cuts might seem to constitute the first wartime tax cut in American history. In fact, though, this was less of a tax cut than a tax restructuring. Concerned that protectionist tariffs lined the pockets of wealthy manufacturers rather than increasing tax revenues, Treasury Secretary Francis Walker argued for a reduction in rates, although not to the levels contemplated by the Clay Compromise more than a decade earlier. Notwithstanding the lower overall rates, tariffs on luxury goods increased substantially, while items like tea and coffee were relieved of tariff burdens altogether. This compromise increased revenues while reallocating the burden of taxation and reducing the tariff subsidy to the rich.[2]

The tariff reforms of 1846 produced a growing federal surplus and helped prompt yet another round of tariff revisions in 1857. These reforms reduced protective tariffs to their lowest level in 40 years. Duties were cut across the board by 20 to 25 percent, with the highest rate set at 24 percent. While the protest from formerly protected industries crossed sectional boundaries, the tide had appeared to turn toward a new era of government finance. Some observers began to suggest that direct taxes might be used to help phase out revenue tariffs entirely.[3]

Unfortunately for its supporters, interest in direct taxation plummeted when opponents blamed tariff reductions for the Panic of 1857. Horace Greeley wrote in the *New York Tribune* that "no truth of mathematics is more clearly demonstrable than that the ruin about us is fundamentally attributable to the destruction of the Protective Tariff."[4] As a result of the depression, imports fell by more than 25 percent in one year, leading customs revenues to drop by a third. Between 1856 and 1861, revenues dropped by almost $25 million while spending dropped by less than $2 million.[5] For the first time in a decade, the federal government ran a deficit.[6]

Bowing to deficit concerns and resurgent agitation for trade protection, Congress considered in 1860 a bill to restore customs duties to their pre-1857 level. But the measure got a hostile reception in the Senate, where a Democratic majority remained committed to tariff reduction. If the Southern states had not seceded at the end of the year, the bill might have failed, forcing Congress to resort to some other mechanism for closing its fiscal gap. But as it happened, secession ended the movement for direct taxation and cleared the way for higher tariffs, as the departure of several Southern Democrats gave GOP senators the majority they needed. In March 1861, the chamber approved a broad upward revision of the Union tariff.[7] This pro-tariff victory, however, would be short-lived; the onset of hostilities prompted lawmakers on both sides of the Mason-Dixon line to revisit the direct tax debate.

The Civil War and Direct Taxation

At the outset of the Civil War in April 1861, political leaders in the North and South minimized the need for fiscal sacrifice. In fact, however, neither government was financially capable of sustaining a conflict that went on for very long. The North was still reeling from the Panic of 1857, and four straight years of budgetary deficits had left the newly elected President Abraham Lincoln with an aggregate debt of approximately $75 million.[8] The South, of course, had to create a government and raise an army from scratch, all without the benefit of established credit or currency. Indeed, the Secretary of the Treasury, Christopher G. Memminger, had to provide a personal guarantee to a local bank in order for the Confederacy to obtain credit initially. While both sides eventually recognized the need to levy new taxes, Confederate lawmakers avoided this unpleasant reality far longer than their Union counterparts. This difference in their approach to taxation and finance may have reflected the divide between the North and South over the nature and desirability of centralized state power.[9]

Confederacy

In the new Confederate states, many observers believed the war would end quickly. One Southern journal predicted that "the strange infatuation by which the people of the North are deluded to believe that it is in their power to subjugate us and force us back into political union with them and under their government, cannot endure very long. A few weeks, or at most a few months more, with the experience they have already had, can scarcely fail to bring them to a sober perception of the insuperable difficulties of an enterprise which has appeared to them to be so easy to be accomplished."[10] This view, which was widely held, convinced Confederate leaders that they could prosecute the war without asking for great fiscal sacrifices. As President Jefferson Davis later recalled,

> At the commencement of the war we were far from anticipating the magnitude and duration of the struggle in which we were engaged. . . . A long exemption from direct taxation by the General Government had created an aversion to its raising revenue by any other means than by duties on imports, and it was supposed that these duties would be ample for current peace expenditure, while the means for conducting the war could be raised almost exclusively by the use of the public credit.[11]

The goal, according to Confederate Vice President Alexander Stephens, was to avoid burdening the people by conducting the war with as little direct taxation as possible.[12]

The Union blockade of Confederate ports in the spring of 1861 drastically reduced tariff revenues, forcing the new government to rely almost exclusively on loans and notes to pay its bills. According to one study of Confederate finances, bonds and treasury notes accounted for 99 percent of total revenues between July 20 and November 16, 1861. This dipped only slightly to 96 percent for the 1862 fiscal year and was still as high as 95 percent for the first nine months of 1863.[13] By relying upon the issuance of unsupported notes at the national and state level, the Confederacy essentially financed the early stages of the war by printing money. This had disastrous effects on the Southern economy. The surfeit of Treasury notes and bonds produced hyperinflation unseen since the Revolutionary War, with the Confederate dollar eventually worth just five cents in gold. There was a corresponding effect on commodity prices. Prices for staples like wheat, bacon, and flour rose by as much as 2,800 percent between 1863 and 1865. A cup of coffee, which might have cost less than 15 cents before the war, cost as much as three dollars by 1864. Local differences in commodity prices encouraged rampant speculation, which only fanned the flames of economic distress.[14]

The lone attempt to impose a direct tax during the first two years of the war was less than successful. After the first Battle of Manassas (or Bull Run) in July 1861, the Confederacy's provisional Congress adopted a direct tax of one-half of 1 percent on all property, including real estate, slaves, and personal property. The levy was necessary to support the borrowing of funds, since the Confederacy otherwise lacked adequate access to capital.[15] Rather than impose the tax on the people directly, however, which would have required the erection of its own collection apparatus, the Confederacy permitted state governments to assume the obligation and pay it themselves. As a consequence, few states collected any tax at all,[16] choosing instead to issue their own treasury notes or to borrow from their local banks. This development further increased the aggregate Confederate debt burden and reduced the value of state and federal treasury issuances. During its two years of operation, only $20 million was received from the states, and little of it came from the imposition of the Confederate tax itself.[17]

The failure of this direct tax appeared to reflect a concern about centralized power. While economic historian Richard Bensel has concluded that Confederate economic and social policies reveal an embrace of a centralized post-secession government,[18] Confederate tax policies, at least during the crucial first half of the war, pointed in the opposite direction. Edwin Seligman, a Columbia economics professor and noted 19th century expert on taxation, observed that "the aversion of the people to direct taxation was so great as to have rendered the [Confederate] war tax practically nugatory."[19] According to Rose Razaghian's analysis of roll call votes in the provisional Congress, this reflected the antebellum concerns about centralized power. "Congressmen who were the most deeply committed to protecting states' rights and slavery were more likely to rely on financial policies that limited the aggrandizement of federal power, issuing loans and notes, and were more likely to oppose policies that empowered the federal government, in particular taxes."[20] The Confederate legislature sought to proceed without requesting deep fiscal sacrifices from its citizens.

Confederate policymakers believed that debt financing could be accomplished with minimal administrative support. Taxation, by contrast, would directly involve the central government in the lives of its citizens through the necessary expansion of its fiscal bureaucracy. Taxes were also more likely to survive the wartime emergency. Alabama's governor, A. B. Moore, epitomized this attitude in a letter to the Confederate Congress explaining why the states should not cooperate in collecting the Confederacy's direct tax:

The State should never concede to the General Government the exercise of powers not delegated to the Constitution, and they should never, except in cases of
absolute necessity, consent to exercise powers or to perform duties which do not
properly belong to them. As a general rule it is dangerous in its tendencies, and
precedents of this character are to be avoided. The collection of this tax by the
State would be an onerous and unpleasant duty, as it imposes upon the State the
necessity of enforcing the laws of the Confederate Government against her own
citizens.[21]

For a people "who had even more than the typical American's resistance to taxation," the initial opposition to taxation was predictable.[22]

Although the Confederacy avoided explicit taxation, it did resort to
two forms of implicit taxation—impressment and conscription—that
provided important resources for the war effort. Much like the direct tax,
however, the appetite for these roundabout fiscal tools was limited.
Under impressment, the government paid a below-market rate for the
goods and property it needed to fund the war effort, which effectively
imposed a tax equal to the difference between the market value and the
amount paid. This practice incited bitter resentment and charges of unequal sacrifice from those it burdened. For example, in the 1862 annual
report of the Milledgeville Railroad Company of Georgia, a company
that had almost all the iron it was using to lay down its tracks seized by
the government, the president tried to walk the fine line between patriotism and protest:

In a time of war, encroachments upon individual rights are often submitted to,
and sometimes necessary; but a just Government, in peace or war, will make these
sacrifices as equal as possible. If the exigencies are so urgent as to justify the
forcible seizure of the property of the citizen, the principle of indemnity should
be recognized, and the public should make just compensation for the injury done.
There is no justice or propriety in making individuals or classes the victims of a
forced economy for the benefit of the rest of their fellow citizens.[23]

The government's seizure had literally stopped the railroad in its
tracks. Even if it could have afforded to replace the iron that had been
seized, the directors predicted that the government would only take it
again. Thus, the Milledgeville Railroad Company chose to cease efforts
to build the new tracks until the war ended. The phenomenon occurred
with even greater regularity in agricultural communities, where the Confederacy obtained the food to feed its armies. Toward the end of the war,
less than a fiftieth of the land in the best corn district in Georgia had been
planted with corn.[24] After suffering under impressment, farmers simply

stopped planting new crops since they knew the Army would seize the crops at a fraction of their real value once they were brought to market.

Not surprisingly, Southerners also resisted conscription. In 1862, the Confederate Congress enacted the first national draft in American history to replace the waves of soldiers who failed to reenlist after their year of service was up.[25] All able-bodied white males age 18 to 35 were required to serve, but men could avoid service by hiring a substitute from outside the pool of those already required to serve. Substitution was a long-standing practice, present in Europe as well as in America during the Revolution, but it became quite controversial during the Civil War.[26] Given the broad reach of the draft, substitutes had to come from a fairly narrow pool of men, including those younger than 18 or older than 35, alien residents, and honorably discharged veterans. Within a year or two, the price for hiring a substitute reached $600 in gold, an amount equal to three years' wages for a skilled man. This exorbitant price led some to call the conflict "a rich man's war but a poor man's fight."[27] In his 1863 annual report to the president, James Seddon, the Confederate Secretary of War, suggested that substitution

> has done more than any single measure to excite discontent and impatience under service among the soldiers . . . the fact that the wealthy could thus indirectly purchase liberation from the toils and dangers necessary for the defence of the very means that gave them the privilege, and of the country itself, naturally produced among the less fortunate and poorer classes repining and discontent.[28]

To combat this, the Confederacy eventually barred substitution. Nevertheless, individuals could still avoid service through a system of occupational exemptions. This allowed men in certain key positions—including government officials, railroad and telegraph operators, teachers, and medical personnel—to avoid military service. Predictably, these professions enjoyed "remarkable growth" during this period.[29]

One of the most controversial exemptions was for overseers in plantations with at least 20 slaves. Confederate lawmakers approved this infamous "Twenty Slave Law" on October 11, 1862, in part to ensure that agricultural production continued without interruption and in part as a response to the fears of slave rebellion after Lincoln's Emancipation Proclamation. Nevertheless, critics decried the measure as "pure class legislation," insisting that it "caused great dissatisfaction, both with the country and army" while pitting the Confederacy's rich planters against its poor whites (who, not incidentally, did most of the fighting).[30] Some historians have suggested that the exemption contributed to the rampant desertion that plagued the Confederate army. As one poor soldier wrote home in announcing his intention to desert,

> Here I was fighting to save their negroes and property and them remaining at home, living in all the luxuries of live, and if a poor soldier went to get anything from them they would charge him. . . . Them are the kind of people that are here in the South.[31]

In North Carolina, one commentator characterized "this flagrant move by the wealthy planters to exempt themselves from actual combat" as "the key factor in turning the mountain counties' initial enthusiasm for the war into hostility toward the Confederacy."[32]

After several years, it became clear that explicit taxation was not only necessary, but much preferable to financing the war through debt, notes, and implicit taxes like impressment and conscription. To be sure, there were a few holdouts: "Let our authorities then fearlessly task and stretch the public credit to the utmost, in order to carry on the war so that taxation may not crush to earth our already overburdened people," counseled the *Wilmington Journal* in the spring of 1863.[33] But most political leaders understood the gravity of the situation. Even some of the most ardent advocates of states' rights pleaded to be taxed. As Governor Joseph Brown of Georgia, a states-righter who had quarreled with President Jefferson Davis over something as basic as the control of Georgia troops in the prosecution of the war, exclaimed, "For God's sake tax us. Nothing else can save us from ruin." Assistant Secretary of State William M. Browne lamented, "If something is not done, we shall have to pay $27,000 for a barrel of flour."[34]

The Confederacy thus began to consider a more comprehensive financial strategy—one that included an income levy and other internal taxes. On April 24, 1863, a year behind the Union and more than four months after Lincoln issued the Emancipation Proclamation, the Confederate Congress imposed a graduated individual income tax, featuring a higher rate on unearned than earned income, as well as a graduated tax on corporate income and a profits tax on speculative commodity transactions.[35] The latter was akin to an excess profits tax, designed to check the speculators who were exploiting price swings caused by the impressment system. These attempts to reach "idle wealth," while not as progressive as when first proposed, were designed to at least symbolically spread the burden of fiscal sacrifice more evenly across the population. Treasury Secretary Christopher Memminger acknowledged that an income tax would be more susceptible to evasion than some of the other taxes in the bill, but he argued that it was necessary to include such a tax: "otherwise the whole profits of speculation and trade, together with those resulting from skill and labor, would escape contribution."[36] In November 1863, Thompson Allan, the Confederate Commissioner of Taxes, justified a proposed tax increase on corporate profits by stating, "While three-fourths, perhaps, of the men of the Confederacy have dedicated their lives or fortunes, in many instances both, to their country's cause, the remaining fraction have no moral right to amass fortunes at their expense."[37]

The Confederate Congress also attempted to use taxation to address more directly the uproar over the unequal sacrifices imposed under conscription. Most significantly, the Confederacy imposed a special $500 tax on exempted overseers in which the revenues were allocated to relief agencies in individual states for the benefit of Confederate soldiers and their families.[38] This very specific and direct act of redistribution, which was part of a general attempt to stem the abuse of the overseer exemption, was one of the most visible efforts during the war to use the tax system to redress the inequality of conscription. It was also duplicated on the state level. In Georgia, for example, a progressive income tax was imposed on the net profits from manufacturing and sales, with its proceeds dedicated to supporting disabled soldiers and the families of soldiers either still fighting or deceased. Similarly, Georgia exempted soldiers with less than $1,000 in property from poll and property taxes, which, according to Governor Brown, was "in consideration of the hardships and privations endured by our soldiers in service, and the necessities of the families of many of them."[39]

These compensatory tax measures failed to mollify poor whites unhappy about conscription. As Albert Moore later described,

> The concessory character of the act of May 1st [1863] did not placate the partisan sensibilities of the common folk; and, of course, any leniency in the enforcement of it was odious to them. Ominous mutterings reverberated through the Confederacy and men began to talk lightly of their obligations to a Government which would so distribute its most painful burdens as to relieve in large measure the upper social structure.[40]

Part of this unhappiness reflected monetary trends; devaluation of the Confederate currency had made $500 too small a price to pay. Thus, in February 1864, the Confederate Congress enacted a provision forcing the plantations of exempted overseers to pay a tax-in-kind and to sell surplus food and other agricultural products to the families of soldiers at below-market prices.[41] Given the damage inflation did to the purchasing power of any cash subsidy, this implicit tax subsidy to soldiers' families may have redistributed more wealth than the explicit tax itself.

In addition to income and profits taxes, the 1863 revenue bill imposed a tax on gross sales, a tax on currency and bank notes, a one-year ad valorem tax on agricultural and luxury products, and license taxes on a variety of professions, ranging from bankers and lawyers to innkeepers and entertainers. It also imposed an in-kind tax on agricultural products grown in 1863, sometimes referred to as a "tithe tax," in order to institutionalize and reform the impressment system. This tax proved particularly controversial, especially in light of its exclusion of any property taxes on real estate, slaves, or livestock due to constitutional concerns. Farmers objected on the ground that the income tax was payable in depreciated Confederate currency while the in-kind tax necessarily was paid the full market value of the agricultural products transferred to the government.[42]

The tithe tax exacerbated tensions over the unequal distribution of fiscal sacrifice. During the summer of 1863, farmers held public meetings and issued resolutions denouncing the tax and the "licensed thieves" who enforced it. One resolution called the tax "monarchical" and "a relic of barbarism which alone is practiced in the worst despotisms." Another complained that "taking from the hard laborers of the Confederacy one-tenth of the people's living, instead of taking . . . currency is unjust and tyrannical, and we solemnly protest against that act." In many of these resolutions, the protesters proclaimed themselves "in favor of a just and equitable system of taxation, so that all classes may bear their burdens equally; we are, therefore, opposed to the tithing system . . . discriminating against and taxing the labor and industry of the agricultural classes."[43] The Confederacy eventually responded to such concerns, enacting exemptions for small farmers and for the families of soldiers.[44] But these revisions did not come until February 1864, when the tax had already wrought much damage to both groups.

Farmers were not the only ones to complain about the burden of taxes imposed under the April 1863 revenue act; urban businesses objected, too. After the act was passed, one southern partnership posted an advertisement in the Richmond *Whig* explaining that "in consequence of the very heavy taxes, we have deemed it best to close our business."[45] The

Richmond Enquirer reported that "the tax bill . . . carries consternation to the whole mercantile community. Half the merchants and manufacturers talk of discontinuing their business."[46]

Notwithstanding such dire talk, many businesses were profiting handsomely from the war. The owners of the Tredegar Iron Works, the chief munitions plant of the Confederacy, reportedly were so successful that "they did not know what to do with their accumulated profits." There were similar stories of high war profits, with a paper mill paying out almost 600 percent dividends during the war, a woolen factory nearly tripling its invested capital, and at least one railroad doubling its dividend payout rate. Blockade runners, who managed to evade Union naval blockades to continue the cotton trade, did even better. John Frasier & Company of Charleston managed to accumulate approximately $5 million in gold by the end of 1862 through this activity.[47]

These high profits were largely untouched by the Confederate revenue system, in large part because the tithe tax was the only levy that was ever effectively enforced. Over the course of the war, only about 1 percent of the Confederacy's cash receipts were raised through taxation: a shockingly small proportion compared with modern wartime governments.[48] The Confederacy had neither the administrative capacity nor the political will given the opposition to centralized power to collect most of the taxes it imposed. Treasury Secretary Memminger, focusing on the first issue, reported,

> the difficulties which are encountered in the collection can only be estimated by any one who will inspect the mass of papers which are required for each return, and the inquiries necessary to be made of each individual taxpayer. The results of the tax will probably confirm the recommendation already made of a resort to a more simple system of taxation. The frauds and evasions, which cannot be discovered under the present system, are a perpetual drain upon the tax, which is necessarily increased by the number of officers who must be employed in its collection.[49]

Not surprisingly, therefore, collections were initially quite slow. Almost a year after passage of the 1863 Act, only $27 million had been received, excluding the value of in-kind payments. Collections eventually rose to more respectable levels as the Confederacy improved its administrative apparatus, but they were still well below expected levels.[50] To augment revenues, the Confederate Congress increased the rates on income when the tax act was extended on February 17, 1864.[51] This came too late in the war, however, to have much effect. Memminger reported in May 2, 1864, that the Confederacy could only be expected to collect the in-kind tax revenues from the tithe tax during the coming year. Surrender occurred before the 1864 taxes could ever be fully implemented.[52]

Union

At the beginning of the war, the Union appeared to suffer from the same excess of optimism that plagued the Confederacy. Salmon Chase, Lincoln's Secretary of the Treasury, suggested "it is hardly to be doubted, moreover, that the great body of the citizens, now involved in the calamities of insurrection, will, ere long, become satisfied that order and peace, and security for all personal and political rights, in the Union and under the Constitution, are preferable to disorder and conflict." "It is not unreasonable," Chase continued, "to expect that with a restored Union will come, not merely renewed prosperity, but prosperity renewed in a degree and measure without parallel in the past experience of our country."[53] The *New York Times* offered a similar picture of the mood in Northern commercial circles, reporting that "the belief is almost universal, among our business men, that in a short time the whole thirty-four States will be, in practical truth, as they are by the letter and spirit of the Constitution, One People."[54] Thus, Chase proposed to reduce the massive deficit through a combination of traditional means: issuing Treasury notes with the assistance of financier Jay Cooke, increasing tariffs to their pre-1857 levels, imposing or raising excise taxes, instituting license fees, and selling public lands.[55]

Chase's optimism took a significant hit with the Confederate victory in the first Battle of Bull Run (or Manassas, as the South called it) on July 21, 1861. Because of the battle's proximity to Washington, D.C., Congress was intimately aware of the defeat. It could hardly have been otherwise, considering that members of the House and Senate had taken to the streets to persuade wild-eyed Union soldiers, who had retreated as far back as the capital, to turn around and fight.[56]

Congress was also well aware of the defeat's implications for Union finances. "I do not know what to call the sort of precipitate retreat from Centreville that some of our soldiers made the other night," commented Republican Senator James F. Simmons, a manufacturer from Rhode Island, "but I believe it is going to make it much more difficult for us to negotiate loans than if they had stood their ground."[57] Indeed, the defeat brought Northern morale to a new low point, but it was perhaps a useful prod. As the *London Times* predicted, "This prick in the great Northern balloon will let out a quantity of poisonous gas, and rouse the people to a sense of the nature of the conflict on which they have entered."[58]

This early turning point in the war became a turning point in fiscal matters as well. On July 23, 1861, two days after the disastrous defeat at Bull Run, Thaddeus Stevens, the "dictatorial" Republican chair of the House Ways and Means Committee, proposed a $30 million direct tax on land, with each state's share to be apportioned by population. Two days later, Senator Simmons proposed adding an income tax provision to the tariff bill passed in the House on July 18.[59] Most observers acknowledged that relying on loans to finance the war would be insufficient. When Stevens introduced his proposal, the New York Times wrote, "It is admitted on all hands that the money to be raised on loan, by the government during the present fiscal year, will fall short of its actual necessities, by at least 80 million—and that taxation, either direct or indirect, or both, must be resorted to, without delay, to provide for the deficiency."[60] The war could no longer be prosecuted without demanding monetary sacrifices from its people in the form of higher taxation:

> Hitherto we have been able to maintain a powerful government at comparatively a small expense raised by indirect taxation; none felt the burden of the government, while all enjoyed its inestimable blessings. . . . No one could have conceived the ridiculous idea of a government undertaking to sustain itself from overthrow against a formidable rebellion, without a most serious drain upon the taxable resources of the people. The cost of our vast military and naval operations necessary to achieve the great ends which the government has in view are enormous, and it rests with the people now to say whether these ends shall be urged forward or whether we shall let the government go to a quiet and ignominious grave.[61]

Stevens argued that "the annihilation of this government is the alternative" to increased taxation.[62]

While lawmakers agreed that some form of taxation was necessary, they differed over the distribution of the burden. Under Stevens' proposal, farmers would bear the brunt of the tax while holders of intangible wealth, such as stocks and bonds, would be virtually exempt. Reduced to sectional terms, the New York Times described the proposal as "operating unequally on the interior states."[63] Thus, the House initially recommitted the bill with instructions to amend it to include a tax on both real and personal property. When this ran into constitutional difficulties, the bill was again recommitted, this time with instructions to replace much of the direct tax with an income tax. The income tax had been used as early as 1799 in England during the Napoleonic wars, thus providing a model for income tax proponents. At the end of July, both the House and

Senate passed bills that, to varying degrees, combined an income tax with a direct tax on land. The full Congress adopted a compromise bill on August 5, 1861.[64]

While the 1861 act appeared to promise a radical change, it initially did little to improve finances. The direct tax produced no short-term revenue, since assessments were not due until April 1862. Moreover, every state but Delaware elected to assume the tax obligation on behalf of its citizens, making the Union's direct tax only slightly more effective than its Confederate counterpart.[65] The income tax fared even worse, as Chase made no effort to assess or collect it. He also failed to nominate anyone to serve as commissioner of taxes, further frustrating the creation of a collection mechanism for internal taxes.[66]

Unlike their Confederate counterparts, Union lawmakers were relatively quick to grasp the gravity of their financial predicament. War expenses were rising steeply, and the national debt was increasing at a rate of 2 million dollars a day. In January 1862, the Union's suspension of specie payments severely hampered the government's ability to secure loans of any kind. In response, Chase asked Congress for $50 million in new revenue. Leaders of the House Ways and Means Committee dismissed the request as far too modest, instead suggesting a hike fully three times as large.[67] But the panel took its time drafting a bill, prompting a barrage of criticism from impatient onlookers.[68] Indeed, foreign observers were surprised at the apparent eagerness for heavy taxation. "I was not surprised to see your young men rushing enthusiastically to fight for their flag," recalled one commentator. "I have seen that in other countries. But I have never before seen a country where the people were clamorous for taxation."[69] When the committee finally introduced a bill in March 1862, the *Saturday Evening Post* emphasized its deliberate creation, describing the measure as "one of the longest of any kind ever before prepared— months of preparation having been bestowed upon it."[70]

The new House bill dramatically expanded the base of taxation, chiefly through a raft of excise taxes and a gross receipts levy. A contemporary observer from Austria commented that under the bill,

> The citizen of the Union paid a tax every hour of the day, either directly or indirectly, for each act of his life; for his movable and immovable property; for his income as well as his expenditure; for his business as well as his pleasure.[71]

In addition to the direct tax and a somewhat broadened version of the income tax adopted in 1861, the bill included excise taxes on everything from alcohol and tobacco to soap and salt; license taxes on everything from bowling alleys and circuses to bankers and commercial brokers; stamp taxes on the full range of legal and commercial documents; and both an inheritance tax and a gross receipts tax on corporations in the transportation and financial industries.[72]

In the Senate, lawmakers replaced the bill's direct tax with a graduated version of the income tax.[73] Opponents of the direct tax insisted, as they had in 1861, that it would unduly burden farmers; since the Constitution required that direct taxes be apportioned according to population, rural landholders in sparsely populated states would pay more than urban dwellers who kept their wealth in intangible form, including stocks and bonds. Such arguments, however, were poorly received in the House, where critics pointed out that intangible wealth was no longer exempt, since its returns would be taxed under the new income tax. If Congress replaced the direct tax on property with an even more progressive income tax, landholding farmers would find themselves undertaxed. As Massachusetts Representative Alexander Hamilton Rice protested, "I am at a loss to know upon what principle of justice one class of industry should be taxed 5 percent upon its industry and another class of industry exempted from such taxation."[74] The Senate and House eventually compromised by agreeing to suspend the direct tax for two years rather than eliminate it altogether.

A similar debate took place over the income tax's graduated rates. While the progressive feature of the income tax served to replace the revenue from the direct tax, supporters also insisted that it would counterbalance the more regressive effect of excise taxes and tariff duties, both of which burdened consumption. As Senator Simmons explained, "The poor people pay as much, and rather more, generally, than rich men on their consumption."[75]

Not everyone agreed. Senator Zachariah Chandler, a Republican from Michigan, argued that the tax rate on income should match the rate on consumption:

> You tax the day laborer moderately on his consumption, three percent, a very small item indeed; and you tax the man of wealth the same way, and if you tax him in the same ratio for his income, he feels the satisfaction of knowing that this is a reasonable burden, a burden which he ought to bear, and thus you induce men rather to enlarge than to diminish their incomes under the feeling of justice, equity, and propriety.[76]

Simmons countered that "the consumption of this country has 25 percent put on it by this bill. . . . We put three-quarters of a cent on sugar last March a year ago, and now it is two-and-a-half cents. The taxes have increased in consequence of the rebellion. I find no trouble in my own mind in levying this income tax." As Senator Timothy Howe, a Radical Republican from Wisconsin, had explained, "the great amount of this revenue is to fall upon consumption, and consumption is not limited to the eastern cities."[77] The implication was that western farmers would indirectly bear their share of the burden through such taxes.

Such arguments proved persuasive, although the Conference Committee reduced the bill's progressivity by striking the top bracket from the Senate's three-rate system. The new income tax also contained some innovative features, including a reduced rate on interest from federal securities (designed to encourage their purchase), a higher rate on income from property in the United States owned by citizens living outside the country (on the theory that they would not otherwise contribute through the internal excise taxes), and withholding provisions for tax due on dividends, interest, and government salaries. Congress passed the bill and President Lincoln signed it into law on July 1, 1862.[78]

While the Union legislature may have embraced explicit taxation earlier than the Confederate Congress, the commitment among Northern taxpayers to the ideal of shared sacrifice was just as uneasy as in the South. Perhaps the most controversial aspect of the new tax bill was a general 3 percent excise tax on all manufactured goods, which was expected to raise more revenue than any other internal levy.[79] Manufacturers argued that this tax, which was based on sales rather than profits, would be "utterly ruinous to them" and would lead to "triple and quadruple taxation" because it was imposed in addition to the excise taxes on raw materials.[80] They argued that it could not be passed on to consumers, at least not right away, and therefore was deducted "wholly from their profits."[81] One letter writer reported in December that "not one manufacturer in a thousand has paid his ad valorem taxes; and this part of the law threatens to become a nullity and yield comparatively no income."[82] The Merchants Magazine and Commercial Review noted that "if [manufacturers] seek to evade it, it is to be feared their example may have a bad influence upon other classes, less interested, perhaps, in sustaining the government."[83] At a convention in Chicago held in June 1863, manufacturers went so far as to develop a circular "urging upon the Commissioner of Internal Revenue to either ignore the law altogether, or to suspend its operation until Congress can meet and repeal the obnoxious feature of the bill."[84] Manufacturers advocated replacing the excise tax with a uniform sales tax.

The manufacturers' noisy protest fell on largely deaf ears. The Office of Internal Revenue responded to the Chicago convention resolutions firmly: "Rest assured that the law is not considered by this office in the light either of a mistake or an accident, and that its provisions will be neither explained away, nor its operations suspended."[85] The inequity of the manufacturers' claims, especially in light of the sacrifices others bore in the same act, helped the Office in its efforts. *The Scientific American* wrote that

> the tax on manufacturers is doubtless heavy, and will fall with great inconvenience on many; but we, as publishers, might as well claim exemption from the onerous burthen as the manufacturers. We pay a heavy tax on paper, the price of which has greatly increased since the war, also upon every other article used in our business.[86]

One attorney had a similar response, writing that the tax,

> both specific and ad valorem, is invariably added to the prime cost of the manufactured article, and ultimately falls either wholly upon the consumer, or is partially shared by the retailer. . . . The income tax complained of is really the only government charge in any shape which touches the pockets of manufacturers.[87]

While these arguments successfully drowned out the complaints about the excise tax, manufacturers did achieve a partial victory when Representative Justin Morrill introduced a bill to increase tariff rates.[88] As an indirect method of countering the effects of an undesirable wartime tax, it was more effective in blunting the force of the tax without calling into question the manufacturers' willingness to sacrifice for the war effort. This would prove a valuable lesson to business in opposing wartime tax provisions in the future.

By 1864, the decline in tariff revenues from the Confederate navy's activities and the pressures of inflation caused by the heavy issuances of Treasury notes once again prompted a call for additional taxation. The *New York Times* demanded "to be taxed to a degree which shall fairly correspond with the vast amount of promissory money afloat."[89] Despite the existing heavy burden, many observers believed the public could bear it. The *Times* opined that "one of the greatest fallacies into which many are beguiled is, that the imposition of taxes in addition to those already imposed will bear too heavily on the people."[90] The *New York Tribune* echoed this point, noting "the reports thus far . . . show an unexpected capacity of our people for taxation."[91]

Thus, in two revenue acts adopted in 1864, Congress increased the tax rates to what were described as "extravagant" levels.[92] Internal excise tax rates were more than doubled on spirits, tobacco, and cigars, and the general excise taxes increased correspondingly. Income tax rates increased as well, with the highest rate topping out at 10 percent on income over $10,000 under the Act passed on June 30, 1864.[93] After realizing this might not be sufficient to cover bounties necessary to recruit and retain soldiers, Congress passed an emergency income tax act only a few days later, on July 4, 1864, which increased all rates another 5 percent for incomes above $600.[94] Despite the patriotic symbolism of the Independence Day tax, there was substantial disagreement about whether this unanticipated fiscal gap should be closed with an income tax rather than a property tax. James Brooks of New York attributed the choice of the former to the power of the farmers' lobby, but Justin Morrill defended the income tax, noting "there is no tax more equal than an income tax. . . . it is in all cases to be paid by those who are able to pay it and who have the most at stake in sustaining the credit of the country."[95]

Part of the rationale for progressive rates was pragmatic—the need for revenue and the appearance of fiscal stability. Augustus Frank, a Republican railroad director from upstate New York, argued for a more progressive income tax on the grounds that it was necessary to reassure private creditors: "The larger the tax we pay at this time, the safer we are and the better will be the securities of the Government." Representative J. B. Grinnell, a Republican from Iowa, concurred with this sentiment, explaining "if gentlemen demand to sustain our credit and prosecute the war with success, I could not advocate anything else in justice to the middle classes in this country."[96]

Yet support for increased progressivity was not merely a function of fiscal pragmatism. It is no coincidence that the 1864 acts, which represent the most progressive tax legislation in U.S. history to that point, came on the heels of bitter and violent controversy over compulsory military service. A year after the Confederacy began conscripting soldiers, the Union enacted its own draft in March 1863. All men between the ages of 20 and 35 and all unmarried men up to age 45 were subject to the draft. According to U.S. Provost Marshall General James B. Frey of the War Department, opposition to this new legislation was swift and bloody, with draft resisters killing 38 department employees and wounding 60 between July 1863, when conscription was first implemented, and 1865:

> Every imaginable artifice was adopted to deceive and defeat the enrolling officers. Open violence was sometimes met with. Several enrollers lost their lives. Some were crippled. The property of others was destroyed to intimidate them, and prevent the enrollment. In certain mining regions, organized bodies of men

openly opposed the enrollment, rendering it necessary that the United States authorities should send troops to overcome their opposition. There were secret societies, newspapers, and politicians who fostered and encouraged this widespread opposition.[97]

The New York Draft Riot of 1863 was the worst riot in American history, with at least 105 people killed. Spurred on by the staunchly anticonscription rhetoric of Democratic leaders, poor white workers feared that blacks would take their jobs if they were drafted.[98] Compounding their frustration was the perception that the rich easily avoided service, free to maintain their "luxurious repose."[99] This was a valid concern. While the Confederacy repealed substitution early on, the Union actually supplemented it by permitting individuals to pay a $300 fee to the government to commute the service obligation until the next draft.[100] In reality, this commutation fee may have made avoiding service more affordable compared with the exorbitant prices substitution brokers charged. In the immediate aftermath of the draft riots, some towns, including New York, took advantage of the commutation provision to buy out their young men from service.[101] Nevertheless, the popular perception, as one newspaper declared, was that "the rich are exempt!" The combination of substitution and the implicit commutation tax meant that wealthy had greater opportunities to avoid service than the poor. More importantly, they took advantage of these opportunities. Of the 207,000 men drafted in the Union, 87,000 paid a fee to have their service obligation commuted and 74,000 paid substitutes to take their place.[102]

In light of this discontent over conscription, many members of Congress sought to demonstrate their commitment to equal sacrifice, and tax legislation became the vehicle for doing so. Representative Grinnell exclaimed that the rich should not escape their civic obligations:

> It is time that extravagance in gewgaws, snobbishness in display, and that large class whose great care is to safely compound their hundreds of thousands, should feel that there is a war and a demand which they have not yet felt on their purses and on their patriotism, which in many cases has been but poorly acknowledged. . . . Let colossal wealth, protected, meet the full share of burdens, which are lighter in this country than in any other civilized country in time of war.[103]

The issue was not simply that the rich had not yet been forced to make material sacrifices, but that they were not sacrificing their lives and the lives of their sons in battle. As Senator Garrett Davis of Kentucky pointed out, when they did serve, it was in a more elevated status than their poor compatriots:

The idea that millionaires and men whose incomes exceed $25,000 as a general rule go into the camp is not supposable. There may be some exceptional cases; but if they go into camp at all it is not by shouldering the musket, unless in very rare cases. They do not send their sons there as a general rule unless the sons go with epaulets upon their shoulders.[104]

Thus, an income tax alone was not enough; rather, a steeply progressive one was needed to reflect the inability of fiscal sacrifice to fully substitute for the sacrifice of human life. Radical Republican James Grimes of Iowa argued, "If there is any class of men that the distinction ought to be made in favor of and not against, it is the very class of men we have discriminated against [in other ways]."[105] The implication was that the higher tax burden on wealthy individuals was justifiable given they were not otherwise sacrificing for the cause.

Although the 1864 acts produced some of the largest receipts during the war, bond sales began to lag and President Lincoln abruptly accepted Secretary Chase's resignation. His successor as Treasury Secretary, former Senate Finance Committee Chair William Pitt Fessenden, engaged Jay Cooke to market several more loan issuances. It was not enough, however, to finance the final military push. Thus, in December 1864, Fessenden recommended once again increasing internal revenue taxes with the goal of raising nearly $300 million. He hoped to satisfy much of this need with increased progressive income taxation, proposing to eliminate exemptions and thereby broaden the base.[106] The increasing reliance on the income tax was particularly controversial, especially in light of the detested, but officially sanctioned, custom of printing individual income tax returns in the local newspaper in an attempt to induce a taxpayer's neighbors to report fraud and underreporting.[107] This publicity feature, called a "most disagreeable and injudicious interference with private affairs" by the politest of its critics, was by no means the only objectionable aspect of the new revenue bill Justin Morrill introduced on February 9, 1865.[108] As Frederic Howe observed, "every possible article which had escaped the scrutiny of the earlier acts was sought out and taxed."[109] Nevertheless, the measure was eventually adopted on March 3, 1865.[110]

As a result of the 1864 and 1865 acts, the percentage of tax revenues derived from internal taxes increased substantially, with income tax receipts more than tripling. These acts marked the culmination of a radical shift in the system of federal financing over a short period. While customs revenues as a percentage of total receipts declined precipitously during the war, other revenue sources quickly filled the gap. Internal excise taxes made up the bulk of the new revenues, but income taxes also became a significant part of the revenue system.

Not surprisingly, until fighting ceased and the soldiers went home, this increase in the size of revenues never kept pace with the even more significant rise in government expenditures. Of course, the largest portion of the rise in expenditures was the combined cost of the War and Navy departments, which amounted to almost $1.2 billion in 1865 alone. Another significant factor, though, was the need to service the mounting debt the Union incurred during the war through the issuance of Treasury notes and other mechanisms. During 1861, in the earliest stages of the war, this amounted to approximately $4 million, or 6 percent of total expenditures. By 1866, however, after the war had concluded, the number has risen to more than $133 million, or more than 25 percent of total expenditures.[111]

From the perspective of fiscal sacrifice, perhaps the most significant added expense to emerge from the crucible of war was the veterans' pensions. These pensions were promised to conscripted soldiers on the same terms as members of the regular army to induce their service and placate their concerns about the inequality of sacrifice. Effectively, they were a form of deferred compensation, financed through the tax payments of future generations. Even before the end of the war, disabled Union soldiers or widows of the deceased began to file for veterans' pensions. While the Pensions Office had existed before the Civil War to administer pensions for veterans of the War of 1812, the costs rose sharply during Reconstruction. Veterans' pensions, which had only amounted to approximately $853,000 in 1862, skyrocketed to over $34 million by 1871, or almost as much as the entire amount spent on the War Department for that year.[112] By 1870, nearly 200,000 pensioners, both former soldiers and their widows and dependents, were on the rolls at the Pensions Office. Far more than just a residual expenditure of the conflict, Civil War veterans' pensions effectively became the first large-scale progressive federal social welfare program, presaging 20th century developments.

The Civil War Tax Legacy

Although the end of the war left the country with mounting debts and continuing obligations to fund veterans' pensions, political support for wartime levels of taxation soon began to wane. Early targets included two controversial taxes—the manufacturers' tax and the income tax. Representative Frederick Pike of Maine reported in 1866 that he had received "petitions from struggling manufacturers . . . from all quarters of the land, asking for relief."[113] The *New York Times* sided with these manufacturers, arguing that "the [3 percent excise tax on all domestically manufactured goods] tax must be abolished at once and completely" on smaller manufacturers and should be phased out over a three-year period on larger manufacturers to "give temporary assistance to the treasury, while our military and naval establishments are gradually being reduced to the peace standard."[114]

Similarly, political support for repealing the income tax gained momentum almost immediately after the war ended. Less than a year following the surrender of the Confederate armies, *Arthur's Home Magazine* wrote

> It is to be hoped that Congress will, at an early date, entirely repeal the income tax, or modify it in many particulars. It was from the very beginning a very unpopular tax, and has been rendered doubly so by the publication of incomes, which we have always regarded as a trespass upon private rights of a very grave character.[115]

While the calls for income tax reduction were not universal, with merchants and importers viewing the income tax as a potential permanent replacement for the tariff, bankers and manufacturers continued their opposition. The calls for reduction were not limited to the manufacturers' tax and the income tax, however, as many internal taxes became sources of irritation when the demands of war financing had subsided.[116]

Thus, Congress systematically reduced and refashioned the size of the postwar revenue system during Reconstruction. Initially, as the nation attempted to struggle with its postwar debt, lawmakers retained the income tax and even broadened it slightly.[117] But they insisted that the tax would only be applied "until and including the year 1870 and no longer." The general sentiment was that when prices returned to their normal levels and the burdens on manufacturers lifted, the income tax could be removed as well. Political economist David Wells, a special commissioner of the revenue, issued a report in 1866 that recommended reducing internal excises taxes and tariffs to address the inflation blamed for postwar economic stagnation.[118] Congress adopted most of these recommendations over the next several years. As Harry Smith observed, "now that a reduction in revenue was possible, almost every member of Congress was interested in having some particular tax reduced or repealed because it affected his constituents."[119] In 1866, many internal excises were reduced or repealed altogether, including all taxes on apparel, sugar, advertisements, and cigars.[120] In 1867, Congress repealed many internal excise taxes while also replacing the graduated rate feature on the income tax with a flat 5 percent rate and raising the exemption to $1,000.[121] This latter move left a mere 0.7 percent of the population covered by the income tax.[122] Congress repealed the controversial excise tax on cotton in February 1868 and, a month later, in a move considered "sudden and unexpected," repealed all taxes upon manufactured goods, except for those imposed on gas, tobacco, liquor, and banks.[123]

In 1870, an odd coalition of income tax supporters and opponents of the few remaining internal duties secured a reprieve for the income tax. It was only temporary, however. While there was some support for continuing the tax, the pressure for additional tax reduction was overwhelming. With internal duties cut substantially, the income tax was the last target for tax reformers. The *New York Times* wrote, "We have reached the time when the income tax can be no further defended. The people demand its repeal with one voice."[124] Anti–income tax associations in such cities as Boston and New York began to explore legal avenues of redress, including efforts to enjoin collectors and to test the constitutionality of the tax.[125] As Representative John Rice admitted, "The question of revenue reform and reduction of taxation is engrossing more of the attention of the people than any other with which this Congress has had to deal."[126] Thus, with the annual budget surplus growing to almost $100 million and prices on nonprotected goods beginning their descent from wartime highs,[127] Congress simply allowed the income tax to lapse in 1872. Returning full circle to the period before the Civil War, the revenue system now consisted of primarily regressive taxes.[128]

Coupled with the repeal of the inheritance tax in 1871 and the removal of most of the remaining internal excises and stamp taxes in 1872,[129] the end of the income tax marked a fundamental retrenchment of the revenue system. These developments not only reduced the size of the federal government, but also reshaped the distribution of taxes, easing burdens on the wealthiest members of society. Nevertheless, the Civil War experience had a lasting effect on the U.S. fiscal regime and laid the groundwork for many subsequent innovations, including the inheritance tax and the income tax. The Civil War also changed the terms of public debate over taxation in the United States. Before the war, the income tax had some proponents, but the idea was never taken seriously in Congress. By contrast, between 1873 and 1879, 14 different income tax bills were introduced in the House. In 1878, the Greenback movement's new party aligned with the Labor Reform Party in adopting a platform favoring a graduated income tax. While none of these bills achieved the two-thirds vote required to overcome the opposition of House leadership, they often were supported by substantial majorities. These new political developments were reflected in developments outside Washington as well. In 1883, Joseph Pulitzer forcefully demanded the return of both the income and inheritance taxes when he took over the *New York World.* The income tax also had near unanimous support in the academic community among both senior economists, such as Amasa and Francis Walker and Arthur Perry, and young colleagues, such as Richard Ely and Edwin R. A. Seligman.[130] The Civil War had effectively legitimized both the income tax and the inheritance tax as potential sources of revenue. Yet political legitimacy would not be enough to ensure the reappearance of the income tax. It would take another war—and the associated need for fiscal sacrifice to counterbalance the human sacrifice on the battlefield—before the income tax would find an enduring role in the American revenue system.

3

World War I

"The people of this country are not only united in the resolute purpose to win this war, but are ready and willing to bear any burden and undergo any sacrifice that it may be necessary for them to bear in order to win it."

—President Woodrow Wilson

Unlike the Civil War, which necessitated the creation of an internal revenue system from scratch, World War I came on the heels of two decades of tax reform and financial preparation. During this period, the country debated tariff reform, enacted an income tax that was struck down as unconstitutional, ratified the Sixteenth Amendment, and reinstated the income tax, complete with progressive rates. Thus, rather than marking the beginning of a period of transition in American finance, the first World War marked the beginning of the end of a transition that had started in the 19th century.[1]

It was the war, though, that brought the income tax to the forefront in modern public finance. The transition from an almost exclusive reliance on customs duties to a substantial reliance on internal revenues, such as the income tax, the estate tax, and excise taxes, could not have occurred without the demand for fiscal sacrifice that accompanied wartime politics. But this process did not flow naturally from the public mood in support of the war. Rather, for the first time, the notion of wartime fiscal sacrifice was cultivated, marketed, and sold to the American public. While this public relations effort was relatively primitive, focused primarily on speeches and public appearances because of the nature of media at the time, it was still a major advance in public finance.

Initially, this mass marketing effort encouraged voluntary fiscal sacrifice. The Treasury hoped to finance as much as half of the war costs through bond offerings targeted not only at the very wealthy but at the untapped wealth of middle-class investors. The hope was that individuals could be persuaded to invest out of patriotic duty. The strategy was an overwhelming success, with most offerings oversubscribed. Still, most contemporary observers recognized that this was only a modest form of fiscal sacrifice. After all, Liberty Bonds, as they were called, not only paid out interest, but the interest itself was initially exempt from income taxation, which in many cases more than compensated for the below-market interest rate.

Eventually, fiscal sacrifice had to be compelled through higher tax rates. This was never a broad-based effort as in the Civil War. Through high income tax rates, estate taxes, and an excess profits tax on businesses, Congress made an explicit choice to focus these calls for fiscal sacrifice on the well-off. Despite the speed with which the system converted to reliance on "soak-the-rich" taxation, the compulsory prong of the fiscal sacrifice campaign was an unparalleled success. After reporting record compliance with the War Revenue Act of 1917, Internal Revenue Commissioner Daniel Roper explained that "national patriotism and solidarity engendered by the war have contributed largely to our success. The way in which the taxpayers have generally assisted and cooperated has been a constant source of inspiration."[2]

Nevertheless, even amidst the patriotic fervor and expressions of support for the war effort, the sentiment for fiscal sacrifice was strained and contested. Business groups, in particular, followed their declarations of unqualified support with pleas for exemptions or protests against provisions targeted at them. They lobbied heavily to eliminate or narrow the reach of the excess profits tax, expressing concern that the taxation of business risked killing the goose that lays the golden eggs. Moreover, while business taxes accounted for a substantial amount of federal revenues during the war, evasion and creative tax planning were rampant. Fiscal sacrifice may have helped fuel the growth of the wartime revenue system, but it did not do so at the expense of self-interest.

Introduction

While the United States returned to its heavy reliance on the tariff at the end of Reconstruction, the Civil War's innovations had demonstrated the country's ability to utilize alternative revenue sources. This emboldened reformers. The income tax was the most prominent Civil War–era tax provision to be pushed for readoption, with income tax bills introduced in Congress almost every year in the two decades after the original income-tax measure expired.[3] Not until the Panic of 1893, though, did the accompanying economic dislocation highlight the inequities of the tariff system and prod Congress to adopt an income tax a year later. The Supreme Court struck the income tax down as a nonapportioned, and therefore unconstitutional, direct tax in the *Pollock* case, but it was clear that the battle for revenue reform was not over.[4]

President William McKinley's victory in 1896 was presumed to represent a mandate for a return to protectionism, and Congress subsequently enacted the Dingley Tariff Act. This erected one of the most highly protective tariff systems in American history, but the resulting increase in prices for foreign goods served only to lower imports and reduce federal revenues. With the onset of the Spanish-American War in 1898, Congress needed to raise revenue, and the tariff was once again not sufficiently nimble for this task. *Pollock* had foreclosed the option of an income tax, but it had left open several alternatives, including "excise taxes on business, privileges, employments, and vocations."[5] Congress first considered excise taxes on the gross receipts of all corporations, under the theory that this would be "a tax on the occupation of privilege of doing business as a corporation,"[6] but eventually settled on excise taxes specifically directed at the sugar and oil trusts, as well as a tax on inheritances.[7]

Although the war revenue taxes were repealed at the end of the Spanish-American war, the pressure for tariff reform remained. Between 1898 and 1907, the cost of living rose between 20 and 25 percent and wages failed to keep pace.[8] Republicans attempted to shift the blame for rising prices from the tariff to "the desire to keep up with the changing styles in clothing and shoes," but, not surprisingly, this backfired.[9] The Panic of 1907, which refocused popular attention on the potentially adverse economic effects from the tariff system and the insecurity of the capital markets, propelled Congress to seek a constitutional amendment to overturn *Pollock*.

The ratification of the Sixteenth Amendment and the enactment of the first modern income tax in 1913 culminated this period of transition in American public finance. While the Civil War provided valuable lessons in the process, the income tax ultimately developed in the absence of wartime pressure. Nevertheless, the income tax was still a relatively minor player in the overall revenue system. The rates were low, with the maximum combined normal and surtax rate only reaching 7 percent, and the exemption was generous, covering the first $4,000 of a married couple's income at a time when the average adult male earned only $578 per year. As a result, the income tax accounted for less than 10 percent of total federal revenues, and only 2 percent of American households were even subject to the tax. In the absence of war, the income tax might have forever remained "like a border to a carpet."[10]

The Outbreak of War

The assassination of Archduke Franz Ferdinand and the onset of World War I did not immediately require a large rise in expenditures. America remained, at least officially, neutral in what was not yet a world war. Nevertheless, the war placed a huge strain on the system by disrupting traditional revenue sources. As American involvement shifted from neutrality to aid of the Allies, the tax system had to adapt accordingly.

"Europe's War" and the War Revenue Act of 1914

Several months after war broke out in Europe, Congress passed the first War Revenue Act in October 1914. Although there had been some concern in the spring about raising preparedness for possible hostilities with Mexico,[11] the War Revenue Act was not intended to fund America's active participation in the war. Indeed, with the tax act coming on the heels of Wilson's neutrality proclamation in August 1914, the United States would not formally enter the war for another three years. Rather, the new act was designed to replace the revenues lost because of the effect of the war, and more particularly German submarines, on imports.[12]

A little over a month into the war, House Ways and Means Chairman Oscar Underwood reported that "commerce on the Atlantic Ocean today virtually has ceased, and with it importations and tariff collections."[13] The United States stood to lose as much as $150 million in customs duties annually, with a total cost of perhaps $1 billion depending upon the war's duration. Thus, the search began for alternatives. The income tax enacted the previous year was both too new and too slow to make up for the daily rise in the deficit. Thus, this first war revenue act relied principally on traditional war taxes, including the stamp taxes and alcohol taxes first enacted during the Civil War, to make up the deficit.

Not surprisingly, there was little popular sentiment in favor of sacrificing to pay for "Europe's war." "Why should the American people, who are not engaged in war, have to pay a war tax?" asked one popular journal. The Pittsburgh *Dispatch* pointed out "the paradox that the one great nation which has kept out of this war must pay additional taxes for its exemption." While most observers expected the tax to be borne "patriotically," the war tax had clearly struck "the American people in the pocket-nerve."[14] One concern was that politicians were still "squandering money like drunken sailors."[15] As a result, the tax was made explicitly temporary, with a scheduled expiration date of December 31, 1915.

Progressive Taxation and the Revenue Act of 1916

Despite optimistic reports that the war would be concluded before the War Revenue Act of 1914 expired,[16] hostilities only intensified. With the German submarines enforcing a blockade against England, customs revenues continued to fall and the deficits mounted.[17] More importantly, however, the war was brought closer to home when a German U-Boat sank the Lusitania on May 7, 1915, killing almost 1,200 civilians, including 128 Americans. While the United States remained officially neutral, the hostile act "aroused deep resentment in the American people."[18] Army and Naval appropriations had already increased dramatically, but President Wilson called for further increases in military preparedness in the event the United States had to enter the war.[19]

Thus, in contrast to the situation in 1914, the country began to consider additional taxation with an eye toward funding military action, rather than merely covering a war-related drop in tariff revenues. One possibility was simply extending the 1914 Act provisions and financing the remainder through loans, but lawmakers made three decidedly more progressive reforms in a bill passed in September 1916: (1) income tax surtaxes were more than doubled from 6 percent to 13 percent, while the exemption was broadened to cover widows and other heads of household; (2) an estate tax was levied for the first time, with rates ranging from 1 percent on estates above $50,000 to 10 percent on estates over $5 million; and (3) a munitions tax was adopted, levying a 12.5 percent charge on manufacturers of items such as gunpowder, firearms, and shrapnel.[20] A House Ways and Means Committee report on the proposed legislation opined that a transition was necessary from the almost exclusive reliance on consumption taxes:

> In meeting the extraordinary expenditures for the Army and Navy, our revenue system should be more evenly and equitably balanced and a larger portion of our necessary revenues collected from the incomes and inheritances of those deriving the most benefit and protection from the Government.[21]

Elliot Brownlee has characterized this move to finance the preparations for war on the backs of the rich and powerful as "the single most important financial decision of the war."[22] Although it was spurred in part by the redistributional demands of Democratic insurgents, and some contemporary observers considered it part of an inevitable shift away from the tariff, it may never have succeeded without the pressures of war.[23] The looming financial demands of battle allowed proponents to cast the progressive reforms as a demand for equal sacrifice. As the *New Republic* explained, "when our common safety is involved, certain principles should be axiomatic. One of these principles is that the sacrifice involved should be equal. . . . An equality of sacrifice involves equality of financial sacrifice."[24] Thus, the Association for an Equitable Federal Income Tax responded to critics of income taxation by noting that "the direct income tax is designed to reduce the inequality of sacrifice involved in our indirect tax system." Similarly, Senator Oscar Underwood defended the measure on the grounds that "increases in the army and navy have come from a demand from the representatives of wealth. They largely will get the benefit and it is but just that they should pay for that protection."[25]

Despite such appeals to sacrifice, there was substantial opposition from members of the business community. While they acknowledged the inevitability of taxation, business leaders sought to shift the burden to the personal income tax, primarily through lower exemptions. This was sometimes cast in the language of fiscal sacrifice. A New York investment banker wrote to Treasury Secretary William McAdoo advocating reducing the income tax exemption to $1,000, suggesting that this would be "patriotic and in line with good politics." Corporations also lobbied to be freed from the responsibility of collecting income taxes at the source on dividends and interest.[26]

In affected industries, the most vigorous opposition was reserved for the munitions tax. Companies manufacturing gun powder and other explosives, such as E.I. du Pont de Nemours & Co. and Hercules Powder Co., complained that the tax was "unjust, inequitable, and discriminatory." Pierre du Pont wrote a letter to the chairman of the House Ways and Means Committee arguing that the tax constituted double taxation and risked harming the nation's war preparedness by threatening the viability of munitions manufacturers. Perhaps to underscore this latter point, Hercules Powder announced that it would probably have to close a newly opened San Diego plant if the munitions tax were imposed.[27] Several companies threatened to test the constitutionality of the tax and several local chambers of commerce adopted resolutions in opposition.[28] This campaign against the munitions tax was levied even though most companies clearly anticipated it. Indeed, many of the largest companies had already tried to protect themselves by contractually shifting the cost of any such tax to the buyer.[29]

Ultimately, business was unsuccessful in its efforts to limit the munitions tax. Although the war had crippled imports and, as a consequence, customs duties, manufacturers reaped huge profits from the exports of war goods and general merchandise. There was substantial concern about the "war brides" by the fall of 1916.[30] Indeed, one of the most significant critiques of the munitions tax was that it targeted only one industry while permitting significant profits from the war trade to go untaxed.[31] As it turned out, the munitions tax was simply a dress rehearsal for a more extensive campaign against war profits that waged the following year.[32]

War Profits Taxes and the Revenue Act of March 3, 1917

Although the Revenue Act of 1916 was only a few months old, the expenses of war preparation quickly outpaced receipts. Several ominous signs suggested the United States would soon enter the war, voluntarily or involuntarily.[33] In late January, the British intercepted a telegram from Germany urging Mexico to enter the war by attacking the United States. Around the same time, Germany announced the resumption of its campaign of unrestricted submarine warfare against commercial vessels in the Atlantic. In response, Congress sought to increase appropriations for military and naval expenses. As Randolph Paul described it, "tax bills were in a losing race with events."[34]

Thus, Congress considered an emergency revenue act in early 1917 to fund the heightened military expenditures. The income tax was a likely candidate for expansion, but there was little sentiment in favor of higher surtaxes. Although the rates would increase exponentially by the fall,

America had still not yet officially entered the war, and the appetite for further sacrifice from the higher-income classes was limited. Typifying the perspective of this prewar period, Representative Henry Rainey, the ranking Democratic member of the House Ways and Means Committee, commented in December 1916 that income tax rates had "already reached the very highest notch."[35]

Since Democrats had rejected a lower exemption for the income tax in 1916, they began to pursue expanding the munitions tax to cover all war profits. This move had great ideological appeal. It reflected the concern of many that American business had been profiting from the war for several years while the rest of the country had been paying a higher price in the form of increased taxes. It also responded to the critique that the munitions tax had been too narrow in targeting only munitions manufacturers. Businesses in many industries had benefited from the war by supplying goods to Europe, replacing European trade with neutral countries', and supplying domestic alternatives to imported goods in the United States.

Following the lead of Canada and several countries in Europe, Representative Claude Kitchin, Chairman of the House Ways and Means Committee, proposed an excess profits tax on all business profits regardless of industry and regardless of whether earned in corporate or partnership form, at rates reaching as high as 60 percent.[36] Rather than limiting the tax to war profits, which would have compared current profits to the average annual profits during some period before the onset of the war, Kitchin's proposal relied on an approach that exempted profits up to 8 percent of invested capital. In effect, it was a tax on high profits rather than war profits. This made it both more broadly applicable across different industries and more easily transitioned to a permanent source of revenue after the war, something T. S. Adams, a Yale University economist and special advisor to the Treasury, advocated for a time.

The excess profits measure elicited significant opposition. Trade groups, such as the Merchants Association and the National Retail Dry Goods Association, publicly announced campaigns to oppose the tax. The *Los Angeles Times* called it "unfair supertaxation" and the *New York Evening Sun* called the proposed taxes "discriminatory" and a "burden on efficiency and prosperity."[37] At a Democratic caucus, Kitchin attempted to mollify Southerners concerned about the effect on business, but reports of his statements only inflamed sectional tensions over the tax:

You can tell your people that practically all of this tax will go north of Mason and Dixon's line. The preparedness agitation has its hotbed in such cities as New York. This bill levies a tax on those who have been clamoring for preparedness and are benefiting because of preparedness appropriations.[38]

Kitchin later defended his statement as an attempt to connect the tax with those reaping the benefits and to mollify those who believed that the sacrifice would fall unequally. He argued that many businessmen were "patriotic enough" to appreciate the equity of the excess profits tax: "Not all the preparedness advocates and clamorists are seized and dominated by the impulse of avarice."[39] Opponents, however, sought to shift the attention from excessive profits to national defense, contending that the latter was something "the whole country should pay for." The intensely partisan debate on this issue only highlighted the extent to which preparedness and excess profits taxation were still considered political and economic tools rather than instruments of national security in this prewar environment.[40]

While the bill was in the House, German submarines sank two American ships, heightening the immediacy of the war and lessening opposition to the tax. On March 3, 1917, Congress passed the Emergency Revenue Act, which also increased the estate tax rates by 50 percent. The excess profits tax satisfied the Democrats' desire to close the deficit without lowering the exemption on the individual income tax. It would soon assume a much greater role, though, as Congress began to grapple with raising revenue in a time of war.

America Enters the War

By late March, the successful German U-Boat campaign against Allied shipping, combined with the public revelation of Germany's attempt to entice Mexico to attack the United States and the abdication by Czar Nicholas II of Russia, convinced the reluctant President Wilson and his cabinet advisors that U.S. involvement in the war was inevitable. At Wilson's recommendation, Congress declared war on April 7, 1917. The immediate effect was to render the previous month's Emergency Revenue Act a dead letter as Congress proceeded to consider a grander plan for financing the war.

There was substantial debate during the ensuing months over the appropriate balance between taxes and loans in financing the war. Initially, the popular assumption was that Congress would raise revenues primarily through taxation rather than borrowing. In his message to Congress, Wilson announced the intention to support the Allies "so far as such support can equitably be sustained by the present generation, by well-conceived taxation."[41] There were dissenting voices, however, with Senate Finance Committee Chair Furnifold Simmons arguing that "it has been the custom of this country to pay war bills by bond issues, and I see no reason for a change in that policy."[42] The notion was that since future generations would enjoy the war's benefits, they should bear some or all of the cost.[43] Nevertheless, the country's disastrous experience with loan financing during the Civil War had led many to conclude that taxation was a necessary guard against runaway inflation.[44] Moreover, given the "wave of patriotism" that had spread in anticipation of the declaration of war, the willingness to endure further taxation was at its height.[45] Treasury Secretary McAdoo announced the intention to draw equally upon taxation and debt in financing the war, which would elevate tax to a higher percentage of revenues than in any prior war.

Liberty Loan Campaign

Even with the decision to rely more heavily on taxation, the government still had to raise funds while Congress was considering a revenue bill. Treasury Secretary McAdoo proposed to resolve the short-term financing problem by borrowing the money. This went against the advice of many members of the banking community who felt the capital markets would be "wrenched out of shape" by the kind of large debt offering required to satisfy immediate revenue needs.[46] Bankers also thought that bonds would have to offer reasonably high interest rates to attract sufficient attention, but this would risk setting off a rate spiral and escalating the cost of the war. Nevertheless, given the length of time necessary to consider a full-fledged tax bill, Congress had to find some means of financing the war. Moreover, McAdoo insisted that he could accomplish this through issuing bonds offering low interest rates.[47] His reasoning appeared to be that patriotism would induce individuals to lend on more favorable terms. Thus, on April 24, 1917, Congress overwhelmingly passed the Emergency Loan Act, which authorized the issuance of $5 billion in bonds at the below-market interest rate of 3.5 percent.

The bond program was named the "Liberty Loan" campaign because, according to the Treasury, the proceeds were designed to aid in "waging war against autocracy."[48] This was the beginning of an overall strategy to sell war finance by linking it more directly to the purposes of the war. McAdoo was convinced that the only way to fund the war successfully was to secure broad-based support. Part of doing this was to seek a new class of investors. "We went direct to the people," McAdoo later wrote, "and that means to everybody—to businessmen, workmen, farmers, bankers, millionaires, school-teachers, laborers."[49] Even the man "with only a few dollars to spare" was targeted. According to McAdoo, "we capitalized the profound impulse called patriotism."[50]

Encouraged by broad indications of popular willingness to support the bond effort,[51] the Treasury launched a mass marketing campaign of almost unprecedented proportions.[52] McAdoo began a nationwide speaking tour and secured the services of such Hollywood celebrities as Douglas Fairbanks and Mary Pickford to speak before huge bond rallies and Liberty Bond parades. Liberty Bonds were advertised on streetcars, in newspapers and magazines, and in promotional spots at movie theaters. Even the Boy Scouts of America were enlisted for the promotional campaign under a slogan of "Every Scout to Save a Soldier."[53]

Over two years and four separate bond offerings, the Liberty Loan campaign assumed an enormous role in war finance, operating effectively as a voluntary, implicit tax on the middle and lower classes. Indeed, critics initially derided it as evidence of politicians' reluctance to force the country to endure the fiscal sacrifice necessary to fight the war. Senator and future President Warren G. Harding referred to the campaign as "hysterical and unseemly," suggesting it was nurtured by Wilson in order to avoid forcing the American public to recognize and bear the true costs of the war.[54] The hope was that "patriotic fervor" would allow voluntary contributions to substitute for compulsory taxation.

By all accounts, the Liberty Loan campaign was a great success right from the start in reaching middle-class investors. The First Liberty Loan was oversubscribed by 50 percent, resulting in an additional $1 billion dollars of revenue from more than four million purchasers. Moreover, 95 percent of the purchasers bought in amounts ranging from $50 to $10,000 dollars, suggesting that the revenues came from more than just wealthy subscribers. Indeed, whereas fewer than 300,000 Americans owned bonds before the war, more than 4 million became bondholders in the First Liberty Loan campaign. As a result, personal savings increased dramatically, almost doubling from $5.56 billion in 1916 to $10.07 billion in 1917, with the rise almost completely attributable to investment in Liberty Bonds and other government securities. As a percentage of gross national product, personal savings rose from 12 percent in 1916 to between 17 and 18 percent in 1917 to 1918.[55]

Although patriotic sentiment may have fueled the sales of Liberty Bonds, contemporary observers argued that it involved "no real sacrifice" when the below-market interest rates were offset by the tax exemption on the interest.[56] Perhaps as evidence of the true motivations of Liberty Bond purchasers, investors reacted negatively to a proposal by Columbia economist Edwin Seligman to subject the interest on Liberty Bonds to taxation. C. E. Mitchell, a banker who served as president of the National City Company, argued that while "patriotism can persuade [the small investor] to buy these bonds," the wealthy were not quite so willing to voluntarily sacrifice investment return. The tax-exempt interest—given the high, and predicted to go higher, surtax rates on large incomes—constituted the principle attraction of investing in tax-free bonds. Another banker, Samuel Untermyer, predicted that "if the exemption is removed, the interest rate must be increased, and we are likely to lose more money in paying the added interest than we shall collect by way of tax on the bonds." While some commentators pointed out that making Liberty Bond interest tax exempt would "result in a certain measure of inequality in taxation . . . [since] all holders of the bonds would not be relieved from the payment of a tax at the same rate upon the income derived from their bonds," most apparently viewed it as imperative to ensure the success of the Liberty Bond campaign. In this sense, the effort to secure subscriptions from the masses was "a tax, without the careful equity considerations generally found in a tax."[57]

Even with the tax exemption, the patriotism of wealthy investors did not cause them to overlook the interest rate. While they were willing to accept below-market, but tax-exempt, interest rates, it was understood that the first Liberty Loan would be followed by others, possibly at higher interest rates. Because of investor agitation, the Treasury thus incorporated a feature in subsequent offerings that permitted holders of earlier bonds to convert to the later higher-rate bonds. This created a potential drain on revenues, however, so the tax-exemption feature was limited in subsequent offerings to the interest from the first $5,000 in bonds. This tradeoff between tax and yield, which was designed to dissuade wealthy investors from converting, reflected the more limited fiscal sacrifice demanded under the Liberty Loan campaign.[58]

The Revenue Act of October 3, 1917

While the Liberty Loan campaign proceeded, Congress began the more difficult task of considering a new tax program to finance the war. The act passed prior to the declaration of war was admittedly insufficient, both in terms of the expected revenue and its apportionment of the tax burdens. There was significant debate about the balance between taxation and debt in financing the war,[59] but there was little question that taxation had to play a major role. Thus, a bill was quickly introduced into the House that increased surtax rates on income, lowered exemptions, doubled the excess profits tax, and imposed excise and sales taxes on certain items and industries.

Taxation was considered necessary not merely as a revenue raiser, but, as the *Nation* declared, as "a vital factor in the equalization of public burdens."[60] This was a particularly salient concern at a time when the economic and noneconomic burdens of the war were mounting. Food, fuel, and other natural resources were in short supply because of the demand from Allied forces. Prices rose as production failed to keep up with demand, in the United States and abroad.[61] As a result of the passage of the Lever Food and Fuel Control Act, a food conservation program was instituted in mid-1917 and its leader, future president Herbert Hoover, promised to "mobilize the spirit of self-denial and self-sacrifice in this country," rather than rely on the food rationing that was prevalent in Europe. Ironically, a legacy of the food conservation effort was that it became a vehicle for the temperance movement to push Prohibition from the state to the national arena.[62]

While these sacrifices were considerable, by far the most notable sacrifice imposed in the early stages of U.S. involvement was the military draft. After relatively muted debate, conscription was authorized in May 1917. Starting on June 5, 1917, approximately 10 million men registered for the draft and 678,000 men were conscripted in its first round. After accounting for deferments and exemptions, more than 2.75 million men were eventually inducted into the military.[63] Mindful of the violent reaction against the draft during the Civil War, the Wilson administration attempted to soften the blow in a variety of ways, using local draft boards staffed by civilians rather than military officers and offering exemptions for skilled workers in the agricultural and industrial areas. Even the program's name—"Selective Service"—was designed, in Wilson's words, to change the draft's image from "a conscription of the unwilling" to a "selection from a nation which has volunteered in mass."[64]

Conscription was often invoked as a justification for taxing those at home. Harvard economist Oliver Sprague, seeking to highlight the financial obligation for those not serving, called for a "conscription of income."[65] In the House, Representative James Collier, a Mississippi Democrat, portrayed this as a broad burden:

> We are going to conscript the dollars necessary to carry on this war. I believe when we send our young men to the front to bear the brunt of battle those who are beyond fighting age and who will not fall within the selective draft should make no complaints when they are called upon to help defray the expenses of the war.[66]

Representative William Borland, a Democrat from Missouri, echoed this sentiment, arguing that the "burden ought to fall and will fall upon those members of the community who cannot offer their bodies, their lives, their health, and their strength as a sacrifice for the redemption of their country."[67]

More frequently, however, the draft was used to justify an explicit focus on taxing the wealthy. This was based not merely on the failure of the wealthy to make sacrifices equivalent to those of the draftees, but also on the benefits they received from the protection of their wealth. Representative Borland continued, "The capitalized wealth that is protected by the fleet and by the Army in the field should make its sacrifice. It is only a question of justice and lack of discrimination between different forms of taxation." Kansas Republican Edward Little reminded Congress "when you conscripted the youth of this country" you promised "that you would conscript the wealth" as well. "Let their dollars die for their country too," Little exclaimed.[68] While no one asserted that this form of conscription effected a sacrifice in any way equivalent to that of military service, there was, as Sprague asserted, the need to demonstrate that no sacrifice, financial or otherwise, was being evaded.[69]

The push for fiscal sacrifice appeared to meet with popular approval. Sprague observed that "readiness to make sacrifices on account of the war is everywhere manifest. There can be no more opportune moment for the imposition of an adequate measure of taxation."[70] The "conscription of income" campaign had garnered significant support in both the academic community and in popular circles. Even the United States Chamber of Commerce announced that it was "undismayed at the prospect of great taxes" and pledged "its full and unqualified support in the prosecution of the war."[71]

Notwithstanding these patriotic expressions of solidarity, there was a significant undercurrent of opposition. As the *Bellman* noted, "paying heavy war taxes is an altogether different matter from subscribing generously to Liberty Loans. The latter involves no real sacrifice; it is merely taking advantage of an opportunity to make a first-class investment."[72] Thus, proposals to tax items such as advertising, transportation, and postal mail were subject to "considerable dissent," with publishers complaining that the taxes would put them out of business. A gross sales tax on the manufacture of certain "luxury" items, such as automobiles, musical instruments, motion picture films, jewelry, boats, and perfumes, was called "unjust and mischievous discrimination that is wholly out of sympathy in a democracy where the whole people should bear the burden equally." As the *New Republic* mockingly explained,

> Those who must pay income or profits taxation complain bitterly, if not in the public press, at least in their private clubs, over their black coffee. Universal is the muttering that arises when it is proposed to levy consumption taxes of wide incidence. Two-dollar coal throws a dark pall upon the patriotic enthusiasm of the mining magnate; two-dollar wheat almost raises sedition in the breast of the farmer, bulwark of democracy.[73]

Many of the bill's targets, while expressing a willingness to pay their fair share, sought to shift the burden elsewhere. Joseph Fordney, the Michigan Republican who later chaired the House Ways and Means Committee, noted that he had not received a single communication from anyone who was satisfied with his tax burden under the bill. "They want it put on some other man or levied in some other way," Fordney explained. Representative Collier told a similar story:

> I have received more telegrams in the last two weeks than I ever received during the consideration of any other bill. I have received telegrams worded patriotically, that each and every person whom we intend to tax is willing to pay his share to carry on the war; but . . . they all think some other fellow ought to pay the tax.[74]

The greatest opposition was reserved for the proposed expansion of the excess profits tax. While business interests expressed the desire to aid in the war effort, they were uneasy about the excess profits tax's potential threat as a peacetime addition to the revenue system. This was a continuation of the debate begun in the first 1917 act about whether to levy a high profits tax or a war profits tax. Business lobbied to revisit the earlier choice of a high profits tax, triggered by profits in excess of 8 percent of invested capital, advocating instead a tax that only reached profits in excess of an average of prewar profits. They charged that a high profits tax would kill the goose that lays the golden eggs by discouraging businesses that were profitable before the war from continuing to earn such profits.[75]

Business opposition was seen as particularly ironic in light of business's lead in the war effort. Senator Hiram Johnson lamented, "our endeavors to impose heavy war profit taxes have brought into sharp relief the skin-deep dollar patriotism of some of those who have been loudest in declamations on war and in their demands for blood."[76]

The controversy over the excess profits tax played a significant role in delaying the passage of the War Revenue Bill. The House sought to impose a steeper version of the high profits tax enacted in March, while many in the Senate favored the war profits tax levy the British government used. Proponents of the war profits tax in the House argued that computing "invested capital" under a high profits tax would be difficult and susceptible to evasion. Critics in the Senate countered that the war profits tax could not be used for firms not in existence before the war and would miss large companies with substantial profits. Both sides claimed that the other type of tax would be inequitable in many cases. As early as June, President Wilson urged the Senate to speed its consideration of this bill and several others so that it might resolve war financing before adjourning for the summer. This hope proved too optimistic. When the Senate appeared headed for radical amendments to the original bill, aimed primarily at the excess profits tax, House members proposed to redraft the entire bill rather than attempt to reconcile their original House bill with the Senate version.[77]

The War Revenue Act ultimately adopted on October 3, 1917, operated as a compromise between the House and Senate positions. Commissioner of Internal Revenue Daniel Roper called it "the greatest tax-raising measure ever enacted," and Edwin Seligman characterized it as "colossal," constituting "the most gigantic fiscal enactment in history."[78] Designed to raise $850 million from income taxes, the act dramatically increased individual surtax rates, with the top rate rising from 13 to 50 percent. In addition, the act imposed a panoply of excise taxes, stamp taxes, and, perhaps most controversially, an increase in postal rates. The act was made retroactive to the period covered by the Revenue Act (adopted in March), effectively overriding that act.

Perhaps the most significant element of the act was in excess profits taxation, where an even larger sum than from the income tax—$1 billion— was expected from taxpayers. Although business managed to secure a small concession for the war profits principle in this tax, it fundamentally remained a high profits tax. This "war excess profits tax," as it was called, exempted the average prewar profits during the years 1911–1913, but the exemption was limited to 9 percent of invested capital. Profits earned above that amount were subject to a tax ranging from 20 to 60 percent.[79] T. S. Adams called the expansion of the excess profits tax "the most revolutionary development in public finance since the introduction of income taxation."[80]

Despite the all-encompassing nature of the act, a conscious effort was made to alleviate some burden from the middle and lower classes. Thus, proposals to tax electricity, heat, and telephone service were stricken from the final bill, as were excise taxes on commonly used items, such as tea, coffee, cocoa, and sugar. Moreover, the base, or "normal," income taxes, while doubled, were still set fairly low at 4 percent on individuals. According to an analysis of the bill by Columbia economist Edwin Seligman, in "striking" contrast with the Civil War tax program, 74 percent of the revenues from the 1917 act were focused on taxing wealth and another 13 percent were focused on "luxurious or harmful consumption." Only 13 percent of the revenues were to be derived from taxes on general expenditures or exchanges. Thus, much like the 1916 act, the focus was on "soaking the rich."[81]

Opposition to the Excess Profits Tax

During 1917, logistical difficulties in transporting men across the Atlantic meant that only 175,000 of the nearly 700,000 conscripted soldiers had actually reached French ports by year's end, and Selective Service inductions had ceased. In the spring and summer of 1918, however, the situation reversed. Heavy Allied casualties, especially by British forces in Passchendaele, coupled with the freeing up of German soldiers on the Eastern Front after the Bolshevik Revolution in November 1917, pushed the army to step up the pace of inductions and troop movements.[82] Consequently, the U.S. involvement shifted from one that had been primarily indirect, consisting of providing loans and producing supplies, to one that was increasingly direct, with American lives at stake.

Despite the increased U.S. involvement in the war, business criticism of the excess profits tax continued unabated in 1918. Indeed, according to one contemporary report, the tax bills passed in 1917 came in "for more criticism than perhaps any other measures passed since the war emergency began."[83] Business leaders argued that it was a fallacy to justify fiscal sacrifice as a counterweight to the human sacrifice now being made by soldiers. C. W. Barron suggested that this rationale was akin to a demand that "the officers in the rear must have like wounds and deaths with the soldiers at the front; that the generals must bear equal human sacrifice." The problem with this reasoning, according to Barron, was that it failed to recognize the important role the general played in the fight. In the same vein, he argued that it was important to recognize "that capital in private hands is a necessary part of the war administration supporting the soldier at the front."[84]

Business leaders tried to balance their opposition and avoid appearing too unpatriotic by issuing loud proclamations in favor of the war effort. At the annual convention of the United States Chamber of Commerce, an organization which counted more than 500,000 members on its rolls, a resolution was passed announcing that businessmen stood firmly behind the government in prosecuting the war "until Prussianism is utterly destroyed." The Chamber of Commerce did not disclaim its opposition to the excess profits tax, but tried to subtly shift this opposition to a call for a provision that was harsher against war profiteering. It adopted a platform plank declaring that "present tax laws should be amended so far as necessary if they prove inadequate to prevent abnormal and unreasonable profits as a result of war."[85]

The Chamber of Commerce's position reflected business's strategy of arguing for a war profits tax, such as the one in place in Great Britain, as a replacement for the "high profits" version of the excess profits tax adopted in 1917. Part of this preference for a war profits tax was that it assured that the tax would be limited to the wartime emergency and repealed thereafter. Activists had already begun to speak of the excess profits tax as a new tool of public finance that not only could supplement the income tax on a permanent basis, but "could be made an equally powerful instrument of social reconstruction."[86]

More practically, the excess profits tax was assailed for its unequal effects between equally profitable businesses. J. F. Zoller, a tax attorney for General Electric Company, called the war excess profits tax a discriminatory tax because of its arbitrary invested capital standard. It imposed an unfair burden in certain industries and afforded an undue windfall in others depending upon the state of profits in that industry prior to the war.[87] For example, members of the manufacturing community protested the exclusion of self-created intangible assets from the invested capital base, such as patents, copyrights, goodwill, and the value of distribution or supply contracts, while railroad corporations expected to pay little under the excess profits tax. Moreover, the definition of invested capital was susceptible to manipulation. "What constitutes invested capital," Edwin Seligman remarked, "is so elusive as to be virtually impossible of precise computation."[88]

To respond to such concerns, the Treasury instituted the Excess Profits Advisory Board. In addition to the problem of defining "invested capital," administrative difficulties beset the excess profits tax. While the bill as a whole had been drafted in six months, the compromise over the excess profits tax principle was developed in days and subjected to only limited debate.

The Advisory Board, charged with applying the new law "in the fairest and most equitable manner,"[89] faced a near-impossible task. Not only had it been saddled with a "multitude of confusing inquiries coming from the bewildered businessmen," but business interests attempted to use the Advisory Board to secure favorable accommodations. According to Samuel Untermeyer, a legal advisor to the Advisory Board, there was "a concerted movement of big industrial interests to discredit" the excess profits tax, in part by lobbying for a midstream change in the methods of calculating excess profits that would create sufficient "chaos" to lead to calls for repeal. While McAdoo largely resisted these efforts to undermine the tax, the Treasury issued several rulings considered favorable to industry and published many of them in a primer on the excess profits tax.[90]

A Treasury investigation of the excess profits tax only confirmed the popular belief that large businesses were resorting to self-help methods of reducing their burden under the tax. Led by T. S. Adams, the study found that corporations had reduced their rates of return for excess profits tax purposes through various means, including capital issues, increased salaries, and increased advertising costs. According to the Treasury investigation, even war contractors earning large rates of return on supply contracts were paying relatively low amounts of excess profits taxes. The highest rates of return were found among smaller corporations.[91]

Given the strength of the business opposition and the administrative difficulties in implementing the tax, it is not surprising that members of Congress began to call for the repeal of the excess profits tax soon after the War Revenue Act was adopted in October. In December 1917, Republican Senator Reed Smoot of Utah opined that "nothing more grotesque has ever been passed by Congress than the excess profits tax in the War Revenue law." He promised to replace it with a "rational, workable substitute."[92] Smoot introduced that substitute at the start of the new year, proposing to impose a tax at graduated rates as high as 80 percent on income in excess of certain percentages beyond the averages of the previous five years, after discarding the highest and lowest year.[93] Smoot claimed that his bill would eliminate the need for the Excess Profits Advisory Board, which he argued was effectively legislating through its interpretations of the law. Most significantly, the bill proposed to change the focus of the tax from high profits, or those in excess of a certain arbitrary percentage of invested capital, to war profits. This became the fundamental divide in tax policy debates over the ensuing 12 months.

Prelude to the Revenue Act of 1918: "Politics [Was Not] Adjourned"

While most of the controversy concerned the interpretation of the excess profits tax and, to a lesser extent, the income tax, the more immediate problem was ensuring that individuals and businesses filed their taxes on time. Internal Revenue collectors relied on some of the promotional techniques devised during the Liberty Loan campaigns to accomplish this. Thus, the Committee on Public Information sent out its "Four-Minute Men" throughout the cities in the week before returns were due to encourage people to file by the April 1, 1918, deadline. The Four-Minute Men, led by Mississippi newspaper editor George Cree, were a squad of volunteers trained to deliver brief speeches on war topics, initially in motion picture theaters (speaking during the four minutes it took to change a reel), but later in churches, public squares, and anywhere people congregated. The goal was as much to dispense propaganda as it was to provide information.[94]

In the case of the income tax, the propaganda campaign relied heavily on connecting the filing of tax returns and payment of taxes due with achieving success in the war. Thus, in New York City, one hundred Four-Minute Men were sent to speak at motion picture theaters. Their message was punctuated by slogans flashed on the screen, such as "Pay Promptly, Punctuate Prussianism," "The passing in of the income tax means the passing out of the Potsdam Gang," and "Help Pershing take the flag to the front by taking your income tax return to the Collector of Internal Revenue."[95] Squads of Four-Minute Men were also sent to lodges, churches, and YMCA centers to preach the patriotic virtues of tax payment.

Despite such efforts, it was clear that revenues would be insufficient to keep pace with the country's burgeoning war expenses. Even when the second 1917 act passed, congressional leaders expected it would only be a placeholder. While the bill was being considered in the fall of 1917, Treasury revised its estimate of probable future war expenses several times. The last such revision came only a few weeks before the bill's passage and substantially increased the estimated needs. Congressional leaders, however, had decided to restrict the tax bill to funding expenses already appropriated and resolved to seek additional taxes in the following session of Congress.[96]

Thus, it should not have been a complete surprise when Treasury Secretary McAdoo advised Congress in May 1918 that new legislation was "imperative to provide revenue to meet the unexpected increase in expenses incident to the vast expansion of the nation's war program." Nevertheless, McAdoo emphasized that the advice was premised on an "unexpectedly heavy" estimate of wartime expenditures for the year, including $15 billion for the army alone, rather than as part of the normal cycle of revenue legislation. Upon receiving the letter, Senate Finance Committee Chairman Furnifold Simmons agreed that the situation had now "materially changed" and the Committee would likely have to consider whether further increases in income and excess profits taxes were necessary.[97]

Part of the reason for justifying new legislation as a response to unexpected increases in projected expenditures was that it appeared to violate a tacit agreement that any new revenue legislation would be pushed back until December 1918. Congressional Democrats feared the political backlash in fall elections if they forwarded additional tax increases, and Treasury officials had agreed that the bill would likely be much worse if subjected to the partisan pressures of reelection politics. After McAdoo's letter to Simmons was made public, Representative Henry Rainey wrote to him explaining that "you cannot find a single Democrat in the North who would consider his place in the House secure if another tax bill is passed at this session."[98] Republicans also were wary of new legislation, with several minority members of the Senate Finance Committee arguing that the bill could wait until December. Even Senator Smoot, who had been one of the loudest congressional critics of the 1917 act, argued that since revenues from a new bill would not be received before the spring of 1919 at the earliest and the most significant of the new expenditures would not be incurred before the beginning of 1919, revenue legislation could wait.[99] Eventually, McAdoo and congressional leaders found themselves at a stalemate, with the Treasury Secretary continuing to call for a new revenue bill, and members of Congress, perhaps emboldened by recent evidence that the Treasury had overestimated expenditures and underestimated revenues for the first nine months of the fiscal year, resisting any tax increase legislation.[100]

The push for a new revenue bill might have stalled completely had not President Wilson stepped in to jump-start the process. In a virtually unprecedented move, Wilson defied the majority leaders of his own party and supported McAdoo's call for a new revenue bill in an address to a joint session of Congress on May 27, 1918.[101] In his address, Wilson famously declared that "politics is adjourned" and emphasized the need for fiscal sacrifice. He explained that "the people of this country are not only united in the resolute purpose to win this war, but are ready and willing to bear any burden and undergo any sacrifice that it may be necessary for them to bear in order to win it. We need not be afraid to tax them, if we lay taxes justly." Wilson recommended "war profits and incomes and luxuries for the additional taxes," noting that "the profiteering that cannot be got at by the restraints of conscience and love of country can be got at by taxation." "There is such profiteering now," Wilson continued, "and the information with regard to it is available and indisputable."[102] His use of the term "war profits" rather than "excess profits" was judged to be a nod in favor of replacing the invested capital base with the war profits base recommended by the Treasury and industry.[103]

Secretary McAdoo followed up Wilson's speech with a letter to House Ways and Means Chairman Claude Kitchin outlining his suggestions for a new revenue bill. With a goal of raising a third of the projected $24 billion in new expenditures through taxes, McAdoo advocated adding a war profits tax to the existing excess profits tax levy, with businesses paying whichever tax was higher. While the 1917 act had incorporated an aspect of the war profits principle in its exemption, it remained fundamentally a high-profits tax and often failed to reach war profits. McAdoo proposed adopting a "real war profits tax at a high rate," perhaps approaching the 80 percent levy applied in Great Britain, plus amending the existing excess profits tax "to remove inequalities." Because, according to McAdoo, "there is a popular demand that all the people should contribute to financing the war," he also recommended taxing unearned income at a higher rate than earned income and subjecting luxury purchases to high excise taxes. Interestingly, his justification for the higher tax on unearned incomes was that this would "exempt the patriotic purchasers of Liberty bonds on their holdings," while "weighing heavily upon the shirkers who have not bought them."[104] Since debt financing would cover two-thirds of the projected expenses under McAdoo's plan, this aspect of his proposal was designed more to motivate bond purchasers than to raise tax revenue.

McAdoo emphasized that his proposals would involve sacrifices, but he characterized these as "sacrifices of a relatively insignificant sort as compared with the sacrifices our soldiers and sailors are making to save the life of the nation."[105] This call for fiscal sacrifice struck a positive chord with the public. One persistent concern during this period was that the war was a "capitalist war"—one designed to promote the welfare of capital rather than spread democracy. While the high surtax rates may have hit the super-rich quite hard—with John D. Rockefeller reportedly projected to owe more than $38 million in taxes as a result of the War Revenue Act of 1917—the popular suspicion was that wealthy businesses and their owners were not ultimately paying their fair share.[106] The consensus was that fiscal sacrifice had to be broadened. As the *New York Times* wrote, "Already the task of war has been faced by America in sacrifices of food, in raising armies, in sending men to the front, in a death list that begins to grow by the hundreds. It is now beginning to be faced in terms of money."[107] The *Bellman* echoed this sentiment, noting that the American people "realize what this involves in financial expenditure and sacrifice, and are ready to face the cost, whatever it may prove to be."[108] Some even suggested a reverse causality—not only were existing sacrifices used to justify fiscal sacrifice, but fiscal sacrifice was justified as a tool to demonstrate the need to sacrifice elsewhere, such as by curtailing the consumption of luxury items.[109]

The endorsement of higher tax burdens on war profits was particularly well-received in many quarters. According to the liberal journal the *Public,* this aspect of President Wilson's address had been "hailed with intense satisfaction by the very large number of citizens who have felt that the one weak spot in our war program was our failure to adequately conscript excess profits and surplus income."[110] In a speech delivered a month or so after President Wilson's address, Secretary of Labor William L. Wilson used the commitment to high surtax rates and a strong excess profits tax as convincing evidence (as far as American wage earners were concerned) that "this is not a capitalist war, but that this is a war for democracy and for the maintenance of the right to work at our own destinies in our own way."[111] Even Food Administrator Herbert Hoover joined the chorus in support of war profits taxation, writing in a letter to Senate Finance Committee Chairman Simmons, "it is abhorrent to all decent people" that any man profits because his products are needed for war or because of the resulting scarcity, especially "when the youth of the nation are being called upon to sacrifice all that they have."[112]

While congressional leaders grudgingly acceded to President Wilson's call for new revenue legislation, "politics," remarked Randolph Paul, "was not adjourned."[113] A substantial rift developed over the nature of the excess profits tax under the bill. House Ways and Means Chairman Claude Kitchin remained steadfast in favoring an excess profits tax relying upon an invested capital base. While McAdoo had attempted to straddle the fence in proposing the retention of a modest excess profits tax alongside a new war profits tax, this compromise was viewed as far from satisfactory. According to Kitchin, the war profits tax could exempt as many as 130 large corporations from tax liability, resulting in a drop in revenue of as much as $500 million. Kitchin claimed that many large, highly profitable businesses, such as Ford Motor Car Company, Standard Oil, and United States Steel, had higher profits before the war than during the war. At the same time, Kitchin argued that higher "war profits" were often the result of inflation and supply and demand rather than "deliberately planned and manipulated profiteering."[114]

Even business interests were not entirely of one mind on the issue of the proper base for profits taxation. James Emery, representing the National Association of Manufacturers, the National Industrial Conference Board, and 19 national trade associations, testified in favor of replacing the excess profits tax with a war profits tax. Under his proposal, the tax would be levied upon profits in excess of the average of the three prewar years selected by the taxpayer between 1911 and 1915 to constitute the base. By contrast, the State Associations of Manufacturers preferred to retain the invested capital base for the excess profits tax.[115]

What united most witnesses testifying before the House, despite paying lip service to fiscal sacrifice, was the desire to cut their taxes under any new legislation. The National Retail Dry Goods Association supported a war profits tax, but at tax rates between 8 and 10 percent. This would have placed them far below even the lowest existing excess profits tax rates of 20 percent. The U.S. Chamber of Commerce supported a war profits tax at rates as high as 80 percent but called for liberal exemptions, including for the amortization of any costs associated with building new plants. The State Association of Manufacturers conditioned its support for the excess profits tax on an increase in the exemption from 8 to 10 percent of invested capital, while others suggested greatly expanding the definition of invested capital. Insurance companies argued that their investment income should be exempt from the excess profits tax because of state-imposed limits on the types of investment instruments available to them, and banking interests argued for the deductibility of interest payments, the exemption of intercorporate dividend payments, and the amortization of goodwill and the removal of borrowed amounts from the excess profits base. On the proposed luxury taxes, the National Automobile Chamber of Commerce sought to shift the burden from manufacturers to automobile owners. Even Hollywood stars got into the act through the testimony of the Motion Picture War Service Association. In stark contrast to the patriotic fashion in which such Association officers as Mary Pickford, Charlie Chaplin, and Douglas Fairbanks promoted Liberty Bonds and the timely filing of income tax returns, the Association contended that the "intangible capital" of its members should be exempt from tax during this period of high surtax rates. Instead, unearned income should be taxed more heavily. Members of the Ways and Means Committee became exasperated by these attempts to avoid or shift the war tax burden, especially since most businesses would likely pass along the cost of the tax to their customers.[116]

Initially, the House Ways and Means Committee sided with Kitchin in favor of maintaining the invested capital base for an excess profits tax. Members indicated that they were concerned a high war profits tax would hinder the expansion of productive capacity and injure businesses at a time they were needed for the war effort. According to Kitchin, "the Ways and Means Committee wishes to write a revenue bill that will get those who profited before the war as well as those who are still profiteering. But the Treasury wants to get only present profiteers, and let those who profiteered before the war escape."[117]

Nevertheless, there was both external and internal pressure to adopt the war profits tax. As Committee deliberations proceeded, McAdoo sent a telegram to Kitchin invoking the fiscal sacrifice theme as a justification for moving to a war profits tax base:

> The patriotic producers of America should be content if one-fifth of their war profits are secured to them, especially when we reflect that the men who are fighting and dying in France to save the liberties of those who stay at home and to make it possible for them to continue in business, are limited by act of Congress to $396

per year for their services and to have to give their blood in the bargain. Should we be more partial and tender to those who are protected in safety at home than we are to those who make the supreme sacrifices for us in the field of battle?[118]

Republican Representative William Green of Iowa, author of one of the war tax proposals then circulating, predicted "Congress will adopt some plan to reach big corporations like the packers, some copper companies, and other concerns very highly capitalized before we started in with the present system of income and excess profits."[119]

A Compromise over Profits Taxation

The pressure in favor of a war profits tax base apparently made an impression. Kitchin eventually conceded that the Ways and Means Committee would accept a compromise that included McAdoo's war profits tax as a complement to the existing excess profits tax, but only on the condition that the excess profits tax rates as applied to lower classes of such profits be raised from 20 percent to between 40 and 60 percent. Under this proposed compromise, the top excess rates would go unchanged, but the profits taxes would apply to corporations only.[120] According to the House report on the bill, this latter restriction was designed to acknowledge that partners and individuals were subject to the high individual surtax rates, while corporate stockholders could avoid such rates by causing the corporation to retain its funds.[121]

Kitchin's face-saving compromise failed to save face. In a letter to Kitchin, McAdoo explained that the higher rates at the lower profit levels were unacceptable because they would work a significant hardship on small businesses. Kitchin reportedly "appeared provoked at the attitude taken by Secretary McAdoo," but he was losing his sway over the Ways and Means Committee. According to one member, "we know perfectly well that Mr. McAdoo is going to have his way, either in the bill we write or in the Senate bill." This member opined that "we might as well bow to his wishes gracefully, rather than keep up the losing struggle against his dictation."[122] Rather than force Kitchin to accept defeat, however, the Committee permitted the matter to proceed to the full House, where the bill was quickly approved on September 20 and sent to the Senate.

While Kitchin ultimately persuaded the House to retain the invested capital base, the Senate was more amenable to a switch to a war profits tax. Insurgent Republican Senator William Borah had insisted that hearings be held immediately after the president's speech to investigate the president's claims of profiteering, advocating that the country "follow the example of Great Britain and fix a tax on war profits of 70 percent, if not more." "The Government ought to help itself to the enormous profit made by corporations out of the war," Borah declared. "The people will not be satisfied unless that is done."[123] There were, of course, critics of both forms of profit tax—most notably Republican standpatter Henry Cabot Lodge of Massachusetts—but such critics were in the minority.[124]

The excess profits tax was not the only object of criticism in the House bill. Some also criticized the bill for targeting the rich almost exclusively. Senator Smoot advocated putting at least some of the tax on consumption, and a variety of publications, including the *New York Times,* suggested it would have been more just to have spread the burden to a larger percentage of the population.[125] The *Journal of Commerce* went so far as to describe the bill as having a "strong flavor of socialism" because of its "apparent disposition to strike at 'wealth.' "[126] Even the proposed luxury taxes drew the ire of some observers. Mary Sargent Potter objected to the taxation of servants, noting that it added "insult to injury" for the "already distraught housewife facing problems in economy and conservation which, if the desired results are to be achieved, tax her time, attention, and ingenuity to the utmost."[127] Similarly, the artist Merton Grenhagen argued that the application of the luxury tax to sales of art works ignores that "art is born of the masses and shall return to them to bless their scant leisure for enjoyment and contemplation."[128]

These attempts to shift the focus from the rich to a broader cross-section of the population provoked an immediate response. As the editors of the *Public* responded, critics

> overlook the burden already borne by the less fortunate and the poor. They still fail to grasp the fact that war means sacrifice, sacrifice by the nation, and sacrifice by the individual citizens; it means death to men and destruction to property. Conscription has in a sense equalized the loss of life; but a percentage tax on the expenditures of the people would by no means equalize the loss of wealth. . . . The poor spend practically all their income for the necessaries of life. The rich spend only a portion of their income, and a large portion of that is for luxuries that could be given up without any hardship.[129]

The *New Republic* also saw the bill as necessary in order to spread the financial sacrifice to those who had not yet felt it:

> The recipients of small incomes have already exhibited a willingness to make sacrifices for the sake of contributing to the Liberty Loans. They will have to make still

more sacrifices if the government is to raise the sixteen billion needed in addition to the maximum revenues we can raise by taxes upon the more prosperous classes. But the sacrifice will appear to be worthwhile now that by its taxation proposals the government is demonstrating again that the spirit of democracy guides it not only in its war aims, but in its domestic policy as well.[130]

There were some efforts to broaden the burden, such as to expand the reach of the profits taxes to cover individuals and partnerships as well as corporations,[131] but the Senate remained fundamentally focused on wealth.

Although there was reportedly little to no organized effort in the Senate to oppose the specific tax burdens imposed under the House Bill,[132] opponents managed to significantly delay the process in the Senate. Initially, the administration's goal was to finish the bill before the end of September, when the fourth Liberty Loan was scheduled to be launched. When that date passed, there was little to prevent Senate Republicans from putting off a vote on the bill until after the November elections. In the meantime, Republicans fulfilled the fears of congressional Democrats by launching an antitax campaign that successfully linked economic problems with the high taxes enacted during the war. As William McAdoo later recalled, "the unpopularity of the [then still-pending] bill, with its proposal to increase taxes generally and to bear heavily on large corporate and individual incomes, was undoubtedly the most potent factor in the defeat of the Democrats."[133] The resulting change in control in Congress had an obvious impact on the course of negotiations over the revenue bill, but its effect was quickly dwarfed by the end of the war.

Armistice and the Revenue Act of 1918

As the election approached, the war appeared to be nearing a conclusion. Allied troops broke through the Hindenburg line—Germany's last line of fortifications at the western front near the border between France and Belgium—at the end of September, and Bulgaria, Turkey, and Austria-Hungary agreed to armistice at the end of October. Despite these early signs, Congress continued to proceed with revenue negotiations as if the war would continue at least through the next year. Thus, when Kaiser Wilhelm II abdicated and an armistice agreement was signed two days later on November 11, 1918, the nature of the revenue debate changed fairly suddenly.

Within days after armistice, McAdoo severely scaled back his revenue request by $2 billion. The resulting scramble for position on issues that appeared to have been settled reflected the decline of fiscal sacrifice as a rallying cry. In January 1919, for instance, leading New York City department stores and retail establishments, such as Gimbels, Saks, and Bloomingdale's, organized petition drives against the proposed luxury taxes, receiving 50,000 signatures in a single day.[134] Senate Finance Committee Chair Simmons explained that "taxes which can be easily borne amid the feverish activity and patriotic fervor of war times are neither so welcome nor so easily sustained amid the uncertainties, the depreciating inventories, and the falling markets which are apt to mark the approach to peace."[135]

Revenue negotiations looked as if they would continue indefinitely. While the Senate Finance Committee had finally voted the bill out on December 6 and the full Senate approved it on December 23, the Conference Committee still had significant work to do. Because of McAdoo's revised revenue request and the end to the war, the committee had approximately 600 changes to reconcile with the House bill. Moreover, McAdoo's revenue request was not uncontroversial, with Kitchin and others objecting to the reduction. Ironically, many opponents of McAdoo's proposals had switched from demanding reduced rates to objecting to the reduction in tax burden. Randolph Paul explained this conversion in partisan terms, resulting from a minority party eager to restore the funds to the Treasury while leaving the blame for higher taxes with the administration and the lame duck majority in Congress.[136]

After a bitterly contested Conference Committee negotiation, a compromise was reached on February 1, and Wilson signed into law the Revenue Act of 1918 a few weeks later. Income and profits taxes were counted on for the bulk of revenues, with the remainder coming from luxury taxes. The normal rate of tax on incomes in excess of $5,000 was set at 12 percent, and a surtax was levied on amounts above that up to a 65 percent rate on incomes in excess of $1 million. This was not only a large increase in the normal and top surtax rates from the 1917 act, but it lowered the threshold for the top rate by $1 million. As with the 1917 act, incomes below $2,000 for married persons were exempt. For corporations, the Conference Committee rejected the House scheme for taxing retained earnings at a higher rate than distributed earnings. Instead, corporations were subject to the normal rate of 12 percent in 1918, although it was scheduled to drop to 10 percent in 1919. Robert Haig, recalling Edwin Seligman's comment that the 1917 act's rates were the highest ever achieved "in the annals of civilization," noted that "the 1918 law far outstrips these rates."[137]

The most closely watched conference deliberations were those concerning profits taxation. The Conference Committee's war excess profits tax compromise more closely resembled the Senate plan, which meant that the war tax component was much more serious than in the 1917 act. Under this compromise war excess profits tax, corporations were exempt on the first 8 percent of invested capital plus $3,000. On amounts in excess of the exemption, corporations were subject to a 30 percent tax up to 20 percent of invested capital and a 65 percent tax on amounts in excess of 20 percent of invested capital. To incorporate the war profits component, the act imposed an 80 percent tax on net income in excess of the war profits credit, with a deduction for any amount paid under the excess profits portion of the tax. The war profits credit was $3,000 plus the average net income of the corporation between 1911 and 1913, with an adjustment up or down for differences between the average prewar invested capital and the invested capital for the taxable year.[138] The entire profits tax scheme was exceedingly complex, but the fact that it applied only to corporations mitigated this complexity.

Corporations took no great solace in the presence of the war profits tax because it was still accompanied by the more threatening excess profits tax. Because of the end to the war, the war profits tax was primarily a backward-looking tax. The excess profits tax was the more relevant provision. Counsel for the Investment Bankers Association of America complained that while a profits tax could be justified as a wartime exigency, "the moment we begin to view such a tax as a possible socialistic or experimental limitation of business profits, we are entirely outside of the field of legal thought or sound principle." One corporate executive argued that "in an effort to be fair to individuals, partnerships, and very large corporations, the bill strikes at the very heart of the great middle class of merchants and manufacturers operating as corporations." The theory was that individuals and partnerships were exempt from the excess profits tax under the Senate bill and act as passed, while large corporations were in a better position to manipulate the "invested capital" standard through watered stock, trademarks, and other intangible assets.[139]

Some observers suggest that the president and the Treasury might have completely replaced the excess profits tax with a war profits base if the war had continued, but the cessation of hostilities undercut the principal motivation for this change. Part of the reason the excess profits tax was not repealed at the end of the war was because the Eighteenth Amendment was ratified on January 16, 1919, and prohibited the sale of alcohol the following year. This was expected to cost the federal government approximately $1 billion in revenues.[140] Thus, unlike the Civil War, where the country relied on excise taxes on liquor to fund much of the postwar activities, Congress had to find another source of revenues after World War I. The continuation of the excess profits tax offered a ready alternative.

Transition to Peace

Tax reform was a frequent topic of conversation during the immediate postwar period. Just like the Civil War, the end of the conflict brought an end to much of the patriotic fervor that had fueled sentiments of fiscal sacrifice. At the same time, however, the cost of the war was still being paid and the government's revenue needs would remain high for several years. As one contemporary publication observed, "No peace for the taxpayer was provided by the armistice which ended the war; indeed, the horrors of war from the viewpoint of the man who pays the bills would seem to be if anything increasing rather than diminishing."[141] The Treasury floated an additional bond offering, called the "Victory Loan," to address short-term fiscal needs, but a more permanent successor to loan financing was necessary. While the tariff theoretically became a viable revenue source once again after the cessation of hostilities, the rapid expansion of the income and excess profits taxes had changed the political inevitability of that source of revenue. As early as 1914, tariff revenues dipped below internal excise taxes for the first time. By 1918, the tariff was a distant third behind income and profits taxes and internal excises in raising federal revenues.[142] Moreover, the end of the war reinvigorated the partisan nature of tax policymaking.

Initially, reformers' focus was on excess profits taxation and the high surtaxes on individual income. These two sources had accounted for the bulk of revenues during the war, and this continued in the immediate postwar economy. In 1920, income and excess profits taxes resulted in $4 billion in receipts, while excises on luxury items only accounted for $1.5 billion. Because of the high exemption levels, the income tax was primarily targeted at the well-off, with only 5.5 million returns filed in a population of 106 million people in 1920.[143] Opponents of income and profits taxation pushed to explore other streams of revenue that would help broaden the tax base and shift the focus from the soak-the-rich campaign of the war.

As part of that search for alternative revenue sources, national trade groups and other business lobbying groups marshaled support for a sales tax during consideration of the Revenue Act of 1921. At the very least, they hoped the sales tax would replace the war excess profits tax enacted in the Revenue Act of 1918. Business leaders had always feared that the excess profits tax would remain a permanent part of the revenue system after the war ended, and some government and academic circles supported continuing the tax indefinitely.

Many proponents, however, hoped that a sales tax could also replace the income tax. Despite the introduction of the first peacetime income tax after the ratification of the Sixteenth Amendment in 1913, the income tax still did not seem anything more than an emergency measure. Sales tax proponents understood the need for an income tax during the war, but as prominent businessman Charles Lord explained in a speech to the National Industrial Conference Board,

> The emergency . . . is past and we should promptly discard a theory of taxation which is both so uncertain and working so many evil results, and should seek a method which will be surer in its incidence, more equitable in its operation [and] simpler in its collection. . . . Can such a way be found? Certainly; as soon as we commence to tax what people spend instead of what they save, we are on the right road.[144]

Ardent excess profits tax opponent Senator Reed Smoot proposed a temporary sales tax in the spring of 1921.[145] This proposal was heavily debated by the Senate Finance Committee, and hearings on it took place over several weeks. After evenly divided witness testimony on the sales tax, it was defeated by only one vote. While many business leaders favored the tax, others opposed it, especially in retail trades, where it could deter sales by raising prices. Walter Liggett, representing the Committee of Manufacturers and Merchants of Chicago, somewhat bombastically declared that "we consider the proposed Smoot sales-tax bill one of the most iniquitous measures that has ever been devised. We consider that the Smoot sales tax is a step backward to the days of the Roman empire."[146]

As an alternative to the income tax, Representative Ogden Mills proposed a graduated spendings tax. Under this proposal, all savings and investments would be deducted from the income tax, leaving only spending to be taxed. According to Mills, the graduated spendings tax "can fairly claim the virtues of the sales tax, being in effect a tax on money spent for consumption, without being regressive in character or laying a disproportionate burden on those least able to bear it."[147] It appeared to be an ideal compromise and certainly had the potential to supply sufficient revenue.

Ultimately, the logic in favor of the graduated spendings tax was unpersuasive to the House Ways and Means Committee, in part because it failed to reflect the principles of the wartime taxes it purported to replace. Representative William F. Stevenson, a Democrat from South Carolina, asked

> I wonder how he [Mills] would think a man like the late Russell Sage was bearing his part of governmental expenses when he was drawing his millions and living on $60 a month or thereabouts, and all of that exempt under the plan of Mr. Mills? . . . I understand very well why he is in favor of this bill. It is because it cuts down the income taxes, it cuts down the big corporate income taxes, it cuts down enormously where he is interested.[148]

Thus, fundamental tax reform, although much discussed, failed to occur. Nevertheless, in the Revenue Acts of 1921 and 1924, Congress repealed the excess profits tax and dramatically reduced the high surtax rates that had been in place during the war. The conventional wisdom is that the decline of fiscal sacrifice as a justification for such measures eased the way for Treasury Secretary Andrew Mellon to implement the major aspects of business's postwar tax program. While this is not inaccurate, it misses the big picture. Mellon persuaded congressional leaders to stick with the income tax rather than adopt the sales tax many business groups pushed. The top rates of the income tax dropped from their wartime highs of 77 percent to a more modest 25 percent by 1925, but this was still more than double the prewar rates for the income tax. Moreover, one of the other wartime provisions that targeted the wealthy—the estate tax—remained a significant feature of the revenue system, and corporate tax rates actually increased during the 1920s. As contested as the concept of fiscal sacrifice may have been during the course of the war, its underlying principles of progressivity and ability-to-pay taxation endured in peacetime tax politics during the 1920s.

4

World War II

"It is our duty to see that the burden is equitably distributed according to ability to pay so that a few do not gain from the sacrifices of the many."
—President Franklin D. Roosevelt

I f there is an ideal model in the American political psyche for what constitutes "wartime fiscal sacrifice," that model derives from the country's experience in World War II. Americans remember World War II as "The Good War," a noble struggle to defend freedom and democracy against the perils of tyranny and dictatorship. In popular recollection, this moral clarity has been extended to the homefront as well.[1] The war unleashed a spirit of cooperation and self-sacrifice, we tell ourselves, uniting the country behind dramatically higher taxes.

To be sure, there is some truth to this popular view. Americans did indeed "rally 'round the flag" during World War II, even when it came to new taxes. A Gallup poll from February 1944 asked, "Do you regard the income tax which you will have to pay this year as fair?" and a remarkable 90 percent answered yes.[2] Upon closer inspection, however, World War II was not quite the heroic episode we like to recall, at least not on the homefront. Tax policy during the war reflected not only sacrifice but self-indulgence. It would be wrong to say the era's tax battles amounted to no more than "politics as usual," yet many of the usual features of tax politics characterize the World War II period as much as any other era. "In America," one commentator recently noted, "war does not override the calculus of politics."[3]

This chapter chronicles the politics of tax lawmaking during World War II. As many scholars have noted, World War II brought a sea change in U.S. fiscal policy. The personal income tax, long confined to the upper strata of American society, became mainstream. Between 1939 and 1945, Congress lowered exemptions repeatedly, converting what had long been a "class tax" into a full-fledged "mass tax." The number of taxpayers increased sevenfold during the war, and by 1945, more than 90 percent of American workers were filing income tax returns. At the same time, lawmakers significantly increased tax rates, with marginal tax rates peaking at 94 percent. Together, these changes made the personal income tax the workhorse of the federal tax system, its revenue soaring from $1.0 billion in 1939 to $18.4 billion in 1945.[4] By the war's end, the tax was raising 40 percent of total federal revenue, making it the largest source of federal funds. World War II also transformed the American system of taxing business. U.S. corporations paid steep new taxes on their wartime profits, including a regular corporate income tax and a special levy on excess profits. Statutory rates for the latter were very high, reaching 95 percent in 1943, and effective rates exceeded 70 percent for many companies. Over the course of the war, corporate taxes provided almost a third of wartime revenue.

Americans accepted the burdens of this wartime tax regime with remarkable equanimity. But the pain of wartime taxation was not unmitigated, and political dealmaking over special tax breaks continued throughout the war. Wartime legislation may have boosted the burden on most Americans, but tax laws also included relief for many taxpayers. For example, debates over the scope and propriety of tax relief figured prominently in a high-stakes controversy that erupted between Congress and the president over the Revenue Act of 1943. On February 22, 1944, two days into the "Big Week" of major U.S. bombing missions over Germany, Roosevelt vetoed the bill, complaining that it was "not a tax bill but a tax relief bill providing relief not for the needy but for the greedy." Roosevelt insisted throughout the war that lawmakers were relying too heavily on debt, avoiding the heavier taxes that sound finance required. He was particularly unhappy with the congressional preference for what he viewed as regressive taxes, complaining that lawmakers were too eager to spare the rich and soak the poor. Like many other political leaders, Roosevelt believed that Americans should dig even deeper to foot the bill for fighting fascism. But the president and Congress increasingly disagreed on precisely which Americans should be making the fiscal sacrifice. Popular accounts of the World War II era underplay these disagreements in favor of themes of unity and shared sacrifice. By contrast, our account highlights the fiscal dissensus of the war years in an effort to put a more realistic frame on the country's experience with wartime taxes.

Our analysis focuses on several key legislative enactments during and immediately preceding the war, including the second Revenue Act of 1940, the Revenue Act of 1941, the Revenue Act of 1942, the Current Tax Payment Act of 1943, and the Revenue Act of 1943. In combination, these acts not only raised much of the revenue required to finance the war in Europe and Asia but reshaped the basic architecture of the American tax system. Understanding the politics that resulted in the passage of these acts opens a window through which one can view what is perhaps the most important episode in the American experience with wartime fiscal sacrifice.

Tax Policy in the Shadow of War: 1940–41

The ratification of the Sixteenth Amendment to the U.S. Constitution in 1913 enabled Congress to impose an income tax unrestricted by the requirement of article I, section 8, that direct taxes be apportioned. As chapter 3 noted, that important legal change set the stage for the transformation of the federal tax base during World War I, when Congress turned to the income tax as a principal source of revenue to fund the war effort. Reliance on the income tax continued through the 1920s during the Harding, Coolidge, and Hoover administrations. Yet throughout this period, the income tax remained a levy reserved for the only the wealthiest members of society. In 1929, on the eve of the great stock market crash, only 3 percent of Americans age 20 and over paid income taxes.[5]

Given the dramatic expansion of the federal government during the New Deal years, one might have expected an increased reliance on the income tax. For most of the 1930s, however, such a change found little support among congressional Democrats. Senator Robert M. La Follette, Jr., a maverick progressive Republican, championed the idea throughout the decade, and he had considerable support among his GOP colleagues. Yet the necessary political support for La Follette's reforms never materialized. Thus, while the New Deal featured important reforms, including steep new income taxes on the rich, heavy estate levies, and a novel tax on corporate profits designed to stem tax avoidance and regulate the size and structure of private enterprise, by late 1938, conservative critics had stymied the New Deal tax agenda and there seemed little chance for expanding the income tax base.[6]

World War II changed all of this. Recent estimates put the overall budgetary cost of the war at $4.8 trillion in constant 2003 dollars.[7] To put this figure into context, consider that this is more than 8 times the cost of World War I (estimated at $588 billion) and nearly 12 times the cost of the Korean War (estimated at $408 billion). Alternatively, consider that in 1940 total federal government outlays accounted for 9.8 percent of gross domestic product (GDP), while in 1943, by contrast, government expenditures equaled 43.6 percent of GDP.[8] Expenditures of this magnitude simply could not be sustained by relying on a single method of war finance. It is not surprising, then, that the U.S. government turned to a mix of financing techniques, including substantial reliance on governmental borrowing and printing money.[9] Yet new taxes played a major role in funding the U.S. war effort.

Financing Rearmament in 1940

Long before the Japanese attack on Pearl Harbor on December 7, 1941, lawmakers began to put the country's fiscal machinery on a war footing. In the first six months of 1940, as German armies swept across Northern Europe, Roosevelt sent Congress a series of military spending requests, each bigger than the last. On May 16, the president asked for $1.2 billion; on May 30, citing the "incredible events" over the prior two weeks, he asked for another $1.3 billion.[10] As lawmakers cast about for ways to pay those bills, the Treasury urged a cut in income tax exemptions, invoking the need for sacrifice. "I am convinced that the public is willing and ready to accept the personal sacrifices of paying the additional taxes that are necessary to provide the country with adequate national defense," Treasury Secretary Henry Morgenthau told Congress. In fact, unsolicited contributions had been arriving at Treasury for weeks, with Americans volunteering amounts from 10 cents to $500.[11]

On June 25, 1940, Congress passed the first of what would prove to be two revenue acts enacted that year. While the most significant wartime tax legislation was yet to come, both of these new laws represented major new tax increases at the time. The First Revenue Act of 1940 cut exemptions by a fifth; individuals were taxed on income over $800, rather than $1,000, while couples paid on anything over $2,000, rather then $2,500. Lawmakers expected the cut to create 2 million new taxpayers and to raise about $75 million. Treasury acknowledged that the lower threshold for returns would raise enforcement costs; each return cost between

$0.50 and $1.56 to process, depending on its complexity. But officials believed that lower exemptions would also boost compliance among those already liable under the higher exemptions. Jolted into awareness by the new exemption cuts, taxpayers previously on the margin of taxability would probably pay up, offsetting the $8 million in new administrative costs.[12]

In addition to lowering exemptions, the first 1940 law raised surtax rates across the board. The biggest hikes in the surtax rates were in the lower and lower-middle brackets, but taxpayers earning between $6,000 and $100,000 also saw major increases. The rate hikes were expected to raise $177 million. Corporate income tax rates were also raised slightly in this legislation. Firms were now subject to three brackets of 15, 17, and 19 percent, with the top rate applied to corporations with more than $25,000 in net income. Finally, the law imposed a special 10 percent "defense surtax" on almost every internal revenue levy. This "supertax" was slated to expire in five years, while the exemption cuts and regular rate hikes were permanent.[13] Altogether, the first Revenue Act of 1940 raised $1.2 billion in new federal revenue, representing 0.91 percent of GDP and 15.3 percent of total federal receipts.[14]

The income tax revisions of the 1940 bill were surprisingly uncontroversial. Almost no one objected to the exemption cuts or the rate hikes. To be sure, business groups warned that steep surtaxes diminished the incentive to work, and labor groups complained about any broadening of the tax base. But most people swallowed hard and accepted the heavier taxes with minimal complaint. Congress had deferred the heavy work, though. The increases had been mostly to existing taxes, and the call for sacrifice was still limited and, in some respects, voluntary. The most controversial provision in the first Revenue Act of 1940—an excess profits tax on business—had been deferred for consideration later in the year.

Excess Profits Taxation, Conscription, and "Taking the Profits out of War"

Excess profits taxation, which had been a staple of World War I finance, was about more than raising sufficient revenues to fund the war effort. It was about transitioning from relying on the public's willingness to sacrifice (as Morgenthau praised) to the first stage of a program of compelled sacrifice—one that specifically targeted those enjoying special benefits as a result of the war preparation. In one of his famed fireside chats, on May 22, 1940, President Roosevelt admonished the country not to see the European war as a source of opportunity: "I don't want to see a single war millionaire created in the United States as a result of this world disaster." In keeping with this sentiment, Roosevelt believed that taxes on war-related profits were a vital weapon in the battle against profiteering, and many lawmakers shared his conviction.

In early July 1940, in the wake of the Nazi occupation of Paris, Roosevelt revived the push for the excess profits tax that had stalled during the consideration of the first Revenue Act of 1940. On Monday, July 1, exactly one week after France's official surrender to Germany, the president submitted his proposal to Congress, seeking approval of legislation for a "steeply graduated" excess profits tax. Worried that Roosevelt's own Treasury would resist the idea, the White House sent Congress a terse, 89-word message requesting the tax. "We are asking even our humblest citizens to contribute their mite," Roosevelt declared. "It is our duty to see that the burden is equitably distributed according to ability to pay so that a few do not gain from the sacrifices of the many."[15]

It is hard to imagine many would disagree with such bromides, and even business leaders accepted the excess profits tax, at least in theory. "To the best of my knowledge, no business executive opposes the principle of an excess profits tax which seeks to return to government exorbitant profits arising directly or indirectly from the war effort," wrote tax lawyer George Douglas.[16] Immediately after deleting it from the bill in June, Congress adopted a resolution recommending the adoption of an excess profits tax "as soon as possible."[17] Yet as with most tax policy, the devil was in the details. The reason it had been deferred in the first bill was to address such details, in particular the important question of exactly which profits should be considered "excess." What portion of a company's income should be regarded as a product of the defense emergency rather than normal operations? Congress and the White House disagreed vehemently on this issue, and that rift had important implications for the nature and operation of the excess profits tax.

There were essentially two schools of thought regarding how to approach the issue. Treasury experts proposed a tax that would define excess profits in relation to a "normal" percentage return on invested capital. This normal return might be arbitrarily fixed by government officials, or it might be derived from the prewar returns a taxpaying company enjoys. Many, but not all, tax experts preferred this method, which was the one employed during World War I. By contrast, congressional leaders favored the "average-earnings" method of measuring excess profit. Under this scheme, earnings during the taxable wartime year that exceeded the average earnings during a three-year, prewar base period would be subject to the new tax.[18] The distinction was effectively between a high profits tax and a war profits tax, with the former providing the basis for a permanent excess profits tax and the latter serving as a temporary wartime measure.[19]

For most businesses, significant money was at stake in the legislative choice of which methodology to follow. The predictable result was a heavy lobbying push to give businesses maximum flexibility in calculating the amount of tax owed. As Carl N. Osborne, vice-chairman of the National Association of Manufacturers Committee on Government Finance, delicately explained in his testimony to the House Ways and Means Committee, business supported an excess profits tax, but only if it was "carefully drawn" and not intended to be imposed permanently.[20] Other business leaders offered less delicate testimony. Edgar Gorrell, president of the Air Transport Association of America, appeared before the committee to request a blanket exemption from the excess profits tax for airlines, given their obligation to carry troops and military supplies. New York lawyer Alfred Jaretzki also sought blanket relief from the tax for closed-end diversified investment companies, arguing for parity of treatment with open-end companies that the bill already exempted.[21]

In September of 1940, the first peacetime draft in American history may have helped break the stalemate. To some, the lengthy deliberative process over the taxation of excess profits had become particularly galling in light of the rush to institute conscription. As Democratic Senator Rush Holt of West Virginia complained, "It will be found that these patriots are willing to conscript boys, but when you start talking about drafting wealth, what does the *New York Times* say? It says that we should go slowly on excess profits taxes, that we should go slowly on drafting wealth, but full speed ahead on drafting boys."[22] According to liberal economist Harold Groves, the excess profits tax "was demanded as a monetary counterpart to the sacrifice being made by persons who entered the armed forces."[23]

Within a month after mandating conscription, Congress adopted excess profits taxation. The symbolism was one of compelled sacrifice, but the reality was more business friendly. Under the bill as passed, taxpayers were permitted to choose their preferred method of assessing the tax, subject to certain rate penalties for those selecting the prewar profits technique. Thus, companies with big profits in the averaging period could choose the prewar earnings method and keep making big profits during the war. Corporations making small profits in the averaging years could choose the invested-capital method and preserve their shot at a good return. Meanwhile, a large exemption left all but 70,000 of the 500,000 companies on the tax rolls entirely exempt. The design of the excess profits tax illustrates an important theme from the early stages of World War II. The notion of "sacrifice" had its limits: lawmakers were eager to allow room for business to prosper.[24] Congressional leaders defended their handiwork. "Our taxes must follow the intricacies of business and not attempt to bend business to the pattern of simplicity we should all like to see in taxation," observed Ways and Means Chairman Robert Doughton (D-NC).[25]

It was soon evident that the administration viewed the sacrifice asked of business as still too small. Just days after Congress completed work on the second Revenue Act of 1940, Treasury Secretary Morgenthau casually observed that any business should be satisfied with a 6 percent return on invested capital. To many in the business community, this sounded like a trial balloon for a 100 percent tax rate on all returns over 6 percent. Treasury officials soon backed off this statement, and Morgenthau later claimed it was a slip of the tongue. But in fact, rates would approach that level within a couple of years. Despite the increase in corporate income tax rates and the $900 million the Second Revenue Act of 1940 was expected to raise from the excess profits tax, Congress had only begun to scratch the surface on what would be required. As prominent economists Roy and Gladys Blakey observed in December 1940, "The great present danger appears to be that nearly everybody thinks that billions for preparedness can be provided without costing him much real sacrifice."[26]

The Revenue Act of 1941

Before the dust had settled on the Second Revenue Act of 1940, President Roosevelt moved to eliminate any perception that the war preparations could be achieved painlessly. "I have called for personal sacrifice," Roosevelt told Congress on January 6, 1941, in what came to be known as the "Four Freedoms Speech." "A part of the sacrifice means the payment of more money in taxes." Roosevelt stressed the need for money, but he also refused to compromise his commitment to progressive tax reform; "the principle of tax payments in accordance with ability to pay," he declared, "should be constantly before our eyes to guide our legislation." For Roosevelt, sacrifice and progressivity were inextricably linked. Heavy taxes on the rich would lend legitimacy to the revenue system as a whole, including its more regressive—but remunerative—components. If lawmakers emphasized progressive reform, then Americans would respond nobly, Roosevelt predicted, "putting patriotism ahead of pocketbooks."[27]

Perhaps part of the rationale for the president's wider plea for sacrifice was the recognition that business was quietly softening even the watered-down version of the excess profits tax adopted a few months earlier. The original bill had been enacted with assurances that certain "liberalizing" amendments would be made in due course.[28] By March 1941, Congress adopted amendments designed to relieve hardships caused by plant expansions, abnormal base-period earnings, and other fluctuations businesses contended should not be taken into account in calculating excess profits.[29] These provisions, which were enacted retroactively to the passage of the Second Revenue Act in 1940, brought a deluge of refund claims. Ultimately, some 10,000 claims ended up costing the government about $388 million. This only exacerbated the leakage arising from the tax's basic flexibility. In May 1941, John L. Sullivan, the assistant secretary for tax policy, complained that the availability of the invested-capital and average-earnings methods was eviscerating the tax; one company with $70 million in war orders had paid no excess profits tax whatsoever. Clearly, he declared, the tax was failing in its stated purpose: some companies were making enormous profits from the war.[30]

Thus, in the spring of 1941, Congress set out to shore up the excess profits tax while seeking other avenues for reaching wartime corporate profits. Some proposals for tightening the excess profits tax were shot down,[31] but excess profits rates were raised across the board, establishing a range from 35 to 60 percent.[32] Moreover, in addition to tightening deductions, lawmakers elevated the normal corporate rate from 24 to 31 percent and introduced a new surtax of 6 percent on net income under $25,000 and 7 percent on amounts over that threshold.[33] Consistent with the president's message, the Revenue Act of 1941 did not stop at reaching business profits. With a mounting deficit and aggregate defense expenditures reaching $50 billion, the individual income tax was targeted for another round of across-the-board rate hikes. They now topped out at 77 percent on incomes over $5 million.[34] Additionally, the 1941 Act further lowered the exemption for the income tax to $750 for individuals and $1,500 for couples.

This base-broadening technique was not solely motivated by revenue needs.[35] In a July 31 letter to Ways and Means Chairman Bob Doughton endorsing the lower exemptions, President Roosevelt wrote: "I am convinced that the overwhelming majority of our citizens want to contribute something directly to our defense and that most of them would rather do it with their eyes open than do it through a general sales tax or through a multiplication of what we have known as 'nuisance taxes.' "[36] Echoing his boss, Treasury Secretary Morgenthau predicted that Americans would welcome a broader tax. "It would enable them to feel that they were participating personally and directly in the defense program," he said. Experts predicted that the lower exemptions would result in 5 million new returns filed the next year, increasing the number of returns showing taxable income by over 2 million.[37] This move to spread the sacrifice across a wider range of incomes foreshadowed later developments in the war.

Pearl Harbor and "Total War" Financing: 1942–43

Looking back on the late autumn of 1941, with an awareness of the tumultuous events that would soon follow, it is easy to lose sight of the significance of prewar tax legislation. The Revenue Acts of 1940 and 1941 were massive, unprecedented tax increases, and by early December 1941, congressional leaders expressed the view that a certain political limit on tax increases had been reached. As the *New York Times* reported on December 5, 1941, Senator Walter George, chairman of the Senate Finance Committee, suggested that "federal taxes have now reached 'near-maximum' levels and cannot be increased much more without weakening the whole economy. A similar point of view has recently been expressed by several other authorities on taxation."[38]

Two days later, of course, such sentiments would vanish completely from American political discourse, as the attack on Pearl Harbor ushered in a period of "total war."[39] Military expenditures, which accounted for a sizeable 17.5 and 47.1 percent of total government outlays in 1940 and 1941, respectively, skyrocketed to 73.0 percent in 1942 and as high as 89.5 percent in 1945. The staggering revenue demands of the war changed the very nature of the debate over taxes. Whereas in mid-October "another heavy tax bill had been cold-shouldered out of the congressional picture," after Pearl Harbor new taxes were a political certainty. Four days after the attack, the *New York Times* opined that "by the time elections roll around next November the people will be in no mood to prefer those candidates who affirm that they opposed war taxation."[40]

Shifting Sacrifice in the Aftermath of Pearl Harbor

The legislative story that follows this dramatic turn of events is well known. Major features of the U.S. tax system that we take for granted today—including most prominently a broad-based, individual income tax with wage withholding—were fashioned in the months following the attack on Pearl Harbor. But this transformation of the income tax—its conversion from a "class tax" to a "mass tax"—was never a forgone conclusion. Indeed, the decision to turn to the income tax as the principal revenue engine to fund the war was not at all settled in early 1942. Most significantly, many politicians and opinion leaders preferred a national sales tax, insisting that it would raise much-needed revenue while also curbing inflation. An often unstated advantage, however, was the ability of the sales tax to shift some sacrifice away from the income tax and its focus on higher brackets.

The movement for a national sales tax gained political traction in early 1942. As lawmakers prepared to tackle the most sweeping revenue bill in the nation's history, business groups bombarded Capitol Hill with calls for a retail sales tax. Most urged that a sales tax be used to forestall further hikes in personal income taxes. Others justified the innovation as a replacement for the motley collection of excise taxes. Petitions and letters piled up in congressional offices, and sales tax spokesmen jammed the witness tables at committee hearings. Advocates insisted that a modest sales tax would raise enormous revenue. The National Association of Manufacturers predicted that an 8 percent tax would produce at least $4.4 billion annually. The National Retail Dry Goods Association called for a retail sales levy, pointing out that such a position was pretty noble for a bunch of storeowners.[41]

Congress seemed to be listening. Throughout the spring of 1942, press reports indicated growing support for some sort of sales tax. House and Senate leaders seemed open to the idea, while the two tax-writing committees were reported to be well along in their planning for such a tax. Talk of a sales tax grew so agitated that some observers managed to convince themselves that the White House was behind it all. "A federal sales tax is in the works," predicted *Time* magazine. "The entire body of New Deal thinking, which long opposed sales taxes as a burden on the poor, has switched completely."[42]

In fact, however, the Roosevelt administration was adamantly opposed to the sales tax. From the Oval Office to the Treasury, no administration official wanted anything to do with it. Together, political leaders and technical officials marshaled a powerful campaign to discredit the idea. Treasury experts had long insisted that general sales taxes were unfair, unnecessary, and unworkable. When levied on consumer goods, a sales tax burdened necessities and luxuries alike. Excise taxes were easier to target at appropriate goods, ameliorating the regressive quality inherent in more general consumption taxes. On April 14, 1942, Roosevelt asked the Treasury to prepare talking points on the sales tax, with an eye toward deflecting the idea. Economist Roy Blough obliged him with a memo on the "Evils of the Sales Tax" that stressed its inequities while scoring the levy for its heavy administrative burden.[43]

While sales taxes promised to raise more revenue than selective excises, they were much less productive than many advocates suggested. "The sales tax advocates were romantics about the amount of revenue the tax would yield," remembered Randolph Paul. While ostensibly levied on all consumer expenditures, the tax actually drew from a much smaller base. Out of more than $80 billion in total annual spending during the war, Paul estimated, roughly $30 billion went to services, which were considered untaxable. An exemption for food reduced the base even further to $30 billion. To raise $5 billion in revenue, then, lawmakers would have to approve a tax of 17 percent—far more than even the levy's champions would support.[44]

Organized labor opposed the sales tax, repeatedly and emphatically. In 1942, Congress of Industrial Organizations President Philip Murray denounced the idea as "shocking," calling instead for a modest expansion of the income tax and steep additional levies on wealth and business income. Sacrifice was all well and good, but labor leaders wanted more of it to come from the nation's elite. Murray stated his feelings in bold terms. "In peacetime, a sales tax is vicious enough," he declared, "but in wartime, when we are trying to assure our war workers of sufficient funds to maintain themselves, the proposed sales tax levy would be the equivalent of a military defeat."[45]

But still, the pressure for sales taxation continued to mount. Experts from the Joint Committee on Internal Revenue Taxation offered several plans, as did the Treasury Department. At least two Democrats on the Ways and Means Committee were sold on the idea. On the Senate Finance Committee, Senators Arthur Vandenberg (R-MI) and Harry Byrd (D-VA) mounted a bipartisan campaign for the tax. The committee chairman reported that more than half his members were sympathetic.[46]

But Franklin Roosevelt never wavered. Time and again, when asked by reporters to reconsider his position, the president expressed his opposition to the idea. Administration officials were not optimistic about their ability to stop the sales tax drive. In the spring of 1942, internal memoranda from the Treasury's tax division took some sort of sales tax as a given. In the end, however, presidential opposition, combined with pressure from labor groups, tipped the balance of political opinion. It was a near thing, especially in the Senate. Randolph Paul later remarked that the absence of a sales tax from the Revenue Act of 1942 was one of the most striking aspects of the law. When forced to make a choice, however, lawmakers lined up with the president, choosing to focus on income, not consumption taxes. It was a fateful decision, shaping the federal revenue system—and the American economy—for decades to come.[47]

P.L. 77-753: The "Greatest Tax Bill in American History"

With the sales tax failing to take hold, Congress turned to the individual income tax as the major source of war revenue. Changes to the income tax during the war years were dramatic. The individual income tax saw its share of total revenue climb from 13.6 percent to 40.7 percent. Between 1940 and 1945, it raised more than $163.8 billion, its annual yield soaring from $13.6 billion to $40.7 billion.[48] Over the course of the war, lawmakers made the income tax broader and steeper. They slashed exemptions repeatedly, bringing millions of new taxpayers into the system. But they also raised rates across the board, especially on high-income households. For many political leaders, including President Roosevelt, these changes formed the crux of a crucial bargain: new taxes on the poor and middle class had to be balanced by heavy taxes on the rich.

Notwithstanding the seemingly inevitable focus on the income tax, Congress did not abandon the commitment to excess profits taxation after Pearl Harbor. Roosevelt himself initially returned to the excess profits tax, calling for more stringent rules to ensure that companies shared the burden of wartime sacrifice. "Excessive profits undermine unity and should be recaptured," he declared in his January 1942 budget message. "The fact that a corporation had large profits before the defense program started is no reason to exempt them now."[49] Perhaps recognizing the need to deflect criticism of unequal sacrifice, even the National Association of Manufacturers endorsed a proposal to abandon the graduated rate structure for the excess profits tax and impose a 90 percent levy.[50] Still, business was restive under the burden. Treasury's top tax official, Randolph Paul, complained that after an initial burst of patriotism, business enthusiasm faded dramatically over the course of the war. And certainly, business leaders were vocal in their support for moving more of the burden onto individuals rather than businesses. Often, they used inflation to bolster their case, cloaking their quest for lower taxes in the mantle of macroeconomic responsibility. Thus, Congress had to find new forms of revenue, and the income tax was the most likely source.

In March 1942, Morgenthau offered Congress a blueprint for income tax hikes on an unprecedented scale. "Our task is more than the raising of a huge amount of new revenue," he told lawmakers. "It is to make the tax program an instrument of victory."[51] Congress agreed, crafting a dramatic and far-reaching bill. Roosevelt later called the Revenue Act of 1942 the "greatest tax bill in American history," and the description may still be apt more than 60 years later. This sweeping measure is often credited with creating the modern U.S. tax regime. While it shares that distinction with several other pieces of wartime legislation, it was certainly the most important tax law of the war.

Initially, Morgenthau declined to recommend further exemption cuts, insisting that Americans making less than $15 a week were already heavily burdened (especially given the range of wartime excise taxes). Moreover, people exempt from the income tax were not a threat to price stability: "Their buying habits are governed strictly by the need of maintaining nutrition and health." The secretary did, however, suggest a series of rate hikes for the income tax, ranging from less than 0.5 percent in the bottom bracket to more than 16 percent in the middle and upper reaches of the levy.[52]

Roosevelt's newfound ardor for sacrifice, however, was not yet exhausted. On May 6, Morgenthau reluctantly suggested that exemptions be cut to $600 for individuals, $1,200 for couples, and $300 for dependents. The reductions would raise about $1 billion in new revenue and add about 7 million taxpayers to the rolls. Inflation worries lay behind some of these changes. "Prices were surging against their controls with the force of an angry sea," recalled Randolph Paul. Leon Henderson told lawmakers than steep new taxes were absolutely vital if the country were to avoid ruinous inflation in the next year, and Treasury experts agreed, urging Morgenthau to demand huge new hikes.[53]

Many observers hailed the exemption cuts as a moral and economic necessity. *New York Times* columnist Arthur Krock mused hopefully on the "spiritual values" that flowed from wartime sacrifice. "In the tales of heroism and fortitude from the battlefronts, in the rationing and confiscation of such accessories to pleasure as gasoline, in the tax plans designed to give every American the privilege of direct sacrifice for the conduct of the war, are the materials of these values," he wrote. Extending the income tax to the middle class appealed to many observers, who worried that too many Americans were escaping this crucial burden of citizenship.[54] Others, however, were more cynical. "All parties in interest—the workers, the farmers, the investors, the business and financial leaders—insist upon a different pattern for distributing the inevitable sacrifices of the war," complained Columbia economics professor Robert Haig.[55]

For his part, Roosevelt preferred broader income taxation to most alternatives, including consumption taxes. But he was still very keen on taxing the rich; his penchant for high-end sacrifice remained intact. On April 27, he added an item to his fiscal wish list, asking Congress for a cap on personal income. "In time of this great national danger," he declared, "when all excess income should go to win the war, no American citizen ought to have a net income, after he has paid his taxes, of more than $25,000 a year."[56] The suggestion caused a firestorm of protest, despite— or perhaps because of—its narrow focus; the lofty income threshold (equal to roughly $300,000 in 2005 dollars) would have left only 11,000 Americans subject to the tax, according to the Treasury. Congress largely ignored the idea, and it soon disappeared from serious discussion. But the income cap demonstrated FDR's powerful commitment to taxing the rich, especially after wartime imperatives forced new burdens on the poor and middle class.[57]

When finally enacted, the Revenue Act of 1942 cut exemptions to $1,200, $500, and $350 for couples, individuals, and dependents, respectively. The "normal" tax increased from 4 to 6 percent, and surtaxes went up in every bracket. The first surtax rate more than doubled from 6 to 13 percent. But at the peak of the income scale, the changes were even more dramatic. The top rate climbed from 77 to 82 percent. Even more important, the brackets were readjusted to make this top rate applicable to a much larger percentage of national income. Under the 1941 law, the top rate kicked in at $5 million in annual income. But in 1942, the new, higher rate started at just $200,000. A single taxpayer earning $1 million would see her tax climb from $655,139 to $809,995. A married couple with the same income would see a similar hike. Clearly, rich Americans were being asked to pay handsomely, even as middle-class Americans were struggling to complete their first round of income tax returns.[58]

"Taxes to Beat the Axis"—Marketing the Mass Tax to the Masses

Officials recognized that the expansion of the income tax base meant they had to undertake a massive public relations campaign to advise new taxpayers of their fiscal responsibilities. Polling data suggested many Americans were blithely unaware of their new fiscal responsibilities. A Gallup poll in early 1943 had found a third to half of respondents were unclear about their obligations.[59] Morgenthau and his staff worried that a wholesale failure to file would threaten not just revenues, but the tax system itself. The "Victory Tax" had been so called to associate fiscal sacrifice more directly with the results on the battlefield, but this was only a small taste of the efforts to encourage people to file returns. They unveiled a broad outreach campaign featuring posters, radio announcements, popular songs, and even a Disney cartoon. "It takes taxes to beat the Axis," the narrator warned Donald Duck in a famous short directed at the movie-going public.

According to Treasury propaganda, patriotic Americans would happily file their returns and pay their taxes, cognizant that lives were on the line. The campaign stressed the connection between tax dollars and war materiel, and the PR campaign was rife with images of planes, tanks, ships, and ammunition. Many propaganda posters used the image of an American G.I. to drive home the need for sound war finance. The campaign also made explicit the connection between mortal sacrifice on the battlefield and fiscal sacrifice at home. As one radio announcement observed, "Well, nobody says filling out these forms is fun. But it's more fun than sitting down in a foxhole, and it's more fun than being shot down in a plane. And it's more fun than waiting for a torpedo to hit."[60]

Tax officials did not confine themselves to pictures. As part of their multimedia campaign, they commissioned songs for radio programs, including a 1941 tune by Irving Berlin. Entitled "I Paid My Income Tax Today," it stressed the fiscal obligations of neophyte taxpayers:

I paid my income tax today.
I'm only one of millions more
Whose income never was taxed before.

A tax I'm very glad to pay,
I'm squared up with the U.S.A.
You see those bombers in the sky?
Rockefeller helped to build them,
   so did I.
I paid my income tax today.[61]

The Treasury campaign occasionally tried to link taxpaying obligations with the battle against rising prices. In a flyer on "How to Check Inflation," item number three was "Pay your taxes . . . including possible increases." Sometimes, this anti-inflation message was even melded with the G.I. appeal, as on posters that featured a camouflaged soldier suggesting "We'll Take Care of the Rising Sun, You Take Care of Rising Prices." Most often, however, Treasury took a more straightforward approach, simply exhorting Americans to heed their responsibilities. "You are one of 50,000,000 Americans who must fill out an income tax return by March 15," hectored one poster. "Do It Now!"

From Voluntary to Compelled Sacrifice: The Advent of Withholding

While propaganda might have helped create what historian Carolyn Jones has called "a taxpaying culture," officials could not rely on it to produce the necessary revenue. Some form of withholding was critical. In any number of ways, collecting wage income at the source would make the income tax more productive and efficient. It would also aid in the wartime battle against inflation. Withholding could withdraw purchasing power from the economy more quickly than voluntary payments, restraining the upward pressure on prices. Indeed, withholding could help transform the federal income tax into a potent tool for managing the nation's economy, allowing officials to regulate economic forces effectively and continually.

In 1942, Congress had experimented with withholding in crafting the "Victory Tax," a short-lived income levy that nonetheless played a key role in the development of the modern tax regime.[62] The tax, according to its champions, would bolster the regular income levy by taxing Americans near the bottom of the income scale. Levied as a flat 5 percent tax on Victory Tax net income, it allowed an exemption of just $624 and allowed fewer deductions from gross income. Most notably, the tax was deducted directly from both salaries and wages, making it effective to collect at much lower incomes. According to contemporary estimates, the tax would fall on 13 million new taxpayers.[63]

But withholding had an even older pedigree. In addition to brief experiments with the technique during the Civil War, the new Social Security taxes enacted prior to World War II were collected directly from wages and salaries. In impressive fashion, and without the use of computers, the Bureau of Old-Age Benefits processed over 312 million wage reports by mid-1940, posting more than 99 percent of them to 50 million employee accounts.[64] Faced, then, with World War II's staggering revenue demands, tax officials saw withholding as a vital component of the new, vastly expanded federal income tax. Despite opposition from the Bureau of Internal Revenue (whose leaders never seemed to encounter an innovation they liked), Treasury officials began agitating for the reintroduction of withholding. The idea, they insisted, was administratively feasible and economically crucial.

Treasury officials believed that withholding was necessary if the federal income tax were to function effectively as a mass tax. Before wartime revenue needs forced Congress to add millions of new taxpayers to the tax rolls, the income tax could be administered without withholding. But with so many millions of new taxpayers, the system needed a mechanism of current, compulsory collection, and withholding seemed the most promising approach. "The 39 million individual taxpayers required to pay income taxes of almost $10 billion for 1942 under the present law must be afforded a way of meeting their tax obligations with a maximum of convenience and a minimum of hardship," Randolph Paul told Congress.[65]

Thus, in 1943, Congress passed the Current Tax Payment Act, requiring taxpayers to stay current on their tax liability through a vast new withholding system applied to wages and salaries. The law represented a victory of sorts for the Treasury Department, where tax officials had been promoting current collection for years. Success, however, was a near thing, and it came at a steep price. Administration officials were forced to accept a tax forgiveness plan—championed by one of America's leading businessmen—that gave a windfall to rich taxpayers.

The Price for Withholding: A Tax Cut in Time of War

Only one serious obstacle remained to implementing a withholding system: transition. Simply dropping withholding into the system would have required taxpayers to spend at least one year making "double" income tax payments. Under the law, every taxpayer was expected to save enough money over the course of the year to cover his or her liability when it came due early in the next calendar year. If pay-as-you-go withholding were superimposed onto this system, then taxpayers would be further required to make simultaneous payments on their current liability.

Some observers saw nothing wrong with doubling up on tax payments during the transition year. The result was not really "double" taxation, they contended, since the lump sum payment and the current payments applied to income received during different years. Nevertheless, many taxpayers did not set aside enough money for their tax payments, making double payments a problematic cash-flow reality. Consequently, almost all policymakers agreed that transition relief would be necessary. Among the possibilities lawmakers and lobbyists floated, most involved forgiving some or all tax liability for the year preceding the introduction of withholding.

Treasury tax officials acknowledged the transition problem, and they set to work on a solution. They refused to consider any blanket forgiveness of 1942 tax liability, arguing that it would disproportionately benefit the nation's richest taxpayers. Similarly, they opposed "doubling up" since it, too, would favor rich taxpayers with savings adequate to pay additional taxes without hardship. The only viable alternatives were either partial forgiveness or postponement of 1942 taxes.

As Treasury officials mulled the options, a powerful and popular challenge emerged from the private sector. For several years, Beardsley Ruml, chairman of the New York Federal Reserve Bank and treasurer of R. H. Macy and Company, had been campaigning for current collection, calling it a "simple" change of tax basis from the past year's income to the current one. Effectively, Ruml was calling for a full year's tax forgiveness. Ruml pointed out that the Treasury would see no reduction in cash flow. "As far as the Treasury and income were concerned, things would move along just the same as time moves on under daylight saving," Ruml contended.[66]

While House and Senate leaders attempted to dampen popular speculation that any tax relief would be forthcoming, Roosevelt rejected the Ruml plan out of hand: "I cannot acquiesce in the elimination of a whole year's tax burden on the upper-income groups during a war period when I must call for an increase in taxes and savings from the mass of our people," he declared. Treasury officials echoed Roosevelt's point, arguing that forgiveness "would bestow the greatest benefit on those best able to pay and the smallest benefit on those least able to pay."[67]

Congress and the administration agreed that resolution of the with-holding issue was vital to the nation's economic health. Treasury officials restated their support for current collection, stressing the administrative need for such a system. But they also stressed their opposition to a full year's tax forgiveness. While acknowledging that revenue flows would be uninterrupted, they insisted that forgiveness was unfair. In its stead, they proposed a scheme of deferred payments, under which taxpayers would be required to pay at least a large percentage of their 1942 tax liability but would be allowed several years in which to do so.

Ruml weighed in against the Treasury plan, arguing that the government could forgive a full year's taxes without unduly burdening itself. The asset loss incurred by tax forgiveness would only be evident when examining the Treasury's position on Judgment Day. At that point, millions of Americans would die owing the government money. "These would be bad debts in any case," Ruml observed wryly, so the government had nothing to lose.[68] While Ruml's original plan did not include provisions for withholding, he now added withholding to the list of reasons for supporting his plan. Collection at the source, he declared, was fully consistent with his forgiveness plan.

The House Ways and Means Committee rejected the bulk of Ruml's argument, with Democratic members insisting that forgiveness was little more than a windfall for the rich. The full House, however, was more sympathetic, and the Ruml plan continued to surface in floor votes. The final bill emerging from the House embodied a modified forgiveness plan directing most benefits to taxpayers in the first income bracket. The Senate Finance Committee, for its part, adopted the Ruml plan and its full-year forgiveness.

As the conference began, House and Senate leaders remained firmly at odds, the former digging in their heels against "excessive" forgiveness. Additionally, the issue had taken a distinctly partisan tone, with Republicans generally favoring the Ruml plan and Democrats denouncing it. Roosevelt wrote congressional leaders to emphasize his strong support for pay-as-you-go legislation and renew his strenuous objection to full-year forgiveness. Excessive forgiveness, he asserted, "would result in a highly inequitable distribution of the cost of the war and in an unjust and discriminatory enrichment of thousands of taxpayers in the upper income groups."[69]

In fact, Roosevelt was well aware of those taxpayers who stood to benefit. In March, he had asked the Treasury to draw up a list of taxpayers likely to reap the greatest benefits; "no names, of course," he added. The Treasury responded with a memo listing the 100 largest federal taxpayers—by name—along with their projected savings under the Ruml plan. The memo read like a roster of Roosevelt's staunchest opponents, although it also included a variety of celebrities and even the odd Democrat.[70] After lengthy delay, the conference deadlock ended when House Ways and Means Chair Robert Doughton changed his vote, allowing a compromise bill to emerge. The final version of the bill included a substantial tax forgiveness—less than Ruml had sought, but considerably more than Treasury wanted. The Current Tax Payment Act of 1943 provided for current payment of all individual income tax liabilities and the cancellation of 75 percent of one year's existing taxes (the lower of either the 1942 or 1943 tax liability). Unforgiven liabilities were payable in two installments, one on March 15, 1944, and the other on March 15, 1945. In effect, Congress had passed a tax cut during a time of war, albeit one that was part of a compromise designed to increase tax revenues overall.

The introduction of withholding and the debate over the Ruml plan are significant for two reasons. First, they reveal the extent to which Roosevelt and his administration were willing to fight for tax fairness. The president and his tax specialists consistently opposed complete forgiveness, complaining that it would provide a windfall to the nation's wealthy. FDR's request for a list of rich taxpayers was consistent with his longstanding tendency to personalize abstract issues of tax justice. He always viewed tax issues in terms of winners and losers, and more often than not, he was willing to identify them. (Although in this case, discretion seems to have won out.)

Second, withholding changed the income tax forever. It made the levy more responsive and flexible, reflecting and facilitating its conversion into a powerful tool of macroeconomic regulation. Moreover, as one legal historian has pointed out, it helped create a taxpaying culture, getting Americans comfortable with regular deductions from their paychecks. No small feat in an era when such deductions were all but unknown.[71]

A Return to "Business as Usual"? 1944–45

The legislation enacted in 1942 and 1943 had transformed the revenue system and demanded broad sacrifice from business, the wealthy, and the lower income classes. This sacrifice was grudgingly accepted, although not without routine attempts to shift the burden to one or the other of the groups. The necessity of huge revenues in the midst of "total war" helped constrain some of the more blatant attempts to evade sacrifice. Even so, the tradeoff for withholding was tax relief on an unprecedented scale. As the tide began to turn in America's favor on the battlefield, however, the patience for sacrifice was growing thin on the homefront.

The Revenue Act of 1943

In late 1943, Henry Morgenthau asked Congress for another tax increase to provide $10.4 billion in new revenue. That figure included $6.5 billion from the individual income tax, $400 million in estate and gift taxes, $1 billion in new corporate taxes, and $2.5 billion in excise tax increases. In an effort to simplify the tax system, the administration also asked for repeal of the Victory Tax on the grounds that it applied to many Americans not otherwise subject to income taxation. Morgenthau framed his appeal, in large part, as an anti-inflation effort. The new act, he argued, must continue the battle against inflation. "Nothing in the economic field can interfere with the war effort as much as an uncontrolled rise in prices," he told the House Ways and Means Committee, reiterating his comments from the year before. "An inflationary price rise is a source of grave social injustice."[72]

Congressional taxwriters did not want to hear such language. Increases for income and estate taxes took much of the heat, but so, too, did the suggestion to repeal the Victory Tax. A repeal would have removed 9 million low-income taxpayers from the rolls, but congressional leaders found little to like in that prospect. "Almost before the Secretary had finished reading his prepared statement," reported *Time* magazine, "the U.S. Treasury's design for extracting another $10,500,000,000.00 from the U.S. pocketbook was mackerel dead."[73]

Various administration officials echoed Morgenthau's call for higher taxes. Federal Reserve Chairman Marriner Eccles asked for even bigger numbers: $13.8 billion, including $4 billion in taxes that would be refundable after the war. Ways and Means Chairman Bob Doughton (D-NC) dismissed the higher figure out of hand. "Amazing, fantastic, and visionary. I don't like it at all. If possible, it is worse than the Treasury program," he declared.[74]

Ways and Means went to work on its own bill, which the House passed on November 24. The legislation bore little resemblance to the Treasury plan. Committee members argued that the need for new taxes had been diminished by revenue already in the pipeline. Coupled with promised reductions in nonmilitary spending, existing taxes would be nearly adequate. As for inflation, the panel declared that it could be controlled through discretionary spending cuts, effective price controls, rationing, and wage limits. Higher taxes were unnecessary.[75] The committee specifically opposed corporate tax increases: "It is vitally important that our corporations be kept in sound financial condition so that they may be able to convert to peacetime production and provide employment for men leaving the armed forces after the war." In fact, complaints about corporate tax burdens were on the upswing by 1943, and by 1944, cuts seemed almost inevitable.[76]

New revenue in the Ways and Means bill came primarily from lower-income taxpayers, including a repeal of the earned income credit and a new minimum tax for the Victory Tax. Excises provided another $1.2 billion, with much of the revenue coming from a 50 percent liquor tax hike. The bill did reduce the excess profits tax's invested-capital credit for large corporations and raised its rates from 90 to 95 percent, but it also increased the exemption for the excess profits tax from $5,000 to $10,000. Postal rate hikes added a little more money, bringing the bill's total to about $2 billion—less than a fifth of the administration's request.

The House bill got a bad reception, both from Roosevelt and the press. Editorials across the country denounced the bill as inadequate. Meanwhile, Morgenthau tried to make up lost ground by working closely with the Senate Finance Committee. While eager to placate conservatives uneasy with the administration's penchant for steep estate and income taxes, he nonetheless urged lawmakers to go easy on the little guy. The bill coming from the House already drew more than 50 percent of its revenue from people making less than $5,000, he pointed out.

Senators were unmoved. People earning less than $5,000 might be paying half the new taxes, but they also received four-fifths of the nation's income, critics pointed out. If the administration was serious about fighting inflation, then low- and middle-income Americans would have to shoulder a bigger share of the tax burden. "The principal congressional objection to the Treasury plan," reported the *New York Times,* "has centered on the administration's apparent unwillingness to increase taxes on low incomes."[77] The Finance Committee endorsed the general approach of the House bill and opposed most additional increases. The panel tinkered with the Victory Tax and put off a long-planned increase in the Social Security payroll tax. The final bill emerging from the conference committee closely resembled the Senate package, and Congress sent it to the president in February 1944.

"Relief Not for the Needy but for the Greedy":
A Presidential Veto

On February 22, Roosevelt vetoed the bill. In explaining his decision, he cited its inadequate revenue yield. The most serious problem, however, was its tendency to compromise sound tax policy for the sake of political expedience. Riddled with numerous loopholes, most directed at business, the law was a travesty. "In this respect," the president complained, "it is not a tax bill but a tax relief bill providing relief not for the needy but for the greedy."[78]

Roosevelt objected to the elimination of planned increases in the Social Security tax, a move that ensured a substantial cut in anticipated revenue. But he particularly scored a variety of provisions offering "indefensible special privileges to favored groups." Those privileges set a bad precedent, even threatening the viability of the tax system; by degrading fairness, they undermined the political consensus so fundamental to wartime tax policy. Roosevelt noted that some of his advisers wanted him to sign the bill, arguing that having asked for a loaf of bread, he should be content with a small piece of crust. "I might have done so if I had not noted that the small piece of crust contained so many extraneous and inedible materials," Roosevelt said.[79]

Roosevelt's caustic veto message enraged legislators. Ways and Means Chairman Doughton declared his intention to seek an immediate override; 19 of the committee's 25 members signed a public letter declaring the Treasury's original plan a threat to the nation's economy. Finance Committee Chairman Walter George (D-GA) opined on the overwhelming burden of wartime taxation. The day after the veto, Senate Majority Leader Alben Barkley (D-KY) resigned his leadership post in protest over the president's action. The president's veto, he declared on the Senate floor, was "a calculated and deliberate assault upon the legislative integrity of every member of Congress." Congress had a simple choice: override the veto or surrender the legislature's role in the tax policy process.[80]

Roosevelt tried to calm things down, asking Barkley to rethink his decision. He also pointed out that Barkley had seen large sections of the veto message before it was released, making the senator's declaration something of a surprise. But Barkley followed through with his resignation, only to have his colleagues immediately reelect him to the same post. The charade made headlines, underscoring Roosevelt's predicament. Within a week of FDR's veto, Congress voted to override it, the measure passing with a large majority in both houses. As enacted, the 1943 Revenue Act failed to satisfy the twin imperatives of wartime tax policy: revenue and inflation control.[81] It succeeded, however, in allowing legislators to duck their fiscal responsibilities, even as it made room for a few special favors.

Compared with the tax legislation of the early 1940s, the revenue laws of 1944 and 1945 were relatively minor. Simplification was the byword for lawmakers working on the 1944 bill. With the income tax now reaching deep into the middle class, its complexities had begun to afflict a large number of voters. In an effort to ease their pain, Congress asked the Treasury Department and the JCIRT to collaborate on a series of simplification measures. The law, passed in late May, relieved some 30 million taxpayers of the need to file detailed returns, allowing many to submit employer withholding receipts instead. It also refined the withholding mechanism to reflect more accurately each taxpayer's particular circumstances. The law abolished the Victory Tax entirely, offsetting the cost with changes in the normal and surtax rates that left total tax burdens largely unchanged. Finally, the Individual Income Tax Act of 1944 included two innovations that eased filing burdens for generations to come: the standard deduction and the tax table. The former eliminated the laborious task of itemizing deductions for many millions of taxpayers, while the latter simplified their calculation of taxes due.[82]

In July 1945, Congress passed the Tax Adjustment Act to ease the tax burden for business as the nation confronted the imminent challenge of reconverting industry to a peacetime basis. The law speeded up tax refunds already in the works and paved the way for more sweeping tax relief. The Revenue Act of 1945, passed in November, cut total revenues by $6 billion.[83] It repealed the excess profits tax for business and reduced individual income tax rates somewhat. But the law left intact the broad array of wartime excise taxes, and Congress showed no legislative inclination to tinker with the fundamentals of the wartime regime.

Conclusion

World War II represented a victory for advocates of broad-based income taxation, who had long maintained that income taxes should take the place of consumption taxes in the federal tax system. Wartime revenue needs made *both* kinds of taxes necessary, but the decision to avoid a new

federal sales tax represented a major achievement for income tax supporters. Absent strong administration leadership, Congress would almost
certainly have opted for some sort of sales tax. Roosevelt's embrace of
low-end progressivity—and the mass income tax in particular—proved
decisive. At the same time, however, FDR did not abandon his preference for heavy, soak-the-rich taxation. He demanded steep rates for both
corporate and individual taxes, firm in his conviction that the rich must
shoulder a heavy burden, especially in the context of collective sacrifice.
In the decades to come, the political resiliency of this wartime regime
would provide a solid foundation for federal finance.

In combination, these changes ensured that the business share of the
overall federal tax burden would reach historically high levels in the early
stages of the war. According to federal budget data, the first three years
of the war represent the high-water mark of corporate income taxes as a
share of federal tax receipts, reaching 39.8 percent of total federal receipts
in 1943.[84] Never before and never again would the corporate sector contribute such a large share of total federal taxes.

But the compromise was not without cost. The wartime tax regime—
and especially its steep rates on the rich—went a long way toward creating
the modern market for loopholes and preferences. Many mid-century
liberals, including tax experts in the Roosevelt Treasury, understood the
dangers inherent in high rates: when they get too high, well-heeled taxpayers will step in to bring rates down. If these taxpayers cannot do it
with a frontal assault, then they will do it incrementally, by poking holes
in the tax base. The resulting legislative dynamic is a tenacious one, giving
lawmakers an incentive to support steep marginal rates even as they offer
narrow loopholes to friends and supporters. For decades after the end of
World War II, this dynamic helped preserve the wartime compromise.
But it also set the stage for long-term dissatisfaction with the revenue
system, as loopholes and other means of legal tax avoidance undermined
the legitimacy of Roosevelt's tax regime.

5

Korea and Vietnam

"I think the boys in Korea would appreciate it more if we in this country were to pay our own way instead of leaving it for them to pay when they get back."
—Senator Sam Rayburn

"Conservative Democrats were saying to me, 'We'll go with you on the tax increase, but only if you wrap it in the American flag as a wartime measure and use the revenue solely for military expenditures.'"
—President Lyndon B. Johnson

The conflicts in Korea (1950–1953) and Vietnam (1964–1975) offer the first instances in our analysis of the role of tax policy in a modern-day limited war.[1] At first blush, the two episodes seem to have much in common. In both instances, U.S. military action was motivated by the containment policy of the Cold War era; neither conflict involved anywhere near the magnitude of fiscal effort required during the Civil War or the two World Wars. Moreover, substantial reductions in the overall tax burden preceded both the Korean War and the Vietnam War. In the years immediately following the end of World War II, Congress introduced major tax reductions with the Revenue Acts of 1945 and 1948.[2] Similarly, the Revenue Acts of 1962 and 1964 substantially reduced the federal tax burden on individuals and businesses.[3] In both cases, therefore, the increased military expenditures required fresh legislative attention, with the reversal of prior years' tax reductions hanging in the balance, to ensure sufficient revenues for the war effort.

Despite these similarities, there are many differences between the two wars that deserve attention. With regard to the financing question, perhaps the most significant difference concerns the timing of presidential requests for new taxes. Like other war-related legislation, increased taxes typically benefit from the "rally 'round the flag" effect often experienced in the early stages of military conflict but then lose popular and political support as the war drags on. Thus, political leaders face a certain window of opportunity during which they must translate the surge of patriotic fervor into legislation. On this score, the conflicts in Korea and Vietnam reveal different historical experiences.

The conflict in Korea enjoyed widespread popular and legislative support—at least at the outset. The North Korean invasion of South Korea on June 25, 1950, came at the height of McCarthyism, when both political parties were eager to earn distinction as fervent anticommunists.[4] President Truman responded quickly to the crisis, requesting across-the-board increases in taxes on individuals and businesses, as well as an excess profits tax. Within six months, Congress responded with two major tax bills—the Revenue Act of 1950 and the Excess Profits Tax Act of 1950. The following year, Congress enacted another tax increase with the Revenue Act of 1951. As a result of these tax measures, the Korean War stands out in American history as the closest the country has ever come to a pure "pay as you go" approach to war financing.

Fifteen years later, President Johnson followed the opposite strategy. Like Truman, Johnson initially enjoyed broad popular and political support for his decision to send U.S. troops to defend against the communist threat in Asia. Yet despite initial support for the war, Johnson refused to seek new taxes for the war effort in 1965 and 1966. Fearing the political consequences for his cherished "Great Society" legislative agenda, Johnson postponed his request for increased taxes until late summer 1967—more than two years after the first U.S. ground troops had arrived in Danang. By that time, however, congressional fatigue had set in, both with respect to the war and the rising cost of Johnson's Great Society programs. The delay weakened the president's hand, giving reluctant legislators the leverage to extract concessions (in the form of reduced domestic spending) to allow the surcharge to go forward. When Nixon later requested an extension of the surcharge, Congress demanded fundamental tax reform in exchange for its approval. The product of that legislative compromise was the Tax Reform Act of 1969 and a host of complex provisions that are still with us today—including the much-maligned alternative minimum tax.

Tax Policy and the "Police Action" in Korea

Between the end of World War II in 1945 and the beginning of the conflict in Korea five years later, Congress enacted two major tax bills—the Revenue Act of 1945 and the Revenue Act of 1948. Both acts were designed to return to peacetime levels those taxes that had been raised during the war. The 1945 legislation repealed the wartime excess profits tax and reduced rates for individual and corporate income taxes. The 1948 act further reduced individual income tax rates while also increasing exemptions and giving married couples the option of splitting their income for tax purposes. Yet the similarities end there. Whereas the 1945 legislation had all the markings of a new postwar fiscal consensus, with Congress and the president joining forces to lower wartime tax burdens, President Truman vetoed the 1948 bill, only to be overridden by a GOP-controlled Congress insistent on rolling back World War II's tax hikes further still. Thus, for only the second time in American history, Congress had enacted revenue legislation over a presidential veto (the first being the Revenue Act of 1943, discussed in the previous chapter). The 1948 act remains the sole instance in U.S. history of a tax cut becoming law without a presidential signature.

Truman's veto of the 1948 tax cut bill, aside from revealing something extraordinary for a politician facing an uphill election battle to retain the presidency, sets the stage for understanding U.S. tax policy during the Korean conflict two years later. On June 25, 1950, North Korea launched an invasion of South Korea at several points along the border between the two countries.[5] In the atmosphere of the early years of the Cold War, many viewed this aggression as not only the beginning of a regional conflict but a possible trigger of World War III. The "fall of China" to the communists less than a year earlier had already raised anxieties in the United States and Europe about communist expansion, and many viewed the invasion of South Korea as part of an overall communist push in East Asia. Indeed, one of President Truman's first actions in response to the North Korean attack was to dispatch the U.S. 7th Fleet to the Taiwan Straits on June 27 to protect the island from communist invasion.[6]

The outbreak of hostilities in Korea brought new uncertainties to the political landscape in Washington. With midterm elections less than five months away, Democrats and Republicans must have viewed the news from Asia as a source of both anxiety and opportunity. On the one hand, a war would almost certainly mobilize support for the Truman administration, perhaps minimizing the loss of seats that a president's party historically suffers in midterm elections. On the other hand, a bungled response to the international crisis would likely multiply GOP gains, possibly even returning to Republicans the control of Congress they had lost in 1948.

On the tax front, the Korean conflict immediately called into question the continued viability of an excise tax reduction bill under consideration in Congress in June 1950.[7] Just six months earlier Truman had called for reform of excise taxes in a special message to Congress on tax policy, insisting that "reductions are most urgently needed in the excise taxes on transportation of property, transportation of persons, long-distance telephone and telegraph communications, and the entire group of retail excises, including such items as toilet preparations, luggage, and handbags."[8] The House took up the issue in early spring and deliberated for three months, approving a final bill, H.R. 8920, on June 29, the same day Truman formally authorized unlimited U.S. air and naval action in North Korea. The House legislation went far beyond Truman's January proposals and would have cut excise taxes by more than $1 billion annually, while raising a comparable amount through various other changes to the tax code.[9]

Had the Senate simply approved the House bill, future historians might have tagged this as an instance of Congress enacting a tax cut during a time of war (though the more discerning observer might label it a "tax shift" during a "police action"). With the developments in Asia, however, the future of the tax bill was in doubt. The *New York Times* denounced the bill, arguing that "it is little less than fantastic to be thinking at this juncture in terms of tax relief."[10] Senate leaders seemed to agree. The bill stalled in committee, with Finance Chairman Walter George (D–GA) observing that certain "readjustments" might be needed, given the uncertainties of the Korean conflict.[11]

Eventually, these "readjustments" amounted to a complete abandonment of the House bill, as the Senate Finance Committee took the lead in reworking the legislation to finance mobilization for war. By mid-July, the House bill had officially been shelved and lawmakers began work on a war taxes package.[12] By the end of summer, H.R. 8920 metamorphosed into a wide-ranging tax bill that raised $5 billion for the war effort. The story of H.R. 8920's late summer transformation is the first important chapter in the history of U.S. tax policy during the Korean conflict.

Fiscal Sacrifice, Swift and Decisive: The Revenue Act of 1950

As Witte explains in his comprehensive history of U.S. tax politics, "only in those early months of almost hysterical reaction to crisis can revenues easily be raised in the United States."[13] This observation holds true for congressional debates over and approval of H.R. 8920 in the late summer of 1950. On July 19, in his first public address to the nation since the beginning of the crisis, Truman revealed his initial budget request of $10.5 billion for the military effort in Korea. To pay for these expenses, while also keeping inflation at bay, Truman declared that "it will be necessary to make substantial increases in taxes. This is a contribution to our national security that every one of us should stand ready to make." While not yet revealing the details of his plan, the president called for a "balanced and fair tax program" that would have "as a major aim the elimination of profiteering."[14]

Truman's demand for new taxes was met with nearly universal acceptance on Capitol Hill. Indeed, even before the president had submitted his official expenditure estimates, "leaders of both parties in Congress had made it known . . . that there would be no quibbling about voting him whatever might be needed to halt the spread of 'Koreanism' to other points of Asia and Europe."[15] Even business leaders whose firms stood to benefit from the House excise tax reduction bill conceded the new reality. Thomas Jefferson Miley, executive vice president of the Commerce and Industry Association of New York, noted that while his association "consistently has advocated elimination or reduction of excise taxes, we are faced with the fact that, if full-scale war should break out in Korea or other troubled areas, an increase in taxes undoubtedly would be required."[16] In short, Americans seemed extraordinarily receptive to Truman's warning that "the mobilization would bring the sacrifices and hardships that the world, less than five years ago, was still fighting to eliminate."[17]

Foreign policy advisor John Foster Dulles drove home the need for fiscal sacrifice in a *New York Times* article published in July 1950.[18] Dulles, who had visited Korea in June as a special representative of the president, wrote that

> The time for sacrifice and discipline is here. In fact it has been here for long, but it took the attack on Korea to open our eyes. Many now will risk their lives before the hard battle of Korea is won. Most of us will have to work longer hours and with more intensity. We shall all have to give up some material enjoyments and be more frugal in our living. There will be fewer automobiles, television sets, and gadgets to buy and there will be bigger tax bills to pay.[19]

A similar sentiment was expressed in August by Richard Nixon, then campaigning for a seat in the U.S. Senate from California. Arguing that "our only course is to adopt now a program of all-out mobilization," Nixon advocated "an increase in the taxes on individuals and corporations."

Nixon even took the further step of joining President Truman in calling for an excess profits tax. "In wartime," he insisted, "there is no excuse or justification for allowing any individual or corporation to increase their profits as a result of war while men are dying on the battlefield."[20] That Truman's call for fiscal sacrifice would be so promptly and urgently echoed by GOP elites reveals the breadth of support for the president's actions and policy proposals in the immediate wake of the North Korean invasion.

This support translated into swift legislative action. The administration's specific proposals were officially submitted to Congress in early August and within 45 days both chambers had approved a tax increase of $5 billion. Truman's proposed "readjustment" of H.R. 8920 involved eliminating all of the excise tax reductions that had been passed in the House, repealing the individual income tax rate reductions introduced in the 1945 and 1948 legislation, and raising the corporate income tax rate from 21 to 25 percent. These proposals, according to Harvard economist Sumner Slighter, would bring in approximately $3 billion from increased personal income taxes, $1.5 billion from higher corporate income tax rates, and $500 million from other miscellaneous changes. On August 17, the Senate Finance Committee reported a new version of H.R. 8920 that incorporated almost all of Truman's proposals.

The only real point of controversy over the bill in the Senate and the House was the question of whether to include an excess profits tax in the legislation or defer the issue until after the election. Though Truman had expressed his interest in an excess profits tax in his July 19 address to the nation, declaring that "this tax program will have as a major aim the elimination of profiteering," his actual proposals to Congress included no such tax. Liberals in Congress jumped at the opportunity to demand more fiscal sacrifice of big business, hoping to get their votes on record before the upcoming election. Representative Hale Boggs of Louisiana spelled out the politics of the issue: "Those of us who go home and say we raised individual and corporation taxes, but didn't have time to act on excess profits—then you have got yourself an issue on the platform."[21] The sentiment was echoed in the upper chamber. Speaking on the Senate floor on August 24, Democratic Senator O'Mahoney of Wyoming proclaimed that "this is not time to defer the profit dollar while we are drafting men."

O'Mahoney joined with Tom Connally of Texas to offer an amendment to H.R. 8920 that would tax corporate profits in excess of 1946–1949 average earnings. Connally made the case for the amendment on the floor of the Senate: "With prices rising, personal income taxes being increased and American boys fighting and dying in Korea, we ought to see that those who make unholy profits out of this conflict also make sacrifices."[22] When the question was taken up in the House, however, Speaker Sam Rayburn took the floor and accused proponents of the excess profits tax of delaying collections that "the government needs desperately." "You cannot get an excess profits tax in this bill," he said flatly.[23] When Truman himself came out against the O'Mahoney-Connally amendment, the issue was finally put to rest. As a compromise, a resolution was attached to H.R. 8920 calling for the excess profits tax issue to be considered during a special lame-duck session of Congress immediately following the elections.[24]

The House vote on the conference report for H.R. 8920 was 328 to 7 on September 22, while the Senate approved the measure by a voice vote shortly thereafter. Truman signed the bill into law the next day. Thus, the first tax increase of the postwar era was marked by extraordinary speed and consensus. Just six weeks before they would face voters at the polls, Democrats and Republicans seemed not only willing, but eager, to raise taxes for the war effort.

What accounts for this remarkable fiscal response to the outbreak of war in Korea? Three related explanations help put the episode in context. First, despite the upcoming election, lawmakers faced nearly ideal conditions for consensus on the question of new war taxes. To be sure, bipartisan support for the Revenue Act of 1950 was partly a product of the "rally 'round the flag" effect so common at the outset of any significant military action. Polls taken by the National Opinion Research Center in July and September showed support for the administration's decision to send troops to Korea at 75 and 81 percent, respectively.[25] Yet there was more behind these numbers than just ordinary patriotism. Adding fuel to the fire was the rise of McCarthyism in the first half of the year, beginning with the Wisconsin Senator's notorious speech in Wheeling, West Virginia, on February 9, claiming that 200 communists were working at the U.S. State Department.[26] Political campaigns across the country devolved into debates over who was tougher on communism, including, most notably, Nixon's bid for the Senate in California against Helen Gahagan Douglas, whom Nixon had labeled "the pink lady" for her supposed communist sympathies.[27] In short, at the onset of hostilities in Korea, there was extraordinary political unity regarding the need to fight global communism, and that unity translated into fiscal consensus on the question of war taxes.

Second, on the question of how to pay for the war, there was a remarkable consistency in the policy preferences of key party elites for a "pay as we go" approach. At a superficial level, it helped H.R. 8920's cause that Democrats controlled not only the White House but also both chambers of Congress. But the swift passage of the tax bill was not just the product of single party control of the legislative process. Key leaders from both parties supported the "pay as we go" approach, most significantly President Truman and Senator Robert A. Taft of Ohio, "Mr. Republican." Truman, of course, prided himself on his concern for "sound public finance," once comparing the federal budget to a family budget that "sets the normal limit of expenses against the expected income."[28] Having vetoed the 1948 tax bill, it surprised no one that he would move quickly to raise taxes to fight the war. However, Taft's position on the need for new taxes had been less clear until late August, when he embraced the idea publicly at meeting of the National Federation of Women's Republican Clubs in Cleveland. Calling for "taxation that would put the nation on a pay-as-you-go basis," Taft announced to the group that it "would be very painful, but I think it must be done."[29]

Finally, favorable military developments in Korea during the first few months of the war greatly facilitated political consensus among lawmakers regarding the need for new taxes. The U.S. military effort, undertaken officially through the United Nations, began with a series of strategic setbacks in July and August 1950.[30] The tide of the war took a dramatic turn, however, with General Douglas MacArthur's spectacular amphibious landing at Inchon on September 15, 1950—exactly one week before the overwhelming approval of the Revenue Act in the House of Representatives. By September 26, 1950, UN forces had retaken Seoul and were poised to destroy the North Korean army. Buoyed by these successes, the Truman administration decided that the next step should be the reunification of the Korean peninsula.[31] With the official backing of the United Nations, U.S. troops crossed the 38th parallel and began repelling North Korean forces toward the country's northern border with China. Given these developments, there was good reason for optimism. At a special meeting at Wake Island in mid-October, 1950, General MacArthur assured Truman that the war would be over by November.[32] What no one knew at the time, however, was that 200,000 Chinese communist troops were amassing north of the Yalu River. The United States would soon face an entirely new war.

Lame-Duck Congress Debates an Excess Profits Tax

While passage of the Revenue Act of 1950 may have been swift and decisive, the new changes were expected to raise less than half of the revenues required to satisfy Truman's initial $10.5 billion appropriations request. Moreover, expenditures for the war were almost certain to increase. According to then Secretary of the Treasury John Snyder, the legislation "was not quite up to what it should have been, but it at least made a step towards meeting the Korean expenditures."[33] With the elections behind them, lawmakers returned to Washington to consider measures to fill the expected shortfall. In a special session scheduled to begin on November 27, the lame-duck Congress would take up the excess profits tax that had been left out of H.R. 8920.

Truman submitted his formal request for excess profits tax legislation on November 14, calling for "immediate action" on "the next step in the tax program required for our increased defense effort."[34] The next day, in hearings before the House Ways and Means Committee, Treasury Secretary Snyder revealed the details of the administration's proposal, which closely followed the form of the excess profits tax that had been repealed in 1945. Under the proposal, as in World War II, firms would be given the option of computing their tax liability under two alternative formulas—one based on profits in excess of a three-year average of pre-war profits and the other based on invested capital. Following Snyder's presentation, Ways and Means Chairman Robert Doughton stirred controversy with a proposal to bar any testimony related to tax proposals other than that proposed by the administration, an idea Republicans lambasted as a "gag rule" representing "the rankest form of steamroller tactics."[35] In a straight party vote of 15 to 10, members approved the rule and limited hearings to one week.

If a week is a long time in politics, as Harold Wilson once said, then two weeks of politics in wartime is an eternity. While the House Ways and Means Committee wrapped up its hearings on November 22, the Senate Finance Committee took up the bill on December 4. In between those dates, however, the military situation in Korea deteriorated, with important consequences for U.S. involvement in the war and the taxes required to finance it. On November 24, General MacArthur announced a final offensive on the peninsula, proclaiming confidently that "this should for practical purposes end the war."[36] But only two days later, Chinese forces began pouring into Korea en masse. Overrun by "unimaginably numerous" troops that "seemed oblivious to danger or death," U.S. forces suffered spectacular losses.[37] During the last three days of November alone, the U.S. 7th Division lost 5,000 men—a third of its total force.[38] Two weeks later, in a special address to the country, President Truman would declare a state of national emergency, insisting that "the future of civilization depends on what we do—on what we do now, and in the months ahead."[39]

The military setback in Korea naturally influenced tax politics in Washington. Most significantly, on December 1, the president requested an additional $17.85 billion in defense funds. The request not only made further tax increases inevitable, but also cast serious doubt on the government's ability to hew to its much-touted "pay as we go" principle of war finance. Whereas in mid-November the excess profits tax might reasonably have been viewed as the final piece in the Korean War finance puzzle, by early December lawmakers began to see it as merely an intermediary step toward further tax increases across the board. Faced with the new budget reality, Senate Finance Chairman Walter George said on December 2 that more tax increases would "undoubtedly" be requested, possibly in the range of $6 billion to $7 billion. Raising that much revenue, George observed, would require raising taxes "all along the line."[40] Senator Harry Byrd of Virginia pushed the idea even further, asserting that "we must tax every dollar to the greatest extent that our private enterprise system can stand."[41]

With U.S. troops engaged in battles characterized as "among the bloodiest in the annals of American military history,"[42] the debate over taxes on the home front once again turned to the sacrifices being made by soldiers on the battlefield. "In the days ahead," President Truman noted, "each of us should measure his own efforts, his own sacrifices, by the standard of our heroic men in Korea."[43] In an editorial titled "The Front Line of Taxation," the *New York Times* supported its conclusion that "corporation taxes and individual taxes will have to be increased" with the following disquisition on the idea of shared sacrifice:

> If this seems a hard prospect, if we have to go without things we want, if the rewards we have been patiently working for over a period of years are curtailed, we might acquire a new perspective by reading the eyewitness descriptions of what is going on in Korea. Most of us are to be taxed in money only. We cannot compare our sacrifices for an instant with the sacrifices of the men who are being taxed in pain and blood. Let us continue to work for a wise and scientific system of raising the money the Federal Government must have. But let us not complain because taxation hurts. It doesn't hurt like fighting in below-zero cold, it doesn't hurt like hunger and weariness, it doesn't hurt like wounds and death.[44]

The call for further sacrifices came from Republican quarters as well. Speaking before the National Press Club, Senator Taft outlined the "the inevitable sacrifices that lay immediately ahead for Americans." Anticipating further tax increases across the board, Taft opined that "everybody would have to cut his standard of living by perhaps 10 per cent."[45]

Renewed emphasis on the theme of sacrifice had concrete implications for the excess profits tax legislation under review by the lame-duck Congress. Whereas before the Chinese offensive, Republicans complained of "gag rules" and "steamroller tactics" that prevented them from offering their own tax proposals, by early December, a consensus had emerged that this was no time to bicker over the details. On December 1, the House Ways and Means Committee reported a bill tracking the administration's proposals, which the full House approved by a vote of 378 to 20 on December 5. In an unusual move, the Senate Finance Committee began its own hearings before the House had completed action on the bill. On December 4, as UN troops began their retreat from Pyongyang and President Truman met with British Prime Minister Clement Attlee, Secretary Snyder appeared as the first witness before the Senate Finance Committee. "The events of the past few days in Korea," he began, "testify to the compelling need for the enactment of additional profits taxes at this congressional session."

Through five days of hearings in the Senate Finance Committee, there was virtually no opposition to enacting an excess profits tax as quickly as possible. To be sure, certain witnesses expressed dissatisfaction with the tax. In one memorable presentation, Beardsley Ruml (of the famed "Ruml Plan" during WWII) called the excess profits tax "an evil brew of iniquity, exception, exemption, and privilege." Such a "conspicuously inequitable" tax, Ruml argued, would "poison the spirit of the taxpayer public" and "destroy the moral compulsions that are needed to make any tax system work."[46]

Ruml was not alone in his dislike of excess profits taxes (though his views on the levy were uniquely venomous). Senator Taft, for example, was dubious about the need for such a tax, though he phrased his misgivings with greater circumspection. While endorsing the idea of "taking more money from profits," Taft doubted that the proper approach was to tax "so-called war profits" or even that there were any such war profits available to tax. Snyder snapped back: "You passed a bill up here to draft boys of 18, to send them to war. I think it is just as important we draft some of the profits to help pay for the expenditures." Taft quickly agreed but sought to clarify his point, carefully insisting that what the administration was characterizing as "war profits" were in fact profits that had increased because of Truman's prewar inflationary policies. But Snyder refused to engage him: "We are trying to meet the expenses of this war, not to get into a political debate as to who did what."

On December 18, the Senate Finance Committee reported a revised bill that included not only an excess profits tax but also higher corporate surtax rates. The Senate report described the legislation as "the second step in the financing of the vastly expanded military program resulting from hostilities in Korea and the critical international situation." The act was expected to raise $3.2 billion in 1950 and an additional $4 to $5 billion in calendar year 1951.[47] On January 3, 1951, Truman signed the measure into law. With the enactment of the excess profits tax, the United States had returned to the tax system in place during World War II.

The 82nd Congress and the Revenue Act of 1951

The 82nd Congress began its first session on January 3, 1951, the same day President Truman signed into law the Excess Profits Tax of 1950. As a result of the November elections, Democrats retained a majority in both chambers, but the Republicans gained a net 5 seats in the Senate and 28 seats in the House.[48] As one of its first actions, the reconstituted body would take up the final piece of major tax legislation enacted during the Korean War—the Revenue Act of 1951. If the Revenue Act of 1950 was the strongest evidence of the "rally 'round the flag" effect in the postwar era, the 1951 legislation was a preview of the contentious politics that would dominate U.S. war tax debates in the second half of the 1960s. Whereas the 1950 legislation was introduced and signed into law within 45 days, the 1951 legislation was preceded by nine months of acrimonious debate on Capitol Hill.[49]

Part of the explanation for the delay, as well as the acrimony, lies in the course of political and military developments in early 1951. With the military setbacks of late 1950, the United States was forced to abandon its strategy of unifying the peninsula. By mid-March 1951, the Truman administration had decided to pursue peace negotiations with the Chinese. General MacArthur balked, issuing his own statement indicating his willingness to meet with the Chinese, but also emphasizing that he was prepared to invade China directly with U.S. troops. For Truman, MacArthur's message to the Chinese was the last straw in what had been a series of increasingly defiant actions on the part of the general. On April 11, the president removed MacArthur from his post, ordering the general to return to the United States. The political effect of these events was disastrous for Truman, while also triggering a groundswell of popular support for MacArthur. The president's approval ratings reached a new low of 26 percent (they would go as low as 22 percent in early 1952), a sure indication the administration suffered from an influence deficit on Capitol Hill.

Meanwhile, public opinion regarding the handling of the war effort also began to wane, as the prospects for a short war grew increasingly dim. In response to the question, "Do you think the United States made a mistake in going into the war in Korea, or not?" the percentage of Americans believing the war was a mistake rose from 19 percent in August 1950 to 49 percent in February 1951. As one academic commentator later noted, "the Chinese intervention seemed to shake from the support ranks the tenuous and those who felt they could support only a short war," leaving only a "a relatively hard core of support."[50] Lawmakers no doubt factored these changes in public sentiment into their decisionmaking when they began work on H.R. 4473, the bill that would eventually become the Revenue Act of 1951.

Truman submitted his fiscal 1952 budget request to Congress on January 15, 1951, estimating expenditures of $71.6 billion and receipts of $55.1 billion. In his tax message to Congress delivered February 2, however, the president sought legislation to narrow the anticipated $16.5 billion shortfall by increasing revenues by $10 billion. As with Truman's previous requests, the principal argument offered in support of the tax increase was "sound public finance," which, he once again insisted, required adhering as closely as possible to "pay as we go" principles. His proposals would raise individual income taxes by $4 billion, excise taxes by $3 billion, and corporate income taxes by $3 billion. Hearings on the bill began in the House Ways and Means Committee on February 5 and continued for six weeks. On June 28, the baton was passed to the Senate Finance Committee, which held its own hearings until early August. In both forums, the administration's proposals encountered stiff resistance and a political climate that had little in common with the "rally 'round the flag" atmosphere of 1950.

If there was a recurring theme from the hearings before the House Ways and Means Committee, it was the old saw, "Don't tax you, don't tax me, tax that guy behind the tree." Absent from the debate were the high-minded calls for shared sacrifice and the bipartisan support for taxes that had characterized the previous year's deliberations. As Committee Chairman Robert "Muley" Doughton explained upon completion of the hearings, witnesses invariably expressed their support for doing "their full part in producing the revenue necessary to finance emergency expenditures," yet "they usually, with few exceptions, claimed they were paying as much or more in taxes than they should and that any additional revenue should be raised from some other source." Not surprisingly, Doughton explained, "we were not given much help as far as the other sources were concerned."[51]

Some of the most artful dodging concerned excise taxes, as witnesses presented creative arguments to shelter their products from increased taxes for the war effort. Clinton Hester, general counsel of the U.S. Brewers Federation, presented testimony claiming that beer was "an essential food" and that increased taxes on beer would erode "public and military morale." Decrying the effect of high taxes, Hester noted that in certain high beer-tax states, "it has become a common sight to witness two persons buying and dividing 1 bottle of beer between themselves." Meanwhile, Thomas Kelley, representing the Vacuum Cleaner Manufacturers' Association, emphasized that in a "defense economy," the "vacuum cleaner is an absolute necessity in every home and nothing should be done to increase its price." At times, Kelley's testimony turned emotional:

> Let us picture a young mother with a baby that crawls on the floor. Do not do anything to force up the price of a vacuum cleaner so that she cannot keep her floor coverings free of disease laden dirt. Are you going to deprive her of buying a vacuum cleaner? We are sure that your answer will be no, and that you will decide not to place an excise tax on vacuum cleaners.[52]

On June 19, the House Ways and Means Committee reported a bill that would raise $7.2 billion in revenue, roughly $2.8 billion shy of the administration's initial $10 billion request. Three days later, the full House passed the bill as reported by a vote of 233 to 160. The bill then moved to the Senate, where it was certain, according to contemporary news reports, to undergo extensive revision. Less clear was whether Senate revisions would generate more or less revenue than the House bill would raise. In his first day of testimony in the Senate, Secretary Snyder urged the Finance Committee to "rush through a $10 billion revenue increase," but committee members responded to Snyder's pleas with a notable lack of enthusiasm.

The tepid reaction was partly due to an important bit of budget news that Snyder delivered during his opening statement. For the fiscal year

1951, scheduled to end on June 30, 1951, the federal government would report a budget *surplus* of nearly $3.5 billion. Just six months earlier, the administration had projected a deficit for fiscal 1951 of $5.1 billion. Now, as a result of the tax legislation that Congress had enacted in the second half of 1950, federal revenues exceeded the January estimates by almost $11 billion.[53] Never before in the nation's history had the federal government maintained a budget surplus during a time of war. With this news, the Senate seemed even less likely to approve Truman's full $10 billion request.[54] Recognizing the risk of asking for higher taxes with a surplus on hand, Snyder emphasized to the committee that "defense expenditures have increased rapidly" and that a return to deficit status by the end of the first quarter of fiscal 1952 was all but certain. As Snyder saw it, the time for fiscal sacrifice had not passed: "Adequate financial support of the defense program requires that individuals accept heavier tax burdens, save more, and generally place the community's needs above their own immediate interests."[55]

Even accepting the administration's bleak budget forecasts, however, Senators remained unconvinced by the argument for $10 billion in new taxes. Following Snyder's initial testimony before the committee, both Democrats and Republicans made the case for spending cuts in lieu of increased taxes. Senator Byrd put the question most directly: "It is better to reduce expenditures than to increase taxes in the same amount, is it not?" When Snyder agreed but expressed doubt as to Congress's willingness to reduce spending, Byrd offered his own assessment of the new political landscape: "I think that Congress will do a little more than you think this time, because the people are demanding it. The people prefer cutting the expenses of the government to paying higher taxes."[56] Taft concurred: "What worries me, Mr. Secretary, is this: we have had a year since Korea, so what is the program, not for this year or next year, but for the next three years? How much money are we going to spend, how many more tax bills will we have after this?" The hearings in the Senate spotlighted a consistent theme: one year into the conflict, the country was beginning to experience tax fatigue. Whereas a sense of urgent solidarity in support of shared fiscal sacrifice marked the 1950 tax acts, by the summer of 1951, a certain weariness had crept into legislative debates.

At times, the Senate hearings on H.R. 4473 turned nasty. In mid-July, roughly two weeks into the hearings, Arthur Schutzer, New York State executive secretary of the American Labor party, appeared before the committee to address the merits of the House bill. Insisting that the bill should be retitled, "An Act for the Relief of Greedy Wealth and for the Further Reduction of the American Family's Living Standards," Schutzer drew the ire of Republican Senator Eugene Millikin of Colorado, who suggested a debate with the gentleman on principles of tax policy. "There's no time like the present," Schutzer replied. At that point Millikin demurred, with the explanation "I don't feel very good this morning, but I will take you on some time and pin your shoulders to the mat after coming out of a sound sleep, only half awake, and with one-half of one lobe of my brain at work."[57] Schutzer left the witness chair repeating, "Any time. Any time . . ." Published congressional hearings note only "(Discussion off the record.)."

On September 18, the Senate Finance Committee reported a bill that would raise $5.5 billion, or $1.7 billion less than the House version that Snyder had declared inadequate for a "soundly financed defense program."[58] When the full Senate took up the legislation, another 29 amendments were added, most of which provided some type of tax relief, including an amendment Michigan Senator Blair Moody offered to exempt vacuum cleaners from the federal excise tax. Despite a personal plea by President Truman for a bill that more closely approximated the administration's initial request for $10 billion, the Senate rejected 31 revenue-raising amendments. On September 28, the Senate passed H.R. 4473 as amended by a vote of 57 to 19, and the bill was referred to conference committee to be reconciled with the House version.[59]

Truman had plainly suffered a humiliating defeat in both chambers, but the final tax battle of the Korean War was not quite over. Over the next two weeks, House and Senate conferees produced a compromise package that would raise $5.7 billion. Then, in what the New York Times called "the greatest surprise of the present legislative session," 64 pro-administration Democrats in the House joined with 139 Republicans and rejected the conference report by a vote of 203 to 157. Lawmakers declared themselves "astonished" and even some opponents of the bill expressed concern that "we may have overplayed our hand."[60] Fearing the possibility that a new bill would not be taken up until 1952, conferees reconvened and approved a slightly modified compromise package. The Senate quickly approved the revised package, but the outcome in the House was still in doubt. In a highly unusual public appeal on the House floor, Speaker Sam Rayburn made the case for the new conference report. The New York Times captured the drama: " 'Let us measure up to our responsibility,' Rayburn told the hushed House. 'Let us maintain the integrity of the finances of this government as far as we can and not add to the great and crushing debt that we now have. . . . I think the boys in Korea would appreciate it more if we in this country were to pay our own way instead of leaving it for them to pay when they get back.' "[61] Then, by a vote of 185 to 160, the House approved the revised conference report. On October 20, President Truman signed the bill, but in doing so highlighted several "unfortunate features" of the new law, including specific provisions dealing with capital gains, family partnerships, and depletion allowances.[62]

With Truman's signature, the Revenue Act of 1951 completed the triad of tax legislation that would finance U.S. involvement in the Korean War. Although fighting continued until July 1953, when the Korean War Armistice Agreement was signed, no significant tax changes were enacted during the final 21 months of conflict. In fact, support for new taxes had evaporated by the fall of 1951. Having enacted three major tax increases, Democrats and Republicans alike expressed the view that "the president would have great difficulty in getting any additional tax increases out of Congress."[63]

* * *

In a recent study of the economic effects of war finance, economist Lee Ohanian emphasizes the uniqueness of the Korean War experience. Whereas financing of every major preceding military engagement (including the Revolutionary War, the War of 1812, the Civil War, World War I, and World War II) depended heavily on government borrowing, expenditures for the Korean War "were financed almost exclusively by higher capital and labor income taxes."[64] Truman's decisive action to seek tax increases for the Korean War effort in the second half of 1950 should come as no surprise. He had earned his national political reputation during his leadership of the famous "Truman Committee" on war preparedness in the early 1940s. In many ways, Truman's push for immediate and significant tax increases in late 1950 and 1951, as well as his relentless insistence on a "pay as you go" war financing policy, bears the stamp of that earlier experience.

In one of history's ironic twists, a similar committee was established in late 1950 to investigate military preparedness for the Korean War. However, that committee's chairman—Texas Senator Lyndon Baines Johnson—took from the experience very different lessons. Whereas Truman saw fiscal responsibility as a crucial ingredient of military preparedness, Johnson seemed largely oblivious to such constraints. Writing in late 1951, Johnson commented on the Korean conflict that foreshadowed his approach to the war financing question. "It is clear," he argued, that "in the limited type of mobilization now under way we can and should have both butter and guns." As if recognizing the potential danger of fiscal overindulgence, however, Senator Johnson qualified his remarks by noting that "someone must realistically determine the proper proportions or run the risk of jeopardizing our security." Fifteen years later, Johnson would pursue a combination of policies that seemed to reject the very idea of "proper proportions" between guns and butter.

Vietnam War and U.S. Tax Policy

As noted at the outset of this chapter, there are several important parallels between the Korean and Vietnam conflicts, particularly regarding the role of tax policy in financing the war. While the Korean War was preceded by two major tax cuts—the Revenue Act of 1945 and the Revenue Act of 1948—the Vietnam War was preceded by what was, at the time, the largest tax cut in American history. Indeed, the Revenue Act of 1964, which President Johnson signed into law on February 27, 1964, would hold that title until President Reagan signed the Economic Recovery Tax Act of 1981.[65]

In addition, during both the Korean and Vietnam conflicts, the Democrats controlled not only the White House but both chambers of Congress. Just as Harry Truman and the Democrats had enjoyed impressive victories in the November 1948 elections, so too would Lyndon Johnson and the Democrats make substantial gains in both houses in the November 1964 elections. Thus, at the start of each conflict, a Democratic president presided over substantial Democratic majorities in the Senate and the House of Representatives.[66] Moreover, during the relevant periods of both conflicts, Southern Democrats controlled the tax-writing committees of both houses of Congress. During the Korean War, Robert Doughton (North Carolina) chaired the House Ways and Means Committee, while Walter George (Georgia) headed up the Senate Finance Committee. During the Vietnam War, Wilbur Mills (Arkansas) served as chair of the Ways and Means, while Harry Byrd (Virginia) and Russell Long (Louisiana) chaired the Senate Finance Committee.

Finally, both conflicts were "limited" wars, motivated by the postwar U.S. policy of containment, and fought in relatively well-defined corners of East Asia. While both conflicts ran the risk of triggering a broader war, with military leaders operating under the constant threat of direct involvement of China and the Soviet Union, neither war entailed the sort of full-scale mobilization of American society seen during World War I and World War II. In many ways, during Korea and Vietnam, day-to-day life back on the home front was "business as usual."

Yet, despite these similarities, the tax policy response to the two conflicts could hardly be more different. Whereas in 1950 Truman sought, and Congress approved, immediate, broad-based increases in the individual and corporate income taxes, Lyndon Johnson steadfastly avoided seeking a tax increase to pay for the war in Vietnam until he was effectively forced to do so in August 1967, when he finally submitted a proposal to Congress for a 10 percent income tax surcharge. Even then, Johnson refused to make the case for the surcharge as a "war tax," choosing instead to justify the levy on the basis of complicated and often confusing economic arguments. Congress would not approve the surcharge until late June 1968, nearly three months after Johnson had announced his intention not to seek reelection. The Revenue and Expenditure Control Act of 1968, which raised taxes and cut domestic spending, would be the only significant act of fiscal sacrifice enacted during the Vietnam War.

Johnson's "Guns and Butter" Policy: 1965–66

In the two years following Lyndon Johnson's ascension to the presidency on November 22, 1963, U.S. involvement in Vietnam escalated rapidly.[67] The U.S. role had originated in the Eisenhower and Kennedy years with the signing of a military and economic aid treaty with South Vietnam and the arrival of U.S. military advisors to the regime of Ngo Dinh Diem.[68] Over the 34 months of the Kennedy presidency, the United States increased the number of military advisors in South Vietnam to more than 16,000. Yet the major push for U.S. involvement would follow the assassinations of Diem on November 2, 1963, and Kennedy three weeks later. At the end of 1963, the number of military personnel in Vietnam was 17,000. In the next four years, that figure increased dramatically to 23,000 by 1965, 184,000 by 1966, 450,000 by 1967, and more than 500,000 by early 1968.[69]

Taken by itself, the increase in defense outlays that accompanied the U.S. escalation in Vietnam would have eventually forced Johnson, like every other wartime president before him, to face the questions of whether, when, and how to request tax legislation in Congress to raise revenue for the war. But Johnson's extraordinarily ambitious domestic policy agenda further complicated his war financing dilemma. Under the "Great Society" banner, Johnson secured the enactment of numerous major legislative programs during his first two years in office, including the Civil Rights Act of 1964, the Economic Opportunity Act of 1964, the Voting Rights Act of 1965, the Social Security Act of 1965 (which authorized Medicare and Medicaid), and the Elementary and Secondary Education Act of 1965—to name just a few. More Great Society legislation would follow in 1966 and 1967.

This avalanche of liberal legislation eventually had a dual effect on the prospects for war-related tax legislation. First, with regard to the federal budget, Great Society programs had to compete with rising defense expenditures for limited federal dollars. More than any other time in American history, the Vietnam era posed the "guns versus butter" trade-off so familiar in debates over wartime government spending. Perhaps just as significant as the explicit budgetary cost, however, was the political cost Johnson incurred in winning passage of Great Society legislation. Because so many of these programs were anathema to conservative Southern Democrats in Congress, they required Johnson to spend down much of the political capital he had accumulated during his first two years in office.[70] Moreover, Johnson had secured most of his early legislative victories while he was simultaneously promoting an aggressive tax cutting agenda. Had these tax cuts not been on the table, the political viability of the Great Society would have been much less certain. In effect, by raising the possibility of a reversal of prior years' tax cuts, Vietnam threatened the fragile political coalition that Johnson had built around the Great Society.

Knowing this, Johnson did everything he could to steer clear of the issue. During 1964 and the first half of 1965, it was easy enough to avoid confronting the guns versus butter trade-off. For most of this period, it was still possible to believe that the war in Vietnam would not require a large-scale financial commitment from the United States. To be sure, the Gulf of Tonkin "incidents" in early August 1964, along with the U.S. bombing response, presaged a broader U.S. involvement, as did the Joint Resolution that Congress enacted on August 7, which authorized the use of "all necessary steps, including the use of armed force" to assist the government of South Vietnam.[71] However, the first U.S. ground troops would not arrive in Vietnam until March 1965 and Johnson's commitment to meet General Westmoreland's requests for more troops would not be announced until July 28, 1965.[72]

Thus, for fiscal year 1965, which ended on June 30, 1965, Vietnam had little effect on the U.S. budget. Indeed, for much of this period (especially during the months leading up to the November 1964 presidential election), there was talk of following up the Revenue Act of 1964 with yet another round of tax cuts.[73] In his annual budget message to Congress on January 25, 1965, Johnson proposed a substantial reduction in excise taxes—coincidentally, the same proposal Truman had made in January 1950 on the eve of the Korean War. Unlike in 1950, however, in 1965 Congress enacted the requested excise tax cuts. On June 21, Johnson signed into law H.R. 8371, which would phase in the reductions over a four-year period at an estimated total cost of $4.7 billion. At the signing ceremony, Johnson expressed his hope "to provide further tax relief to those in our nation who need it most—those taxpayers who now live in the shadow of poverty."[74] As late as July 21, 1965, the week before Johnson would sign the landmark Medicare legislation into law, Treasury officials were still publicly discussing the possibility of another income tax cut "aimed at helping lower- and middle-income groups."[75] Clearly, in these early stages of the Vietnam conflict, the idea of wartime fiscal sacrifice was absent from American political discourse.

All of this changed during the second half of 1965. Following Johnson's July 28 decision to give Westmoreland the 44 battalions he requested, the U.S. commitment to Vietnam and its corresponding costs rapidly began to mount.[76] In early August, Congress approved an administration request for supplemental defense appropriations for Vietnam, and estimates soon began circulating that fiscal year 1966 defense spending could reach $54 billion—$5.2 billion more than originally requested in January (the final figure would be $56.8 billion). The increases prompted an immediate political backlash, but not because of opposition to the war. In fact, the backlash occurred for just the opposite reason: Republicans and conservative Democrats began pressing Johnson on the "guns or butter" issue, typically with rhetoric expressing the view that guns should be strongly favored over butter. Gerald Ford, then a representative from Michigan in the House, put the issue plainly: "I urge that [the president] take the lead in cutting back new domestic programs to marshal the nation's strength for the military effort." Several other Republicans in the House and the Senate joined Ford, including Senator Thurston Morton of Kentucky, who argued that "war abroad and the Great Society at home . . . could only be financed by deficit spending and the Siamese twin of huge deficit financing is inflation."[77]

As Johnson was beginning to feel the heat from Capitol Hill, White House economic advisors began pushing the president to confront the guns/butter trade-off. During the Kennedy administration and the first two years of Johnson's presidency, the influential Council of Economic Advisors (CEA) had been promoting its "new economics" calling for expansionary fiscal policies, including higher government spending and tax cuts, as a means of stimulating growth in the economy. Throughout the early 1960s, the new economics had been treated as the gospel in the White House, as the economy grew (and revenues increased) following the tax cuts of 1962 and 1964. By late 1965, however, the economy was showing signs of overheating, and Johnson's advisors began to express concerns about inflation. In a memorandum to the president dated December 17, CEA Chairman Gardner Ackley made the case: "there is little question in my mind that a significant tax increase will be needed to prevent an intolerable degree of inflationary pressure." Walter Heller, who had previously served as chairman of the CEA, gave Johnson the same advice, arguing that "what we really need is a surtax on the individual income tax." Joseph Barr, undersecretary of the Treasury, returned from a trip to Vietnam only to note that "we really had a bear by the tail. I recommended to [Treasury Secretary] Fowler . . . that we consider getting our taxes up and do it quickly."[78]

The message Johnson was getting in late 1965, from political opponents as well as his closest advisors, was that something had to give—some sort of fiscal sacrifice had to be made to sustain the war effort in Vietnam. Johnson faced a fork in the road: to avoid inflation, either domestic spending would have to be cut or taxes would have to be raised. In a decision with far-reaching economic and political consequences, Johnson chose neither path. In his State of the Union address in January 1966, Johnson proclaimed, almost defiantly, that

> this Nation is mighty enough, its society is healthy enough, its people are strong enough, to pursue our goals in the rest of the world while still building a Great Society here at home . . . Time may require further sacrifices. And if it does, then we will make them. But we will not heed those who wring it from the hopes of the unfortunate here in a land of plenty. I believe that we can continue the Great Society while we fight in Vietnam.[79]

What explains Johnson's refusal to ask for fiscal sacrifices at this crucial juncture? In perhaps the best known journalistic account of the period, David Halberstam suggests that Johnson was indeed "receptive to the idea of the tax increase," but feared the political consequences for Great Society legislation, especially among conservative Democrats who controlled the tax-writing committees—most notably Wilbur Mills, who chaired the House Ways and Means Committee.[80] "I don't know much about economics," Johnson said,

> but I do know Congress. And I can get the Great Society through right now—this is a golden time. We've got a good Congress and I'm the right President and I can do it. But if I talk about the cost of the war, the Great Society won't go through and the tax bill won't go through. Old Wilbur Mills will sit down there and he'll thank me kindly and send me back my Great Society, and then he'll tell me that they'll be glad to spend whatever we need for the war.[81]

With the decision to increase taxes indefinitely postponed, Congress considered two relatively minor tax bills in 1966. In early February, as Senator William Fulbright, chairman of the Senate Foreign Relations Committee, began televised hearings on the U.S. role in Vietnam, Congress took up H.R. 12751, the Tax Adjustment Act of 1966. As far as war tax measures go, the act was not exactly a model of shared sacrifice. The bill, which Johnson signed into law on March 15, 1966, derived the bulk of its $5 billion revenue not from increased taxes but rather by accelerating certain corporate income tax payments and instituting a system of graduated withholding for individuals.[82] Moreover, as a result of an amendment Republican Winston Prouty offered on the Senate floor, the bill extended social security benefits to an additional 1.8 million persons at a cost of $760 million per year. Deriding the bill as a "bland" and "relatively painless form of fiscal restraint," the *New York Times* criticized Congress for its "appetite for milk toast, especially when it can add some sugar coating of its own."[83]

The second tax bill, H.R. 13103, fared worse among congressional critics. Officially labeled the "Foreign Investors Tax Act of 1966," P.L. 89-809 eventually came to be known as the "Christmas Tree Tax Bill" for the myriad special interest tax breaks it incorporated.[84] The bill, intended to reform the tax treatment of foreign investors in the United States, was approved by the House in late April at a negligible cost of $1 million per year. However, by early October, not long after the Defense Department announced that American combat deaths in Vietnam had passed the 5,000 mark,[85] the Senate approved a revised tax bill with an annual revenue loss of $460 million, mostly due to numerous "baubles" added to the "Christmas tree" in the form of nongermane amendments. While many of these amendments were dropped in conference, the compromise bill left plenty to criticize, including new tax benefits for swap funds, an extension of the investment tax credit to machinery purchased for use in U.S. possessions, and more generous depletion allowances for targeted industries. Numerous organizations, including a group of tax law professors whose views were embraced by the *New York Times* and the *Wall Street Journal,* urged Johnson to veto the bill. However, Johnson refused. On November 13, five days after suffering significant losses in the midterm elections, the president signed the bill into law.

As 1966 drew to a close, Johnson seemed to be making good on his promise to pursue both guns and butter without asking for any fiscal sacrifice in the form of higher taxes or spending cuts. Just ten days before signing the Christmas tree tax bill, Johnson had signed eight new Great Society bills, authorizing nearly $15 billion in new domestic spending programs.[86] One month later, budget officials revealed that the cost of the war in Vietnam during fiscal year 1967, anticipated at $10 billion, would in fact exceed $20 billion. With revenues slightly higher than expected as well, the budget deficit for the fiscal year was now projected at $10 billion rather than the previously anticipated $2 billion. Yet if Johnson were to pursue a tax increase, he faced an uphill battle—indeed, a battle that, as a result of Democratic losses in Congress and waning popular support for the war in Vietnam, would be waged on a hill of ever-increasing slope. In a poll of the new members of the 90th Congress by United Press International, 80 percent indicated their opposition to "any increase in taxes either to finance the war in Vietnam or to combat inflation." Johnson's window of opportunity to raise taxes for the war was already beginning to close.

Five Dollar Sacrifice: The Battle over the Vietnam Surtax, 1967–68

By New Year's Day 1967, U.S. combat troops had been fighting in Vietnam for more than a year and a half. Within the same amount of time following the outbreak of hostilities in Korea, President Truman had already pushed three major tax increases through Congress. Yet Johnson, who enjoyed larger Democratic majorities in the House and the Senate than Truman ever faced, still had not requested increased taxes for the war effort. In many ways, the bleak budget news of late 1966 set the stage for Johnson finally to act on the tax question. But whereas a year earlier the economy was overheating, prompting near unanimity among leading economists regarding the need for a tax increase, by late 1966 the economy was showing signs of sluggishness. The effect was greater equivocation among Johnson's economic advisors regarding the economic case for new taxes. On December 23, 1966, Joseph Califano cabled Johnson with his assessment of the CEA's views. Of the three economists, Arthur Okun preferred no tax increase at all, while James Duesenberry and Chairman Gardner Ackley favored a small tax increase with an effective date no earlier than July 1, 1967.[87]

Johnson heeded the advice of Ackley and Duesenberry. In his State of the Union address on January 10, 1967, Johnson proposed a 6 percent surcharge on the corporate and individual income taxes "to last 2 years or for so long as the unusual expenditures associated with our efforts in Vietnam continue." Even as Johnson raised the idea of surtax, however, he took pains to emphasize how minimal the burden would be. "For example," Johnson explained, "a person whose tax payment, the tax he owes, is $1,000, will pay, under this proposal, an extra $60 over the 12-month period, or $5 a month. The overwhelming majority of Americans who pay taxes today are below that figure and they will pay substantially less than $5 a month."[88] He explained that even with the tax increase, Americans would be paying less than they had been when he took office in late 1963.

More importantly, Johnson explained, the new tax burden could never match the sacrifices of American soldiers in Vietnam:

> I think you know that our fighting men there tonight bear the heaviest burden of all. With their lives they serve their Nation. We must give them nothing less than our full support—and we have given them that—nothing less than the determination that Americans have always given their fighting men. Whatever our sacrifice here, even if it is more than $5 a month, it is small compared to their own.[89]

The immediate congressional reaction to Johnson's surtax proposal was positive. Front page headlines in the *Wall Street Journal* pronounced, "Legislators Seem Likely To Back Johnson's Plan For 6% Income Tax Rise." While expecting "prolonged hassling over the wisdom of the move," key lawmakers saw "the President's call for 'sacrifice' to support the war effort overwhelming all arguments against an income tax rise." "There is a moral element involved here," noted one leading House Republican, "You come down to the question of whether responsible action doesn't require some tightening of the belt by increasing taxes while we're fighting this war." Another House Republican agreed: "I just don't see how we can be hawks on the war and then vote against taxes to pay for it." Even if economists were to come out against the idea of a tax increase, the article noted, "lawmakers feel they would have to succumb to the political pressures to 'back the boys' in Vietnam."[90]

Despite these expressions of support from anonymous "key lawmakers," support from the lawmakers who mattered most—including the chairmen of Congress's two tax-writing committees—was not forthcoming. House Ways and Means Chairman Wilbur Mills pointedly refused to take a position on the tax increase, noting that he wanted "to be sure the votes to pass a bill are there before taking it to the House floor."[91] Meanwhile, Russell Long, chairman of the Senate Finance Committee, was more explicit in his opposition, saying that "at the moment there is no economic case for the proposed tax increase" and "the Congress is disposed to make reductions in new domestic programs and even in old domestic programs before it votes another tax increase." Asked about Johnson's argument for shared sacrifice, Long replied that a "tax increase of ten times the size recommended by the President would still not begin to equate the sacrifice of our courageous young men fighting and dying in the swamps and jungles of Vietnam with Americans who are enjoying income and prosperity greater than they have ever known."[92]

Given the cool reaction from Mills and Long, as well as the proposed mid-year effective date, administration officials were in no hurry to put a concrete proposal before Congress. In fact, Johnson would not submit his official request for the surcharge until August. By that time, however, the budget picture had deteriorated further still, and a 6 percent surcharge was viewed as inadequate. In a message dated August 3, 1967, Johnson urged Congress to adopt a temporary 10 percent surcharge with an effective date of July 1 for corporations and October 1 for individuals. As with his January speech, Johnson again took pains to emphasize how little he was asking of Americans, calling the proposed levy "a small burden, a small inconvenience, compared to what is borne by our men in arms who put their lives on the line in Vietnam."

Johnson's emphasis on the minimal sacrifice involved in his proposed tax plan presents an interesting contrast to the political rhetoric of fiscal sacrifice during the Korean War. In late 1950 and early 1951, both Democrats and Republicans argued for "substantial tax increases," suggesting that the sacrifices required to pay for the war would be "very painful." By taking the opposite tack, insisting that his plan involved only minor inconvenience, Johnson was desperately hoping to shield his cherished Great Society programs from legislative demands for domestic spending reductions. As Johnson saw it, adopting the "painful sacrifice" rhetoric of Truman, Taft, and others would have been an invitation to dismantle the Great Society, a course he refused to follow. As he later explained in an interview with Doris Kearns Goodwin, "I knew from the start that I was bound to be crucified either way I moved. If I left the woman I really loved—the Great Society—in order to get involved with that bitch of a war on the other side of the world, then I would lose everything at home. All my programs. All my hopes to feed the hungry and the homeless. All my dreams."[93]

Perhaps the best evidence of the "crucifixion" Johnson saw coming was the delay in the House of Representatives in acting on his surcharge proposal. Hearings before the House Ways and Means Committee began on August 14, 1967; yet not until May 6, 1968, more than a month after Johnson announced his intention not to seek reelection, did the committee approve the surcharge. Chairman Wilbur Mills held up the proposal in committee, insisting on domestic spending reductions before the committee would act. Standing by his commitment not to cut back the Great Society, Johnson refused to budge. On October 3, 1967, the committee voted 20 to 5 to set aside the proposal until "the President and Congress reach an understanding on a means of implementing more effective expenditure reductions." The committee's vote infuriated Johnson, who declared in a press conference that Mills would "live to rue the day" he decided to oppose the surcharge proposal. Following the committee's decision, Johnson ordered a freeze on public works projects, one of the first of which was a new post office slated to go up in Conway, Arkansas, Mills's home district.[94]

The Ways and Means Committee continued its hearings on H.R. 15414 in late 1967 and early 1968. Finally, on February 23, 1968, three weeks into the Tet offensive, the committee reported a bill without Johnson's income tax surcharge. The bill, which postponed scheduled reductions in certain excise taxes, was then approved by the full House the following week and taken up by the Senate Finance Committee in mid-March. Despite the opposition from the committee's chairman, Senator Russell Long, several committee members supported the administration's tax proposal, viewing it as necessary to control the deficit and dampen consumer demand in order to control inflation. Senate action on the surcharge was forestalled, however, because of the constitutional requirement that revenue legislation originate in the House. The committee's staunchest supporter of the surcharge, Florida Senator George Smathers, insisted that the Senate should vote on the bill without prior House approval: "I cannot believe that it was the intention of the founders of this Government that the great mass of the Members of the Congress should be left helpless to act. . . . I do not believe anybody has a higher regard for Wilbur Mills than do I, but on the other hand I represent Florida. They did not send me up here to ask Wilbur Mills what I ought to do." Despite Smathers's plea, the Finance Committee reported H.R. 15414 on March 15 without the administration's surcharge provisions.

On April 2, the Senate approved H.R. 15414 by a vote of 57 to 31. The vote was concrete evidence of Johnson's political demise. Two days after the beleaguered president shocked the nation with his announcement that he would not seek reelection, H.R. 15414 arrived before the Conference Committee without Johnson's surcharge proposal. Indeed, the fiscal impasse would not be broken until late May, when Johnson grudgingly agreed to reduce fiscal year 1969 spending by $6 billion to get the votes for his surcharge. On June 20, 1968, the House approved the compromise package, with the Senate approving the bill the next day. One week later, Johnson signed the bill into law. It was a clear defeat for Johnson and his Great Society. As two historians of the period noted, in "June 1968 the Great Society, already badly wounded at the hands of its friends and enemies alike, lost its forward movement and its inner spirit."[95]

As enacted, the Revenue and Expenditure Control Act of 1968 represented the largest single-year tax increase in U.S. history since the end of World War II, outstripping each of the three tax bills enacted during the Korean War as well as all other postwar tax increases.[96] Still, the Vietnam surcharge had little effect in controlling inflation, which worsened in the following months and years. As an anti-inflationary device, the surcharge was simply too little, too late. To have worked, the surcharge had to have been enacted much earlier—perhaps as early as 1965 or 1966.

Could Johnson have secured enactment of his Vietnam surcharge at that early stage? In retrospect, the surcharge proposal might have enjoyed popular and political support had President Johnson followed Truman's strategy of requesting painful fiscal sacrifice at the earliest possible stage in the conflict. Commenting on the surtax controversy and the congressional delay in acting on Johnson's proposal, Representative John W. Byrnes, then the ranking GOP member of the House Ways and Means Committee, criticized Johnson for selling the surcharge on the basis of complex economic arguments instead of linking it clearly to the war in Vietnam. "It was impossible to sell that kind of economic argument to the gas station operator," Byrnes noted. Wilbur Mills offered a similar argument for his committee's delay, suggesting that if the surcharge proposal had been labeled a "war tax," then "it would meet few obstacles in Congress."[97]

Such comments seem to be what Johnson was referring to in his own postmortem on the surtax: "Conservative Democrats were saying to me, 'We'll go with you on the tax increase, but only if you wrap it in the American flag as a wartime measure and use the revenue solely for military expenditures.'"

These comments suggest that an alternative outcome—bipartisan support for an early and explicit "war tax"—may have been available, if Johnson had opted for it. However, sensing that Congress would exact too great a price for that support, Johnson chose to postpone the tax decision and refused to make the case for his surcharge as a "war tax." In effect, Johnson's refusal to follow the Truman strategy of asking for wartime fiscal sacrifice was a tactical decision within his broader strategy of preserving, to the maximum degree possible, government spending on the Great Society.

Surcharge Extension and Tax Reform: 1968–69

The income tax surcharge enacted as part of the Revenue and Expenditure Control Act of 1968 was limited to one year and was therefore set to expire at the end of June 1969—midway into the first year of the new president, Richard Nixon. Significantly, however, the 1968 legislation also contained a provision, introduced in the Senate as an amendment to the bill by Senator Jacob Javits (R-NY), that required the administration to submit to Congress by December 31, 1968, proposals for tax reform. The Treasury Department, under the leadership of Assistant Secretary for Tax Policy Stanley S. Surrey, had been working on tax reform proposals for two years, but with little interest or leadership from an increasingly beleaguered White House. The Javits amendment created an opportunity for tax reform to find a more secure footing on the legislative agenda. Later in 1968, however, Johnson decided not to forward the proposals.[98] Instead, an agreement was reached that the Treasury proposals would be released at the beginning of the New Year. Any tax reform would have to await the new administration of Richard Nixon, scheduled to take office on January 20, 1969.

What happened next is a chapter in U.S. tax history that has often been repeated in recent years. Appearing before the Joint Economic Committee of Congress just three days before Nixon was sworn in as president, outgoing Treasury Secretary Joseph Barr warned of an impending "revolt" of middle-class taxpayers against a tax system that allowed many high-income individuals to pay little or no federal income taxes. "Our income tax system needs major reforms now," Barr told the committee. "We face now the possibility of a taxpayer revolt if we do not soon make major reforms in our income taxes." To drive the point home, Barr cited 155 "extreme cases" where individuals with adjusted gross income in excess of $200,000 paid no federal income tax whatsoever.[99]

As has been commonly noted in recent treatments of this period, the Barr revelations created a groundswell of political support for tax reform that ultimately lead to the enactment of the Tax Reform Act of 1969. Less well known is the precise political connection between the legislative consideration of tax reform in 1969 and the continuation of the Vietnam surcharge, which was scheduled to expire on June 30, 1969. In effect, the Barr revelations pitted Congress, now urgently interested in some sort of liberal-minded tax reform, against Nixon, whose primary concern in early 1969 was to control inflation. As the consumer price index continued to rise during the first three months of the year, extending the income tax surcharge became a central plank of the new administration's anti-inflationary strategy. On March 25, just days after Nixon authorized the secret bombing of Cambodia, the White House disclosed for the first time that Nixon would recommend the surcharge continue for another year at the full 10 percent rate. "I am convinced," noted Nixon in his message to Congress the next day, "that the path of responsibility requires that the income tax surcharge, which is expected to yield $9.5 billion, be extended for another year."

However convinced Nixon may have been regarding the need to extend the surcharge, congressional liberals saw the president's announcement as an opportunity to extract administration support for tax reform. On May 14, as U.S. troops were engaged in fierce combat at Hamburger Hill, where 45 Americans were killed in what would be the last major search and destroy mission of the war, 54 Democrats in the House of Representatives asked Ways and Means Chairman to "delay extension of the 10-percent surcharge until there is assurance of passage of a major tax-reform bill."[100] In addition, the executive council of the American Federation of Labor and Congress of Industrial Organizations (AFL-CIO) issued a statement on the same day indicating that it would not support surcharge extension "until it is combined with immediate, substantial and equitable reform of the federal income tax structure."[101] In the Senate, Edward Kennedy had taken a similar view, insisting that "the fundamental logic of the surcharge demands that it be coupled with tax reform."[102] In effect, liberal Democrats were holding the Vietnam surcharge hostage until Nixon agreed to throw his support behind their tax reform agenda. On June 12, 1969, Nixon reached an agreement with House leaders that traded tax reform for an extension of the surcharge.[103] The following week, the House Ways and Means Committee reported H.R. 12290 and on June 30 the full House approved the bill by a margin of 210 to 205.

That was not, however, the end of the story. Following the House action, the bill moved to the Senate, where liberal Democrats were even more suspicious of the administration's commitment to tax reform. Leading the charge in the upper chamber was majority leader Mike Mansfield, who insisted that surcharge extension was dead unless it could be explicitly tied to tax reform. Despite repeated pleas from Nixon, the Democratic Policy Committee, which Mansfield chaired, refused to schedule floor action on the surcharge bill until a House bill on tax reform was also ready for Senate floor action. Finally, on July 30, as Nixon visited U.S. troops in Vietnam, the deadlock was broken with a compromise to break the surcharge extension into two parts.[104] A new bill, H.R. 9951, would extend the income tax surcharge at a rate of 10 percent for only six months, until December 31, 1969, while a second bill, H.R. 13270, would extend it for another six months at a rate of 5 percent. H.R. 13270 would be the legislative vehicle for the most sweeping reform of the nation's tax system to date.

The Tax Reform Act of 1969, signed into law by President Nixon on December 30, 1969, incorporated several major structural reforms to the income tax, including repeal of the investment tax credit, reduced oil depletion allowances, a new "minimum tax," a revised income-averaging provision (originally enacted in 1964 and eventually repealed in 1986), new rules for private foundations, increased personal exemptions, an increased standard deduction, and new rules for capital gains taxes. On balance, this mixture of tax cuts and revenue-increasing provisions was estimated to cost the Treasury roughly $2.5 billion per year when fully effective.[105] The bill cleared both houses of Congress on December 22, 1969, and was signed into law by the president on December 30.

Tax Cuts during the Vietnam War, 1969–71

Coming at the height of the Vietnam War, during a year in which 11,616 U.S. troops were killed in action,[106] the Tax Reform Act of 1969 meets the literal definition of a "tax cut during a time of war," undermining the claim various pundits would make in 2003 that the Bush wartime tax cuts were unprecedented.[107] To be sure, unlike the Bush tax cuts, the 1969 act was enacted principally to reform the tax system rather than reduce federal tax burdens. Moreover, scoring the 1969 legislation as reducing revenues is somewhat artificial given that the surcharge extension was divided into two parts. Including the first half of the extension in the Tax Reform Act of 1969, rather than in a separate bill, would have increased fiscal year 1970 receipts $5.6 billion. Nevertheless, because it resulted in a net reduction in federal tax receipts, the Tax Reform Act of 1969 was a wartime tax cut—indeed, a wartime tax cut championed and brought to fruition by liberal Democrats in Congress.

Perhaps a better analogy to the tax cuts during the early stages of the War in Iraq would be the tax cuts enacted as part of the Revenue Act of 1971, in the final stages of the Vietnam War. By August 1971, when President Nixon first submitted his proposed tax legislation to Congress, the Vietnam War was nearing its final stages. U.S. combat deaths dropped significantly in the early 1970s, from 6,081 in 1970 to 2,357 in 1971,[108] as Nixon pursued his policy of "Vietnamization" and more troops returned home. Thus, unlike tax legislation introduced in the early 1950s or the mid-1960s, the tax program Nixon proposed in August 1971 came at a time of military de-escalation. What makes the 1971 story relevant to recent tax cuts is that the country had entered a recession in 1970 and policymakers saw tax cuts as providing a fiscal stimulus to the economy. The politics of the 1971 tax cut, however, were quite different than in 2003. On June 29, 1970, Nixon announced that he would not propose any tax cuts that year. Two weeks later, however, 13 Democratic senators wrote to Nixon asking him to reconsider his decision, insisting that the "income tax cuts presently scheduled for 1972 and 1973 should be moved up to this year."[109] When Nixon agreed, proposing accelerated tax reductions in an August 15 speech, Democrats complained that the cuts were "inadequate" and "much too little and too late."[110]

Not surprisingly, given these comments, deliberation over the tax bill in the fall of 1971 essentially became a debate over how to structure the tax cut, rather than whether cutting taxes was advisable. Nixon's initial proposal, which would have cost $27.3 billion over a three-year period, was amended in the House and the Senate to provide $25.9 billion. The principal difference between the administration's initial proposal and the final legislation concerned how the overall reduction was allocated between individual and business taxes. Roughly three-quarters of Nixon's initial reductions were slated for business taxes, while the final bill allocated slightly more than half of the tax cuts to businesses. The bulk of that cost was attributable to the reintroduction of the investment tax credit, which had been repealed as part of the Tax Reform Act of 1969. The legislation also codified (and modified) changes to certain asset depreciation rules that Nixon had established through his administrative authority earlier in the year. As for the individual income tax, the 1971 legislation increased the minimum standard deduction and accelerated increases in the personal exemption and standard deduction that were scheduled to take effect in 1972 and 1973. Overwhelming majorities in both chambers approved the bill on December 9, 1971, and Nixon signed it into law the next day.

Conclusion

If a lesson is to be learned from examining U.S. tax policy and war financing during the Korean and Vietnam conflicts, it is that political leaders must "strike while the iron is hot" if they hope to enact tax increases to fund military efforts abroad. President Truman displayed the advantages of this approach in the six months immediately following the North Korean invasion of South Korea on June 25, 1950, acting quickly and decisively to raise capital and labor income taxes. By contrast, President Johnson refused to follow this approach.

The history of Johnson's struggle to get the Vietnam surcharge enacted between January 1967 and June 1968 may be usefully contrasted with Truman's request for tax-financed appropriations for the Korean conflict in the late summer of 1950.[111] It is tempting to explain the difference in outcome with the observation that Korea was a popular war while Vietnam was unpopular. But this simplistic view overlooks the initial popularity of the Vietnam conflict.[112] As historian James Patterson notes, "Until 1968 Johnson enjoyed considerable bipartisan support in Congress for his support of the war."[113] Of course, enjoying bipartisan support for the war does not necessarily mean enjoying bipartisan support for *tax increases to pay for the war,* as the 18 months it took to get the Vietnam surcharge enacted show. Still, Johnson had several opportunities during the early stages of the Vietnam conflict to act with decisive fiscal leadership as Truman had in 1950.

Two episodes in particular might have provided Johnson the opportunity to seek a tax increase to pay for the war in Vietnam. The first was in August 1964, immediately following the incident in the Gulf of Tonkin; the second was from February to March 1965, in the wake of Viet Cong attacks on U.S. facilities in Pleiku and a subsequent attack of the U.S. embassy in Saigon. In retrospect, however, neither situation offered the right mix of political circumstances for Johnson to act. The Tonkin Gulf incident in August 1964 did generate a burst of public and political support for U.S. military action in Vietnam. However, given the pending election, in which Johnson faced Arizona Senator Barry Goldwater, the time was particularly unpropitious for raising taxes. Aside from opening himself to charges of wanting to increase taxes, any movement on the tax front in August 1964 would have indicated that Johnson was interested in expanding the U.S. effort in Indochina. Having successfully painted Goldwater as a warmonger, Johnson was keen on pursuing only "a limited and measured response."[114]

The second opportunity Johnson faced to increase taxes for Vietnam was in February and March of 1965, just a few months after his victory over Goldwater. On February 6, 1965, Vietcong guerrillas attacked a U.S. air base at Pleiku, killing eight American soldiers and wounding another 129. Later that spring, on March 29, Vietcong forces bombed the U.S. embassy in Saigon, killing six and wounding dozens more. Like the Tonkin Gulf incident, these events generated broad public and political support for Johnson and his policies toward Vietnam. Shortly after the Pleiku attack, opinion polls showed 70 percent approval for the president and an 80 percent approval rating for U.S. military involvement in Vietnam. As with the Tonkin incident, Johnson again refused to capitalize on the "rally 'round the flag" effect by seeking increased taxes for the war. In this instance, however, the reasons were quite different. Two major Great Society bills—the legislation enacting Medicare and the Voting Rights Act—were under consideration at precisely the same time. Both bills—indeed, Johnson's entire Great Society agenda—depended critically on the support of conservative Democrats, especially representatives from the South. Any movement in the direction of increasing taxes in the spring and summer of 1965 likely would have jeopardized the political coalition that Johnson was relying on to ensure passage of these domestic programs.

In the final analysis, Johnson simply placed a greater value on his domestic spending priorities than he did on the war in Vietnam. Not surprisingly, therefore, he exhibited extreme reluctance to ask for the wartime sacrifices so common in previous conflicts. On this score, Johnson may be fairly criticized for his failure to provide effective leadership as the nation's commander in chief. The country ultimately paid a heavy price for Johnson's refusal to confront the inevitable fiscal trade-offs associated with its simultaneous pursuit of guns and butter. At the same time, however, some of the most important legislative accomplishments of the 20th century may not have come to fruition had Johnson taken a strong stance in support of higher taxes for the war in 1965 or 1966. Like a protective father, Johnson safeguarded his newborn Great Society programs from the ongoing political hazards they faced during those early years. However one feels about the wisdom of Johnson's chosen course of action, his decisions established a historical precedent for relegating war taxes to the back burner. Whether or not one believes that "shared sacrifice" through higher wartime taxes was ever an important American value, by the end of the war in Vietnam, that principle had plainly suffered a setback.

6

9/11 and the War in Iraq

"Americans are sacrificing. I mean, we are. You know, we pay a lot of taxes. America sacrificed when they, you know, when the economy went into the tank. Americans sacrificed when, you know, air travel was disrupted. American taxpayers have paid a lot to help this nation recover. I think Americans have sacrificed."

—President George W. Bush

Having examined the American experience with tax policy during the country's major wars, we turn now to a discussion of more recent history and the apparent anomaly of Congress and the president joining forces to substantially *reduce* federal tax burdens during a time of war. As noted in the introduction, commentators have criticized the Bush wartime tax cuts as "unprecedented" and a "break from our patriotic tradition" of wartime fiscal sacrifice. Each of the previous chapters has sought to evaluate the historical claim implicit in these critiques. Our analysis has suggested that claims of a strong U.S. tradition of wartime fiscal sacrifice are not unfounded, but that this tradition derives principally from the first half of the 20th century, and more specifically from the U.S. experience in World War II and, to a lesser extent, World War I and the Korean War. In conflicts both preceding this period and following it, one detects a noticeably different tenor in U.S. wartime tax politics, one characterized by a less obliging attitude toward wartime fiscal burdens. Outside the first half of the 20th century, the voice of resistance, reluctance, and opposition to wartime tax burdens occupies a more prominent role in American political discourse.

In this chapter, we aim to situate the Bush wartime tax cuts within these broader historical patterns. By way of background, we begin with a discussion of tax policy in the George W. Bush administration, including the chief progenitor of those policies, the GOP's 1994 "Contract with

America." We examine the politics surrounding the enactment of the major tax cuts of the Bush era, with a principal focus on the Economic Growth and Tax Relief Reconciliation Act (EGTRRA) of 2001, enacted three months prior to the September 11th attacks, and the Jobs and Growth Tax Relief Reconciliation Act (JGTRRA) of 2003, debate over which occurred roughly simultaneously with the initiation of "Operation Iraqi Freedom" in March 2003. We then turn to debates in Congress in the fall of 2003—a crucial juncture in the U.S. commitment in Iraq, as conditions on the ground were beginning to deteriorate—and a proposal advanced by Senator Joseph Biden to repeal the reduction in the top marginal tax rate to raise the $87 billion that the administration had requested in supplemental appropriations for the war in Iraq. The Biden amendment was handily defeated on the Senate floor, but the controversy deserves attention as the most high-profile instance since the beginning of the Iraq conflict of a serious legislative movement for increased taxes to pay for the war. The chapter concludes with a brief discussion of tax legislation enacted during Bush's second term and a summary of the federal government's fiscal condition in the final year of the Bush presidency.

Background of the Bush Tax Cuts: 1994–2000

The push for the tax cuts that President Bush would eventually sign into law began with the Republican "Contract with America" in 1994. In an effort to distance themselves from the 1990 and 1993 tax increases in preparation for the November 1994 midterm elections, Republicans in early 1994 issued their "Contract with America," which proposed various tax cuts designed to "create jobs," "enhance wages," and "restore the American dream."[1] Among other things, the Contract with America promised a 50 percent cut in the capital gains rate, a new $500 child tax credit, repeal of the so-called marriage penalty, and a host of new tax incentives.[2] The strategy worked. In November 1994, Republicans enjoyed significant gains in the House and the Senate. At the time, many viewed the election as a rejection of Clinton policies and a mandate for the GOP legislative agenda.

Over the next several years, congressional Republicans sought to deliver on their promises with tax-cutting legislation. While President Clinton eventually approved some tax relief legislation during this period, those parts of the Republican tax agenda that most favored wealthier taxpayers typically fell victim to the president's veto. In 1995, Republican leaders secured the passage of a measure incorporating many of the Contract's tax objectives, but Clinton vetoed the bill in early December, arguing that the bill gave "unnecessarily large income tax relief and other tax relief to those who need it least."[3] Two years later, Clinton signed into law the Taxpayer Relief Act of 1997, which offered a package of tax cuts targeted at middle-class families, including the Contract's child tax credit. When Republicans pushed again in 1998 and 1999 for deeper tax cuts, this time at a cost of $792 billion over 10 years, President Clinton once again vetoed the legislation on September 23, 1999.[4]

President Clinton's veto of the more aggressive Republican tax-cutting legislation sets the stage for understanding Bush's calls for substantial tax cuts during the presidential campaign in 2000. For each of the three fiscal years leading up to the November 2000 presidential election, the federal government enjoyed a budget surplus, largely due to surging income tax receipts arising from capital gains and stock options of the dot-com boom.[5] By fiscal year 2000, the budget surplus had reached 2.4 percent of GDP, making it the largest federal budget surplus as a percentage of GDP since 1948, a year in which a GOP-controlled Congress overrode President Truman's veto of tax cut legislation. While Clinton and other Democrats touted the fiscal year 2000 surplus as evidence of the federal government's fiscal discipline under their watch, Republicans charged that surplus revenues should be used to reduce federal tax burdens. In an essay published in early 2000, Lawrence Lindsey, who would later become one of President George W. Bush's chief economic advisors, argued that "the best way for Congress to 'spend' the trillion dollars is not to spend it at all. It is to give the money back to the people who earned it in the first place."[6]

The idea that "tax cuts should go to those who pay taxes" would eventually become a central plank of the Bush campaign for the White House in 2000. Haunted by the political repercussions suffered by his father in 1992, who had famously issued a pledge of "no new taxes" in the 1988 presidential campaign only to sign into law tax increases as part of the 1990 budget agreement, George W. Bush promised an aggressive tax-cutting agenda on the campaign trail. Speaking in Durham, New Hampshire, in January 2000, just a month before that state's primary, Bush explained that his plan "is not only no new taxes. This is tax cuts, so help me God."[7] True to his word, Bush promised $483 billion in tax cuts over five years, the bulk of which would be targeted to high-income families. Bush advisors later revised their estimates so that by May 2000 the tax cut proposal had become a promise for $1.3 trillion in tax cuts over 10 years.[8]

At the center of the Bush tax plan were across-the-board rate reductions in the individual income tax, a doubling of the child tax credit for most families, and a repeal of the estate tax.[9] It was a bold and ambitious tax-cutting agenda, one that many observers had initially characterized as associated with the far-right fringe of the Republican Party. Indeed, when House Republicans voted on budget legislation in March 2000, they envisioned tax cuts in the $150 to $250 billion range over a five-year period, an amount substantially lower than the package Bush was touting on the campaign trail.[10] Over the next year, however, the Bush tax plan would gradually move from the fringe to the center of tax-policy debates in Washington.

The First Bush Tax Cut: EGTRRA 2001

In the wake of the disputed 2000 presidential election, public opinion regarding the proper course of tax policy was highly ambiguous, suggesting that the electorate was potentially receptive to a wide range of policies. For example, when asked whether they considered the amount of money Americans pay in taxes to be a problem, 63.1 percent of respondents indicated that tax levels were either a "serious" problem (41 percent) or an "extremely serious" problem (22.1 percent). At the same time, however, 70.8 percent of respondents indicated opposition to the idea that the taxes of higher-income Americans should be reduced. In addition, 69 percent of respondents said that "strengthening the Social Security system" was more important than cutting taxes. Based on these polling data, there appeared to be little basis to conclude that the November 2000 election delivered a mandate in favor of the Bush tax-cutting agenda. Nevertheless, the incoming administration proceeded to govern without regard to the disputed nature of the election or the ambiguities in the electorate's tax-policy preferences. Indeed, Vice President Cheney remarked that "From the very day we walked in the building, a notion of sort of a restrained presidency because it was such a close election, that lasted maybe thirty seconds. It was not contemplated for any length of time. We had an agenda, we ran on that agenda, we won the election—full-speed ahead."[11]

Nowhere was the Bush-Cheney "full-speed ahead" strategy more in evidence than on the tax front. Upon taking office in January 2001, President

Bush moved quickly to push for enactment of his tax proposals advanced during the campaign.[12] In his February budget submission to Congress, the president proposed a host of tax changes tracking his campaign proposals at an estimated cost of $1.62 trillion over 10 years. Among the highlights were across-the-board reductions in tax rates for the individual income tax, a doubling of the child tax credit, marriage penalty relief, and a repeal of the estate tax.[13] Democrats and moderate Republicans responded by proposing a more modest tax cut, with the benefits accruing to low- and middle-income families.[14] In short order, however, the political equilibrium shifted in favor the Bush plan, giving the president's tax cuts an air of moderation and restraint.

This effect had several sources. Federal Reserve Chairman Alan Greenspan's testimony in Congress on January 25, endorsing broad-based tax reductions of some sort, almost certainly emboldened those with the most aggressive tax-cutting agenda. As Ways and Means Chairman Bill Thomas explained, "All of a sudden the president went from an extremist to a reasonable kind of guy after the Greenspan testimony."[15] Three weeks later, Jack Kemp published an op-ed piece in the *New York Times* concluding that "it would not be unreasonable for Mr. Bush to seek tax rate reductions twice the size of what he has proposed."[16] Not long after that, a group of conservative Republicans in the House, including Dick Armey, Tom DeLay, and J. C. Watts Jr., proposed legislation increasing the tax reductions to $2.2 trillion over 10 years. As DeLay explained, "the Bush plan is a great beginning, but it's a floor not a ceiling."[17] As one GOP strategist explained in early February 2001, "the more the debate rages on the poles of both parties, the more solidly Bush is in the middle."[18]

What the Republican strategy lacked in subtlety it made up for in effectiveness. Less than a month into the Bush presidency, the *New York Times* was reporting that the Bush tax plan had taken on "a mainstream air."[19] Indeed, the president himself, who by then was pushing for a $1.6 trillion tax plan, began admonishing legislators for their fiscal recklessness: "Some in Congress view this as opportunity to load up the tax relief plan with their own vision. I want the members of Congress and the American people to hear loud and clear: This is the right-size plan, it is the right approach, and I'm going to defend it mightily."[20] On June 7, 2001, as a Marine Corps band played "Hail to the Chief," President Bush signed his promised tax cut into law.[21] The final version of the bill, estimated to cost $1.35 trillion over a 10-year period, incorporated nearly all of the main provisions of the initial Bush plan.

Passage of EGTRRA 2001 was a clear victory for Bush, but the celebration was short lived. As work on the bill neared completion, a stunning development in the Senate was about to turn Washington politics upside down. Two weeks before the president signed the tax cut into law, Senator Jim Jeffords of Vermont announced his intention to leave the Republican Party "once the conference report on the tax bill is sent to the president." The Jeffords defection left the GOP with only 49 seats in the Senate, one vote shy of the majority required (with Vice President Cheney as the tie-breaking vote) to maintain their control of the chamber. On June 6, Senator Tom Daschle took over as Senate Majority Leader, while Max Baucus took control of the Senate Finance Committee. At the time, these political developments were viewed as a "historic shift" and a "dramatic transformation of the political landscape."[22] Yet like the headlines of December 6, 1941, the political clatter of summer 2001 would soon be drowned out by the roar of subsequent events.

September 11th and the Prospect of War

The attacks of September 11th came roughly three months after President Bush had signed EGTRRA 2001 into law. Almost immediately, talk of war began. Four days following the attacks, in a press conference at Camp David, President Bush declared flatly "We're at war. There's been an act of war declared upon America by terrorists, and we will respond accordingly. My message is for everybody who wears the uniform to get ready."[23] The *New York Times* expressed the same view in its opinion pages: "There is no doubt that this week's terrorist attacks on New York and Washington were the opening salvos in the first American war of the 21st century."[24] Echoing the thoughts of many observers at the time, author and journalist Thomas Friedman wrote of the parallel to the Japanese attacks that drew the U.S. into World War II: "if this attack was the Pearl Harbor of World War III, it means there is a long, long war ahead."[25]

Contemporaneous polling data reveal that the country was indeed prepared to go to war. Like the attacks 60 years earlier, the events of September 11th triggered broad-based popular support for a military response.[26] In a poll taken on the day of the attacks, 94 percent of respondents indicated their support for military action against those responsible for the attacks, while 84 percent supported military action against countries that either assisted or sheltered terrorists.[27] The prospect of high U.S.

casualties had little effect on these levels of support. Polls taken in the days following the attacks showed 77 percent of respondents supported military action against those responsible, even if "U.S. forces might suffer thousands of casualties."[28] In addition, Americans seemed to be under no illusions regarding the nature of the conflict the country would face; almost all respondents indicated that they believed a war against terrorism would be "long" (92 percent) and "difficult" (94 percent).[29]

While perhaps confirming the obvious, these polling data help put the attacks into historical perspective. Like the events of December 7, 1941, the attacks of September 11th triggered a strong "rally 'round the flag" effect, as Americans readied themselves for the sacrifices of war. Unlike Pearl Harbor, however, there was almost no talk in the wake of the September 11th attacks of a need to increase taxes to mobilize for war. Of course, the nature of the conflict that the country faced in 2001 bore little resemblance to what confronted the United States in World War II. Few would suggest that the United States was on the brink of a full-scale mobilization for "all-out war" in the wake of the September 11th attacks. Rather, as President Bush noted in the days following the attacks, the war that the country was about to embark upon would be a "conflict without battlefields or beachheads." Thus, it was not obvious that a dramatic build-up in military capabilities following September 11th was necessary, much less that increased taxes would be required to finance the country's as yet undefined military response. Moreover, for the fiscal year ending September 30, 2001, the federal government enjoyed a surplus of $128 billion, representing 1.3 percent of GDP, whereas the government had been running deficits for the 10 years leading up the U.S. entry into World War II. Of course, the FY 2001 budget surplus quickly vanished (by FY 2002, there was a deficit of $158 billion), but the fact that September 2001 marked the culmination of four years of federal budget surpluses suggests that U.S. lawmakers simply did not face the same sense of fiscal urgency following the September 11th attacks as they did in previous conflicts.

To be sure, there were calls for increased taxes—or, more accurately, less aggressive tax cuts—in the wake of the attacks. For example, Laura D'Andrea Tyson, chief economic advisor in the Clinton administration, argued in an October 8 op-ed that the Bush tax cuts had "become just another luxury item for the wealthy that a country at war can no longer afford."[30] Similarly, the nonprofit organization Citizens for Tax Justice issued a press release just one week after the attacks calling for a "freeze on the future phase-ins of the Bush tax cuts."[31] Apart from these isolated proposals, however, there was little serious talk in the weeks following the attacks of suspending already enacted tax cuts or otherwise increasing taxes. In fact, as the country braced for the first major battle in the war on terrorism, Operation Enduring Freedom in Afghanistan, the focus of debates in Washington was not on increasing taxes but rather enacting new tax cuts.

The main argument for tax cuts in the wake of the September 11th attacks was that some fiscal stimulus was needed to jolt the economy out of the recession that had begun in March and that now, following the attacks, threatened to worsen.[32] Thus, debate in the fall of 2001 focused not on *whether* to cut taxes, but rather on *how* taxes should be cut.[33] Perhaps the most controversial proposal was advanced by conservative Republicans in the House, including majority leader Dick Armey and whip Tom DeLay, who argued in favor of reducing capital gains taxes as a means of stimulating investment. According to press accounts at the time, the White House was cool to this idea (though Vice President Cheney is said to have pushed for it) and preferred an across-the-board reduction in corporate income tax rates and other tax cuts. Meanwhile, Democrats in Congress favored tax cuts that would benefit low-income households who had not qualified for the rebates issued in connection with the June legislation.[34] When House Republicans announced plans on October 10 to pursue their own tax cut plans, incorporating a capital gains tax cut and a wide array of other proposals, Democrats promised a "food fight."[35] Less than a month after the attacks and just three days into Operation Enduring Freedom, the idea of a bipartisan fiscal response to the attacks of September 11th, whatever shape it would take, had completely collapsed.[36]

As a result of these partisan divisions, Congress would not enact a post-9/11 economic stimulus package until early March 2002. In its final form, the Job Creation and Worker Assistance Act of 2002 provided expanded unemployment benefits and limited business tax breaks, including changes to depreciation rules and an extension of the net operating loss carryback period from two to five years. While the final product reflected a bipartisan compromise, it left unsatiated the appetite for deeper tax cuts among many within the GOP, especially conservative Republican "growth hawks" in the House. Hoping to showcase their fervor for cutting taxes in anticipation of the November 2002 elections, House Republicans adopted what came to be known as the "flaming arrow strategy." Through a series of actions taken during the first half of 2002, House Republicans approved legislation making permanent various features of the 2001 Bush tax cuts, including the reduction in individual income tax rates, the increase in the child tax credit, estate tax repeal, and marriage penalty relief. With the Senate controlled by Democrats, none of these bills became law.

The House and Senate did agree, however, on one significant matter. On October 10–11, 2002, both chambers approved a Joint Resolution authorizing the president to use force to "(1) defend the national security of the United States against the continuing threat posed by Iraq; and (2) enforce all relevant UN Security Council resolutions regarding Iraq."[37] That historic vote, along with mid-term elections one month later, which allowed Republicans to regain control of the Senate and retain control of the House, set the stage for Congress to consider, for the first time in American history, major tax cuts during a time of war. Thus, the spring of 2003 would mark the convergence of what Treasury Secretary Paul O'Neill later referred to as two "big, sweeping ideas that were in collision with reality."[38]

JGTRRA 2003 and Operation Iraqi Freedom

At 10:16 p.m. on Wednesday, March 19, 2003, President Bush appeared in a televised address to the nation to announce that the U.S. military had launched Operation Iraqi Freedom "to disarm Iraq, to free its people, and to defend the world from grave danger."[39] Two days later, on Friday, March 21, both the House and the Senate voted to adopt FY 2004 budget resolutions that would cut taxes by $726 billion over 11 years.[40] With these developments, the third week of March 2003 ushered in a combination of policies without precedent in American history: tax cuts during a time of war.

The novelty of the moment was not lost on the editors of the nation's major newspapers. Over the next six weeks, a flurry of editorials appeared in papers throughout the country.[41] In one representative passage, *The Virginian-Pilot* out of Norfolk (home to Naval Station Norfolk, the world's largest naval installation) echoed an argument that Speaker Sam Rayburn had made on the House floor in October 1951: "President George W. Bush is attempting to simultaneously wage wars against Iraq and taxes. As a result, the Iraqi war is being fought on the nation's credit card. Young soldiers and sailors will fight it, and their children will pay for it . . . It is unseemly for a nation to ask so much sacrifice from its troops in Iraq while treating its civilians at home to indulgences that they cannot afford."[42]

Congressional Democrats seized the opportunity to paint the administration as reckless tax-cutting ideologues willing to jettison the country's longstanding patriotic tradition of wartime sacrifice in favor of tax cuts for the wealthy. The rhetoric, while sometimes overcooked, was not without basis. The centerpiece of the administration's 2003 tax package was the elimination of taxes on corporate dividends, a change in the law estimated to reduce federal revenues by $396 billion over 11 years. Not surprisingly, given the skewed distribution of stock ownership among income classes, higher-income households stood to benefit the most from the Bush proposal. Based on a study using data for taxable year 2000, 17 percent of families received dividend income, with the amount of dividends received rising sharply with income. Households with income in excess of $200,000 per year received 47 percent of all dividend income, while households with income in excess of $100,000 per year received 72.2 percent of all dividends.[43] Thus, what the president's plan promised was not merely a tax cut during a time of war, but a highly regressive tax cut during a time of war.

In addition to eliminating the taxation of dividends, the president's plan promised to accelerate a number of tax cuts that were being phased in as a result of the 2001 legislation. Among the main provisions to be accelerated were reductions in individual income tax rates not scheduled to take effect until 2004 and 2006, increases in the amount of taxable income to be included in the new 10 percent tax bracket, marriage penalty relief not scheduled to take effect until later years, increases in the child tax credit slated to take effect between 2005 and 2010, and an increase in the exemption for the alternative minimum tax. The administration's budget documents argued that, in combination, these provisions would have "powerful, positive effects on the economy." The administration also made much of the fact that "92 million taxpayers would receive a tax cut averaging $1,083 in 2003" and similar amounts in future years. Critics pointed out that the use of "average" figures had the potential to mislead. Under the president's plan, almost half of all tax filers (49 percent) would receive tax cuts of less than $100, while the top 1 percent of tax filers would receive an average tax cut of $24,100.[44]

Democrats had long opposed the Bush tax cuts, which they viewed as unfairly benefiting the wealthy. This time, however, the basis for Democratic opposition to the tax cuts would not be the regressive nature of those cuts (or rather, not *only* the regressive nature of those cuts) but also the argument that the government should not be cutting taxes during a time of war. At the time, public opinion seemed to support the Democratic view. An NBC News/*Wall Street Journal* poll from March 29–30 revealed public apprehension about the Bush tax cuts now that the country was at war. According to the survey, 52 percent of respondents agreed that Congress should not pass Bush's tax plan since "the federal budget is now in deficit and the costs of the war are unknown."[45] Echoing this sentiment, Minority Leader Tom Daschle criticized the Bush plan as "way too much, given the need for sacrifice in this country." Still, many Republicans disagreed, including Jack Kemp, who replied to Daschle's comment in an April 1 op-ed piece: "Sacrifice? What, and to what purpose? Daschle doesn't seem to comprehend that by keeping tax rates too high and 'sacrificing' economic growth, we don't help the war effort, we hinder it; we don't get more revenue, we get less."[46]

The Daschle-Kemp exchange offers an opportunity to examine an important milestone in the evolving history of wartime fiscal sacrifice in American political discourse. As we have shown in previous chapters, the argument that Daschle was making—that is, "we're at war and should therefore prepare for sacrifices, including higher taxes"—is a longstanding refrain throughout American history. In nearly every military conflict from the founding of the Republic onward, we see political leaders making the Daschle argument. By contrast, in the Kemp statement, we see an argument that is truly unprecedented in American history for the simple reason that the supply-side economics Kemp and other Republican "growth hawks" embraced did not gain political acceptance until the 1980s. Indeed, most accounts of the history of supply-side economics begin with a reference to the famous curve that Arthur Laffer drew on the back of a napkin in a Washington restaurant in 1974. In effect, March 2003 marks the first instance in the country's history of political leaders advancing the arguments of supply-side economics during a time of war. Indeed, Laffer himself, in a *Wall Street Journal* op-ed with Club for Growth president Stephen Moore, argued that the full Bush tax cut would be "the perfect wartime boost."[47] Other GOP leaders made the case for wartime tax cuts with even greater vigor. In a comment almost certainly intended to provoke political "shock and awe," Representative Tom DeLay declared on March 12 that "nothing is more important in the face of war than cutting taxes."

Significantly, however, not all Republicans accepted the supply-side argument. Concerned about the fiscal uncertainties of the war in Iraq, a handful of moderates in the Senate balked at the new round of Bush tax cuts. Among those expressing reluctance were Senators Olympia Snowe

(ME), George Voinovich (OH), and Lincoln Chafee (RI).[48] Yet the most vociferous GOP champion of the traditional argument in support of wartime fiscal sacrifice was Vietnam veteran and former POW, John McCain. Both McCain and Chafee refused to support *any* tax cuts during a time of war, yet McCain, perhaps because of his background, grounded his position explicitly in themes of sacrifice. Commenting on the Bush plan a year later, McCain argued that "throughout our history, wartime has been a time of sacrifice" and that the Bush plan's "huge tax breaks for the wealthy" were "far and away from sacrifice."[49] Largely as a result of the influence of these moderates, the Senate voted on March 26 to significantly reduce the size of the Bush tax cut. The surprise action left a significant gap between the House ($726 billion) and Senate ($350 billion) versions of the "growth package," setting the stage for contentious negotiations in conference.

While the administration struggled to defend its tax cut package in Congress, U.S. troops ran roughshod over their Iraqi counterparts. On April 5, U.S. tanks rolled into Baghdad and four days later the Iraqi capital fell, along with a 40-foot statue of former Iraqi President Saddam Hussein. On the homefront, proponents of the Bush tax cuts launched an aggressive ad campaign to persuade House–Senate conferees to favor the more generous House version. In one controversial development, the anti-tax group "Club for Growth" began running ads in Ohio and Maine, home states of GOP moderates George Voinovich and Olympia Snowe, equating the Senators' opposition to the Bush tax cut with France's opposition to the war in Iraq. The ad in Maine began with this dramatic announcement: "President Bush courageously led the forces of freedom. But some 'so-called' allies like France stood in the way. At home, President Bush has proposed bold job-creating tax cuts to boost our economy. But some so-called Republicans like Olympia Snowe stand in the way." The implication, denied in subsequent public statements by those sponsoring the ads, was that a refusal to support Bush's wartime tax cuts was somehow unpatriotic. Similar ads ran against Voinovich in Ohio, which the president visited in late April in support of his plan. Without specifically mentioning Voinovich, Bush told workers at the Timken Company in Canton, Ohio, that "some in Congress say the plan is too big. Well, it seems like to me they might have some explaining to do. If they agree that tax relief creates jobs, then why are they for a little bitty tax relief package?"[50]

Bush's campaign for something more than "little bitty tax relief" corresponded with what was, at the time, thought to be the final stages of combat operations in Iraq. Exactly one week after his speech in Canton, the president made a tailhook landing (in the copilot's seat of a U.S. Navy S-3B Viking refueling plane) on the aircraft carrier U.S.S. Abraham Lincoln. With a large "Mission Accomplished" banner prominently displayed behind him, Bush announced that combat operations in Iraq had ended. Back in Washington, however, the battle over the administration's tax cuts continued. On the same day as the president's tailhook landing, House Ways and Means Committee Chairman Bill Thomas declared that he didn't have the votes to enact the administration's proposal to eliminate the taxation of dividends could not be enacted. Thomas was now advancing a compromise proposal that would tax dividends at the same rate as capital gains, 15 percent. The Thomas announcement was a clear defeat for Bush, who had banked on using his strong wartime approval ratings to secure approval for the dividend tax cut proposal.[51] At the same time, however, the tax package taking shape in the Senate, which included over $100 billion in increased taxes to offset the cost of a complete (though temporary) elimination of dividend taxes, raised the specter of the president repeating the mistakes of his father, who had agreed to tax increases in connection with the 1990 budget deal. Moreover, there was still a $200 billion gap between the House and Senate versions of the tax package.

In a compromise brokered at the White House on May 19, the president agreed to a package that would reflect the language of the House bill, including Thomas's compromise on dividend taxes. However, to keep the overall cost within the Senate's $350 billion ceiling, the president also agreed to more restrictive phase-in and sunset provisions, including an expiration of the dividend tax cut for years after 2008. On May 28, just over two months into the war in Iraq, President Bush signed into law the Jobs and Growth Tax Relief and Reconciliation Act of 2003. At an estimated cost of $350 billion over 10 years, the package was the second largest tax cut of his presidency and the third largest tax cut in American history.

More significantly, however, the enactment of JGTRRA marked the clearest instance in American history of a "tax cut during a time of war." Coming nearly a month after the announced end of combat operations in Iraq, one might be tempted to quarrel with this characterization. As we now know, however, the president's "mission accomplished" announcement hardly marked the end of U.S. military involvement in Iraq. In the month following the announcement, 37 members of the American military were killed in Iraq. Then, on May 28, the same day that President Bush signed JGTRRA into law, American military commanders in Baghdad announced plans "to keep a larger force in Iraq than had been anticipated and to send war-hardened units to trouble spots outside Baghdad."[52] Thus, by mid-summer 2003, difficulties in Iraq were already foreshadowing a much longer and costlier U.S. occupation than had been anticipated. Despite the deterioration of conditions on the ground in Iraq, and the correspondingly greater likelihood of increased military expenditures, conservative Republicans pledged to continue their push for deeper tax cuts. Commenting on the compromise package that Bush signed into law, House majority leader Tom DeLay announced, "This ain't the end of it—we're going to have some more. Our budget says we're going to have $1.3 trillion in tax cuts, and you bet we're coming back for more."[53]

Paying for the War: The Debate over Supplemental Appropriations

One of the key features of the Bush administration's prosecution of the war in Iraq has been its refusal to account for the costs of the war through the regular budget process. The result is that the war has been financed primarily through emergency supplemental appropriations legislation, an approach strongly criticized in the Iraq Study Group Report released in late 2006.[54] The first appropriations bill for the war, authorizing $78.5 billion of spending and enacted as a supplement to the FY 2003 budget, was signed by President Bush on April 16, 2003.[55] At the time, the Pentagon indicated that the supplemental would cover operations in Iraq through the fiscal year, which would end on September 30, 2003. As conditions in Iraq deteriorated, it became apparent that the administration's initial estimates regarding the cost of U.S. involvement were unrealistically low. On September 7, in a televised address to the nation, the president announced his intention to request an additional $87 billion in supplemental appropriations. In a statement with striking parallels to President Truman's December 1950 request for appropriations following the Chinese invasion of Korea, the president declared that the war in Iraq would "take time and require sacrifice." Echoing his predecessor from a half-century earlier, Bush announced that "we will do what is necessary, we will spend what is necessary, to achieve this essential victory in the war on terror, to promote freedom, and to make our own Nation more secure."[56]

Coming as it did just three months after the JGTRRA tax cut, at a time when estimates put the FY 2003 budget deficit at nearly half a trillion dollars, it is no surprise that the president's $87 billion request generated "sticker shock" both in Congress and among voters.[57] In a *USA Today/CNN/Gallup* Poll taken following the president's speech, 57 percent of respondents indicated that they were opposed to the budget request for Iraq, while only 41 percent approved.[58] Thus, unlike the first Iraq supplemental request, which Congress was eager to pass in the early stages of the conflict, this time the administration faced greater resistance on the Hill.

The main political story regarding the supplemental appropriations bill was the unsuccessful attempt by some members of Congress to structure the reconstruction aid to Iraq as a loan rather than a grant.[59] Yet the president's request prompted another controversy, underplayed in press accounts at the time, that is more germane to our analysis. Almost immediately after Bush submitted his $87 billion request, Congress began to discuss tax increases (or, more precisely, repealing scheduled tax reductions) to cover the cost. Having failed to prevent the enactment of JGTRRA the previous spring, Democrats saw the rising costs in Iraq as an opportunity to reopen the tax debate.[60] Not surprisingly, the Bush administration strongly opposed any movement toward reducing or repealing its tax cuts. Addressing the issue at a press conference on September 10, Bush reiterated the growth hawks' mantra on tax cuts: "I heard somebody say, well, what we need to do is have a tax increase to pay for this. That's an absurd notion. You don't raise taxes when an economy is recovering. Matter of fact, lower taxes will help enhance economic recovery."[61]

In mid-September, Senator Joe Biden joined with Democrats Jon Corzine, John Kerry, and Diane Feinstein to introduce a bill "to provide funds for the security and stabilization of Iraq by suspending a portion of the reductions in the highest income tax rate for individual taxpayers."[62] Republican Senator Lincoln Chafee later joined the bill as a cosponsor. The basic idea of the Biden proposal was to repeal only so much of the reduction in the top marginal tax rate as would be necessary to generate $87 billion in increased revenues. At the time, this was estimated to require an increase in the top marginal rate from 35 to 38.3 percent, a figure slightly lower than the 38.6 percent top marginal rate prior to the enactment of EGTRRA 2001. The Biden proposal stands as the most high-profile instance since the beginning of the U.S. involvement in Iraq of legislative movement to raise taxes for the war.

More to the point for our analysis, sponsors of the legislation grounded their arguments in the theme of wartime sacrifice. Speaking on behalf of the bill on the Senate floor on October 2, Senator John Kerry, a Vietnam veteran, criticized the president for refusing to ask Americans to share in the sacrifice of the U.S. troops in Iraq:

> The President has talked a lot about sacrifice in recent weeks. In an address from the White House, he said of Iraq, "This will take time and require sacrifice." In his weekly radio talk, he warned that, "This campaign requires sacrifice." Even in his State of Union address, the President issued a call for sacrifice, saying, "We will not deny, we will not ignore, we will not pass along our problems to other Congresses, other presidents, and other generations."
>
> And there can be no doubt that the President has demanded most of this sacrifice from the men and women in uniform. More than 300 troops have given their lives in Iraq. The Army is stretched too thin for its duties in Iraq, and troops who were promised they'd be home long ago remain in Iraq. . . . And yet—despite all we're asking of the men and women in uniform—the bill we now debate appropriates $87 billion simply by increasing the federal deficit—it asks no sacrifice of anyone living today. This is an off budget, deficit spending free ride.
>
> The amendment that Senator Biden and I are offering will change that. It will pay the cost of this bill—the entire $87 billion—by simply repealing tax cuts for the wealthiest Americans. The Biden-Kerry amendment will ask those who can afford to pay this burden to do so—it is a fair plan. . . . We should not abandon our mission but we must also demand that whatever we spend in Iraq be paid for with shared sacrifice, not deficit dollars.[63]

At the time, the public appeared to favor the idea of freezing parts of the Bush tax cuts to pay for the war in Iraq. According to a September 2003 NBC News/*Wall Street Journal* poll, when asked how to pay for the administration's $87 billion request, 56 percent of respondents preferred to repeal the 2001–2003 tax cuts for individuals in the "upper income brackets." By contrast, 12 percent preferred financing the additional $87 billion expense through increased borrowing, while 13 percent preferred to cover the cost through reductions in other spending programs.[64] Despite the apparent popular support for the Biden amendment, it was handily defeated on the Senate floor. A motion to table the amendment was approved by a vote of 57 to 42 on October 2, with all but seven Democrats voting against the motion and all but one Republican (Lincoln Chafee, RI) voting in favor.[65]

With the defeat of the Biden amendment, the $87 billion for Iraq would be financed through a larger FY 2004 budget deficit and a corresponding increase in federal debt. Yet for those advocating fiscal responsibility, a legislative development of potentially greater significance came in December 2003 when Congress narrowly passed the administration's Medicare prescription drug plan. Under the new program, individuals eligible for Medicare would be able to buy government-subsidized insurance offering prescription drug coverage.[66] At the time of enactment, the administration was estimating a total cost for the program of $400 billion over 10 years, a figure that administration critics challenged as unrealistically low. As it turned out, the administration itself knew the figure was unrealistically low. Just a few months after the law passed, it was revealed that administration officials threatened to fire Medicare's chief actuary, Richard Foster, if he disclosed his estimate that the program could cost as much as $600 billion over 10 years. Eventually, the administration conceded the program's higher cost, revising its estimates to reflect budgetary outlays of as much as $1.2 trillion between 2006 and 2015.[67]

With the war in Iraq, the new round of tax cuts and the prescription drug plan, the developments of 2003 wreaked havoc on the old "guns versus butter" metaphor. As originally conceived, the "guns and butter" reference captured the inevitable trade-offs societies face in deciding between military and nonmilitary spending. During the Johnson years, the question was whether the administration could have both guns and butter without increasing taxes; ultimately, it decided that it could not. Now, as 2003 came to a close, the very idea of a guns versus butter trade-off seemed to have lost its meaning. In the political climate of late 2003, "taxes," "trade-offs," and other such concrete manifestations of wartime fiscal sacrifice were simply not on the table. Heading in to the final year of his first term, President Bush was presiding over a combination of policies without precedent in American history—guns *and* butter *and* tax cuts. And still there was more to come.

War and Taxes from 2004 Onward

From 2004 through the first years of his second term, George W. Bush stayed the course on the two major policy initiatives of his presidency—tax cuts and the war in Iraq. The period from 2004 to 2006 is perhaps best described as a continuation of the political dynamics that characterized 2003, with Congress and the president enacting a seemingly constant stream of tax cuts as conditions on the ground in Iraq deteriorated. U.S. forces experienced several grim milestones during these three years, with the death toll for American soldiers reaching 1,000 in September 2004, 2,000 in October 2005, and 3,000 in December 2006. The rising death toll in Iraq corresponded with the enactment of several new tax relief measures, including the Working Families Tax Relief Act of 2004, the American

Jobs Creation Act of 2004, the Tax Increase Prevention and Reconciliation Act of 2005, and the Tax Relief and Health Care Act of 2006. None of these acts had the same importance as EGTRRA 2001 or JGTRRA 2003; in fact, they are perhaps best understood as spin-offs of those earlier measures, often extending temporary provisions set to expire under the terms of the original legislation.

One exception is the American Jobs Creation Act of 2004, a bill described as "the biggest corporate tax overhaul since 1986."[68] The legislation was motivated by the need to repeal a controversial trade subsidy that had led the European Union to impose trade sanctions. As the bill worked its way through Congress, however, numerous corporate tax breaks were added, including a significant new deduction for domestic manufacturing activities (defined very broadly), which effectively reduced the corporate income tax rate from 35 to 32 percent for a wide range of businesses.[69] The president signed the bill into law on October 22, 2004, less than two weeks before the November election in which Bush won a second term, defeating Democratic Senator John Kerry of Massachusetts. That Washington politics would produce an election-year tax cut should surprise no one. Indeed, legislation doling out special benefits, through the tax code or otherwise, is a longstanding beltway tradition, even during times of war. As discussed in chapter 5, a Democrat-controlled Congress enacted the infamous "Christmas Tree Tax Bill" in the months leading up to the mid-term elections of 1966, just as U.S. fatalities in Vietnam passed the 5,000 mark. If there was novelty in the Bush strategy, however, it was his continued invocation of the rhetoric of sacrifice, even as he insisted on pursuing deeper tax cuts. In an October 2005 speech to military spouses at Bolling Air Force Base in Washington, D.C., Bush returned to these themes. "A time of war is a time of sacrifice," Bush noted. "The sacrifices made by you and your loved ones in uniform are always on our minds and in our prayers. All of you also understand that sacrifice is essential to winning war, and this war will require more sacrifice, more time, and more resolve."[70]

As the president predicted, the wars in Iraq and Afghanistan have indeed required more sacrifice. By early March 2008, more than a year into the administration's "troop surge" strategy to stabilize conditions on the ground in Iraq, combined U.S. fatalities for Operation Iraqi Freedom and Operation Enduring Freedom had reached 4,452. In addition, spending for the war and related activities has continued to climb, with the administration maintaining its practice of securing war appropriations through emergency supplemental appropriations. According to a Congressional

Budget Office analysis from late October 2007, Congress had appropriated $604 billion for military operations and other activities related to Operation Iraqi Freedom, Operation Enduring Freedom, and the war on terror.[71]

In combination with the tax cuts described previously, increased spending on the wars in Iraq and Afghanistan has lead to a substantial deterioration in the country's near-term budget outlook.[72] A study released in December 2006 showed that legislation enacted between 2001 and 2006, in combination with the resulting increase in interest on the federal debt, totaled $2.3 trillion. Put differently, had the government simply maintained the policies in place as of January 2001, federal debt at the end of 2006 would have been $2.5 trillion rather than $4.8 trillion. According to the study, more than half of the $2.3 trillion difference ($1.2 trillion) was attributable to tax cuts enacted since 2001, while another $767 billion derived from increases in defense and homeland security appropriations, including the wars in Iraq and Afghanistan. In other words, fully 84 percent of the deterioration in the budget picture from 2001 through the end of 2006 was attributable to the administration's combination of tax cuts and increased spending on defense and homeland security.[73]

Political changes in Congress have had little influence on these larger trends. As a result of the mid-term elections of November 2006, Democrats reclaimed majorities in both the House and the Senate. Yet despite the changing of the guard, there has been little talk in Washington on the question of how to pay for the wars in Iraq and Afghanistan. One exception was a proposal advanced in early 2007 by Senator Joseph Lieberman (I-CT) for a "war on terrorism tax." Noting that "we're not asking a sacrifice of anybody but our military," Lieberman argued that "we need to ask people to help us in a way that they know when they pay more it will go for their security."[74] On a few isolated occasions, Democrats have also proposed raising taxes for the war effort. Most notably, in early October 2007, Representatives David Obey (D-WI), James McGovern (D-MA) and Vietnam veteran John Murtha (D-PA) proposed a "war surtax" designed to raise $150 billion to help pay for operations in Iraq and Afghanistan. In an open letter to their colleagues seeking support for the legislation, the congressmen also invoked the idea of shared sacrifice:

> When it comes to fighting this war, there is no sense of shared sacrifice. The only families being asked to sacrifice are military families and they are being asked to sacrifice again and again. Meanwhile, even the most fortunate of the rest of us are being asked to make no sacrifice whatsoever. Americans who make more than a

million dollars a year, instead of being asked for sacrifice, are being asked to accept well over $50 billion a year in tax cuts, like the war itself, paid for with borrowed money.

As you know, to bring a greater sense of balance and proportion to the debate surrounding these issues, we have drafted legislation to impose a progressive war surtax to pay for the cost of the effort in Iraq.

Some people are being asked to pay with their lives or their faces or their hands or their arms or their legs. If they are being asked to do that, it doesn't seem too much to ask the average taxpayer to pay $112 for the cost of the war so we don't have to shove it off on our kids.[75]

Perhaps sensing little appetite in the American electorate for tax increases of any sort, whether for wartime spending or otherwise, the Democratic leadership in the House quickly distanced itself from the proposal. House Speaker Nancy Pelosi and Majority Leader Steny Hoyer both indicated that they would not back the measure, while a spokesman for the House Ways and Means Committee noted simply that "there is no expectation that this proposal will come before the committee."[76]

Instead, Democrats focused their legislative attention on providing their own brand of tax relief, including tax breaks included in the Small Business and Work Opportunity Tax Act of 2007, a new one-year "patch" enacted as part of the Tax Increase Prevention Act of 2007 to extend relief from the alternative minimum tax, tax relief for homeowners facing foreclosures contained in the Mortgage Forgiveness Debt Relief Act of 2007, and the Economic Stimulus Act of 2008. While these acts differ significantly in their details from the legislation enacted during the first six years of the Bush presidency, they nonetheless exhibit a remarkable continuity with the tax legislation approved by the Republican Congress. In short, despite the change in Congress, we have not observed any meaningful departure from the now well established practice of deepening the U.S. financial commitment to the wars in Iraq and Afghanistan without regard to how to pay for those increased costs.

Conclusion

However one feels about the Bush-era tax cuts, they plainly constitute an extraordinary episode in the history of American war finance. While large-scale borrowing is a common feature of most of the country's major military conflicts, the idea of consciously and aggressively reducing federal tax revenues while simultaneously pursuing a war abroad is new to the

American experience. As previous chapters have shown, in every major conflict except the current one, the country has raised taxes to fund increased military expenditures. Why does the war in Iraq represent such a sharp departure from past practice? That is, what explains the difference between the tax *cuts* enacted during the war in Iraq and the tax *increases* during every other major U.S. conflict? We address these questions in a final concluding chapter.

Conclusion

Based on the history reviewed in the previous chapters, there can be little debate that the wartime tax cuts of the Bush era represent an abrupt departure from the customary U.S. practice of increasing taxes during times of war. In every major conflict except the current one, the country has raised taxes to fund increased military expenditures. Nevertheless, as we have argued, claims that the United States has a strong tradition of wartime fiscal sacrifice simply do not square with the historical record. To be sure, evidence for such a tradition can be found in the extraordinary tax changes wrought by World War II and, to a lesser (though still significant) extent, during World War I and the Korean War. Yet to focus on that tradition alone is to miss a large part of the story. In many of the wars we examined, the tradition is better described as one of reluctance, resistance, and opposition to the higher tax burdens brought about by war. Still, even in conflicts where this alternative tradition appears more prominently—including, most notably, the War of 1812, the Civil War (especially in the Confederacy), and the Vietnam War—eventually policymakers embraced higher wartime taxes. Why hasn't this happened in the current conflict? That is, what explains the difference between the tax cuts enacted during the war in Iraq and the tax increases of every other major U.S. conflict?

Before addressing these questions, we emphasize the difficulty involved in making historical judgments across time. Consider the problem viewed from the broadest perspective: why might a policy outcome observed at one point in time differ from a policy outcome of a different era? A moment's reflection reveals a vast number of potential explanatory variables. The country may be at a different stage of economic development, political and cultural institutions may be radically different, and the country's significance in global politics and the world economy may vary between eras. The list is so long as to cast doubt on the worthiness of the inquiry. Nevertheless, we believe that certain core features of the current economic and political environment deserve to be highlighted when attempting to put the Bush wartime tax cuts into historical perspective. Three key aspects of the modern policymaking environment differentiate it from previous conflicts, making wartime tax *cuts* possible for the first time in American history.

First, the chief economic justification for wartime tax increases—fear of ruinous inflation—has been an insignificant factor during the war in Iraq. Without that economic imperative, policymakers have been free to consider unconventional wartime fiscal policies, including tax cuts. Second, significant political changes, including the increased polarization of partisan elites, have marginalized deficit concerns and decreased the influence of "deficit hawks." As a result, the political constituency for pay-as-you-go war financing has been weaker in recent years than during any other military conflict in the nation's history. Finally, the elimination of the military draft in 1972 removed one of the most compelling moral arguments for wartime taxes. Previous generations of politicians frequently invoked the rhetoric of "shared sacrifice," citing the mandatory service of American soldiers as an argument for higher taxes. While such arguments have continued to surface from time to time in recent years, their political purchase has diminished substantially with the advent of the modern all-volunteer force in 1973. The result has been a general shift in the political equilibrium on questions of war financing and a new willingness to entertain the possibility of tax cuts, even as U.S. soldiers are fighting a war abroad.

In this concluding chapter, we discuss these three issues in turn, drawing comparisons between earlier conflicts and the war in Iraq where necessary to substantiate our claims.

Inflation and the Economic Imperative of War Taxes

As earlier chapters have shown, in every major military conflict in U.S. history, policymakers have faced the war financing decision with the prospect of disastrous inflation ever present in their deliberations. No major U.S. war has been exempt from these pressures. Reliance on currency finance during the Revolutionary War lead to a collapse in the new continental currency; the War of 1812 forced commodity prices sharply upward; both the Confederacy and the Union faced pressure to increase taxes to stave off inflation during the Civil War; and during each major conflict of the 20th century, political concern over uncontrollable price increases prompted policymakers to turn to current taxation to fund a substantial share of war expenditures. As economic historian Claudia Goldin has observed, "Every major war fought by the United States has been associated with price inflation. In fact, there are no extreme price peaks [between 1775 and 1975] that are not accompanied or preceded by a war."[1]

Given the historical record, one might even go so far as to suggest that preventing inflation has been the core concern of wartime tax policy in U.S. history. Over the past quarter century, however, the threat of inflation—and its corresponding influence on tax policy—has substantially abated. There are many reasons for today's relatively benign inflation environment, including the downward pressure on prices exerted by the increased globalization of the economy. In addition, many attribute the low inflation rates of the past quarter century to the introduction of significant changes in the country's monetary policy ushered in by the chairman of the Federal Reserve Board, Paul Volcker, in the early 1980s.[2] In part because of these policies, inflation has remained low even in the presence of large federal budget deficits, most notably during the years of the Reagan defense build-up.

We offer no commentary on whether the country has achieved an optimal mix of fiscal and monetary policy viewed from the perspective of aggregate social welfare. However, the political consequences of these policies are unmistakable. By keeping inflation low, the Federal Reserve has effectively reduced the political cost to policymakers of deficit financing. In the past, lawmakers who opposed wartime tax increases ran the risk of being blamed for inflation and the havoc it wreaked on the economy. During most of the nation's conflicts, the prospect of ruinous inflation buttressed calls for tax increases. Today, however, there seems to be little fear among those crafting fiscal policy that their choices might endanger price stability. In one sense, therefore, there is a very simple answer to the question of why policymakers have not raised taxes to fund the war in Iraq—because, as yet, they have not been forced to do so.

Indeed, having been freed from the economic imperative of avoiding inflation, policymakers have been able to reduce taxes in the face of rising war expenditures.

Political Polarization and the Marginalization of Deficit Concerns

A second differentiating feature of the current policymaking environment, not unrelated to the discussion of inflation above, is the political marginalization of concerns about federal budget deficits in recent years. In the country's previous conflicts, there has always been a strong constituency in favor of fiscal discipline and against excessive reliance on deficit financing. Concern for budget deficits reached its peak during the Korean War, when lawmakers from both parties, having experienced high inflation during World War II, were keen to avoid what they viewed as the fiscal mistakes of the past. Recall that for the fiscal year 1951, the federal government recorded a budget surplus, in large measure because of the tax increases enacted via the Revenue Act of 1950 and the Excess Profits Tax Act of 1950. In today's vernacular, President Truman would be considered the ultimate "deficit hawk." In the history of American war finance, that "deficit hawk" perspective has always been given voice.

This is not to suggest that concern over budget deficits always prevailed in the formulation of tax policy during all of the country's major conflicts. Indeed, more often than not, the country relied heavily on deficit financing during wartime. During World War II, for example, deficits reached as high as 30 percent of GDP, a level unlikely to be seen again. Yet even in World War II, policymakers took extraordinary measures to reduce the government's reliance on deficit financing. By contrast, recent tax policy has been marked by a specific rejection of deficit concerns, even as the country prepared to go to war. As Vice President Dick Cheney famously quipped in late 2002, in response to Treasury Secretary Paul O'Neill's expression of concern about the country's fiscal soundness, "Deficits don't matter. We won the midterms. This is our due."[3]

The Bush administration's repudiation of deficit concerns has a number of possible explanations. Most prominently, administration officials argued that its tax cuts were necessary to provide stimulus for economic growth. This argument seemed to have the most political traction in the aftermath of the attacks of September 11, when concern for the nation's economic recovery was at its peak. The argument was also advanced in connection with JGTRRA 2003 during the early stages of the war in Iraq, although by that time the case for stimulus policies was weaker, given improvements in the economy over the intervening period. According to the Business Cycle Dating Committee of the National Bureau of Economic Research, real GDP had been growing since September 2001 and reached its highest point ever in July 2003.[4] The point here is not to adjudicate the validity of the administration's stimulus arguments, but rather to highlight the different economic policymaking milieu of recent years compared with earlier conflicts. If one believes that tax cuts stimulate the economy and that the threat of an economic slowdown warrants such policies, then the case for deficit-enlarging wartime tax cuts comes plainly into focus.

The question remains, however, why deficit concerns have continued to play such a marginal role in the formulation of tax policy during the Bush years. What changes in American society account for the apparent decline in the influence of "deficit hawks," who might have pushed tax policy in the traditional direction of tax increases during war? On this point, attention should be given to the substantial political changes the country has undergone since the mid-1970s. As political scientists have observed, the country's political establishment has grown more polarized in the past three decades, with liberals becoming more liberal and conservatives becoming more conservative. This is not a loose "gestalt"-type judgment made by pundits, but rather an empirical observation based on lawmakers' roll call votes in Congress. Recent research by political scientists has shown that the policy positions of the average Democrat and the average Republican have become more widely separated since the mid-1970s. The result, as one recent study put it, is that "the moderates are vanishing from Congress."[5]

The consequences of a more polarized political environment for war financing decisions should not be underestimated. Because deficit hawks come disproportionately from the moderate ranks in both parties, their influence has suffered a decline that roughly corresponds with the rise of partisan polarization.[6] Indeed, the story of the Bush-era wartime tax cuts is perhaps best understood as the triumph within the GOP of conservative "growth hawks" over the more moderate "deficit hawks."[7] The effect has been more pronounced in the House of Representatives than in the Senate. Recall that in connection with JGTRRA 2003, moderate Republicans in the Senate, including most notably Senators John McCain, Olympia Snowe, George Voinovich, and Lincoln Chafee, were able to hold down the overall cost of the administration's second tax cut to $350 billion. There was no similar movement in the House, which, because of redistricting, is more susceptible to the polarizing trend.

In combination with the economic factor of historically low inflation rates, the political developments of increased partisan polarization and the corresponding marginalization of deficit concerns produced something of a "perfect storm" of conditions for wartime tax cuts. It would be wrong, however, to characterize the debate over war taxes strictly in economic and political terms. For more than two centuries, Americans have seen in the war financing question a moral dimension as well. Shouldn't U.S. taxpayers share in the sacrifices borne by those who have been conscripted into military service? And if our moral intuitions lead us to answer yes, should we feel differently about our wartime fiscal obligations when military service is voluntary?

Conscription and the Moral Argument
for Shared Sacrifice

As we have emphasized at various points in our analysis, a major difference between the war in Iraq and previous conflicts is the absence of mandatory military service and the corresponding effect on the politics of wartime tax policy. Shared sacrifice has been a major theme in the politics of wartime taxes throughout the country's history. However one feels about the costs and benefits of conscription, the drafting of ordinary citizens into military service has profoundly influenced the way the country talks about the costs of war.

Conscription adds an unmistakable moral force to the arguments of those who advocate wartime tax increases and obliges opponents of higher taxes to reframe, or perhaps even abandon, their arguments. Recall how Representative Edward Little of Kansas framed his argument at the outset of American involvement in World War I: "You promised when you conscripted the youth of this country that you would conscript the wealth as well. . . . Let their dollars die for this country too."[8] Truman's Treasury chief, James Snyder, issued a similar admonition to the Senate Finance Committee during the Korean War, alluding once again to the conscription of wealth as well as men: "You passed a bill up here to draft boys of 18, to send them to war. I think it is just as important we draft some of the profits to help pay for the expenditures." Opponents of higher wartime tax burdens have likewise reformulated their arguments to appear more sensitive to the burdens upon those drafted into military service. For example, consider Senator Russell Long's awkward argument that a "tax increase of ten times the size recommended by the president would still not begin to [equal] the sacrifice of our courageous young men fighting and dying in the swamps and jungles of Vietnam."[9]

Given the frequent invocation of conscription as a justification for wartime tax increases, it seems reasonable to conclude that Americans are more willing to accept higher taxes when those burdens are framed in the context of the sacrifices of American soldiers. If so, it would appear that the elimination of the draft in 1972 and the introduction of the all-volunteer force shortly thereafter worked an unexpected transformation on the politics of wartime taxation. Whereas conscription made wartime taxes more likely, or at least provided an obvious and compelling argument in their favor, the introduction of a professional volunteer military force eclipsed those arguments completely. From 1973 onward, arguments for the "conscription of wealth" simply no longer have the same moral force they once did.

To probe the issue further, consider the following thought experiment. Over the past several years, Representative Charles Rangel (D-NY), a Korean War veteran, has proposed legislation to reinstitute the draft. The crux of Rangel's argument is that "military service should be a shared sacrifice" and that we should "not allow some to stay behind while other people's children do the fighting."[10] The Rangel bill has never passed and, given strong popular opposition to the draft, it is unlikely to pass any time soon. But imagine for the moment if the Rangel bill were to pass and Congress began requiring individuals to fight in Iraq against their will. Would Congress in such circumstances enact tax cuts of the EGTRRA/JGTRRA variety? Is it possible to imagine repealing the estate tax or reducing the taxation of capital gains or dividends in an environment where Congress has mandated military service? Perhaps—in politics, one should never say never. However, we submit that debates over how to pay for war are cast in very different terms when soldiers on the frontline include not only those who have volunteered for the assignment but also those who are there under force of law.

Some may regard this as an unfortunate commentary on the politics of war financing in the 21st century. Perhaps arguments for "shared sacrifice" *should* carry as much political weight when the country's military efforts are carried out by professional volunteers as when ordinary citizens are drafted into service. Over the past several years, however, there has been little evidence that arguments for shared sacrifice continue to resonate with the American electorate.

* * *

Throughout this book, we have attempted to provide a thorough and balanced account of the politics of U.S. tax policy during wartime. As noted in the introduction, our chief objective has been to put the tax cuts enacted during the war in Iraq into historical perspective. Because the Bush tax cuts represent such a significant departure from the usual wartime practice of raising taxes, commentators have understandably asked whether current policies mark a break from a longstanding patriotic tradition of wartime fiscal sacrifice. Have we entered a new era of fiscal self-indulgence, where even in the face of mounting losses of blood and treasure, American voters demand fewer burdens from their government? As the previous chapters have shown, strands of that mode of thinking about wartime tax policy have surfaced throughout American history.

What is different about the current period is the constellation of circumstances making possible a more extreme manifestation of our nation's latent instinct to oppose the burdens of taxation. The three factors described above—historically low inflation rates, a political environment that has marginalized deficit concerns, and the elimination of the draft—have transformed the politics of wartime taxation in the United States. These changes not only have influenced observed policy outcomes (wartime tax cuts rather than wartime tax increases) but have begun to change how we talk about our collective responsibilities during war.

Throughout American history, lawmakers made the case for higher taxes as an expression of support for U.S. troops. Indeed, in every conflict we examined, support for higher taxes was viewed as a defining feature of being a "military hawk." As one GOP Senator put it in January 1967, "I just don't see how we can be hawks on the war and then vote against taxes to pay for it." There is scant evidence of any remaining life in this point of view. At times, lawmakers have turned the argument upside down, arguing that only by *reducing* taxes can we truly support the troops. Speaking in April 2003, for example, Kentucky Senator Jim Bunning made the case for the administration's tax cuts, arguing that "When our troops come home, I hope they have jobs. The Reserves and

Guardsmen coming back, their jobs are on the line."[11] Senator Bunning's argument stands in stark contrast to the political rhetoric of a half-century earlier, when House Speaker Sam Rayburn admonished his colleagues by noting, "I think the boys in Korea would appreciate it more if we in this country were to pay our own way instead of leaving it for them to pay when they get back."

It is impossible to know how events will unfold over the next several months and years. Most commentators view the elections of November 2006 as a repudiation of the administration's policies in Iraq. The fact that Democrats now control both chambers of Congress will no doubt affect the future direction of the U.S. military's role in that country, as will future changes in the White House, especially if a Democrat wins the presidency in November 2008. Even so, it is worth remembering that, with regard to the war financing question, Democrats have so far shown little interest in reversing the administration's simultaneous pursuit of war and tax cuts. Indeed, if anything, Democrats seem intent on introducing their own brand of tax cuts, even as the war in Iraq continues.[12] If this happens, it might signal that wartime tax cuts, which so many commentators initially decried as a historical anomaly, have found a more secure footing in American politics.

Notes

CHAPTER 1

1. Julian E. Zelizer, "The Uneasy Relationship: Democracy, Taxation, and State Building since the New Deal," in *The Democratic Experience,* edited by Meg Jacobs, William J. Novak, and Julian E. Zelizer (Princeton: Princeton University Press, 2003).

2. Max M. Edling, *A Revolution in Favor of Government: Origins of the U.S. Constitution and the Making of the American State* (New York: Oxford University Press, 2003), 150.

3. E. James Ferguson, "Currency Finance: An Interpretation of Colonial Monetary Practices," *William and Mary Quarterly* 10, no. 2 (1953): 174 and passim.

4. Edling, *A Revolution in Favor of Government,* 151.

5. Edling, *A Revolution in Favor of Government,* 152; Roger H. Brown, *Redeeming the Republic: Federalists, Taxation, and the Origins of the Constitution* (Baltimore: Johns Hopkins University Press, 1993), 25–26.

6. Edling, *A Revolution in Favor of Government,* 153.

7. E. James Ferguson, *The Power of the Purse: A History of American Public Finance, 1776–1790* (Chapel Hill: University of North Carolina Press, 1961); Edling, *A Revolution in Favor of Government,* 153–54.

8. Robin L. Einhorn, *American Taxation, American Slavery* (Chicago: University of Chicago Press, 2006), 126–32.

9. Brown, *Redeeming the Republic,* 11–12.

10. Brown, *Redeeming the Republic,* 32–138. Brown emphasizes the political constraints on state lawmakers, rather than their ostensible parochialism or lack of foresight.

11. Brown, *Redeeming the Republic,* 11–12, 24–28.

12. Brown, *Redeeming the Republic,* 17–19.

13. Brown, *Redeeming the Republic;* Frederick W. Marks, III, *Independence on Trial: Foreign Affairs and the Making of the Constitution* (Baton Rouge: Louisiana State University Press, 1973).

14. Einhorn, *American Taxation, American Slavery,* 155–56.

15. Brown, *Redeeming the Republic,* 20–28; Edling, *A Revolution in Favor of Government,* 154–55.

16. *Documents Illustrative of the Formation of the Union of the American States,* edited by Charles C. Tansill, 69th Congress, 1st Session, House Document no. 398 (Washington, DC: Government Printing Office, 1927).

17. "Federalist No. 31: The Same Subject Continued: Concerning the General Power of Taxation," January 1, 1788, http://thomas.loc.gov/home/histdox/fed_31.html.

18. "Federalist No. 30: Concerning the General Power of Taxation," December 28, 1787, http://thomas.loc.gov/home/histdox/fed_30.html.

19. Einhorn, *American Taxation, American Slavery,* 150–55.

20. W. Elliot Brownlee, *Federal Taxation in America: A Short History,* 2nd ed. (New York: Cambridge University Press, 2004), 21–23.

21. Robert E. Wright and David Jack Cowen, *Financial Founding Fathers: The Men Who Made America Rich* (Chicago: The University of Chicago Press, 2006), 93–95; Dall W. Forsythe, *Taxation and Political Change in the Young Nation, 1781–1833* (New York: Columbia University Press, 1977), 41–42. For the best treatment of the Whiskey Rebellion, see Thomas P. Slaughter, *The Whiskey Rebellion: Frontier Epilogue to the American Revolution* (New York: Oxford University Press, 1986).

22. Brownlee, *Federal Taxation in America: A Short History,* 24; Randolph Evernghim Paul, *Taxation in the United States* (Boston: Little Brown, 1954), 5–6; Forsythe, *Taxation and Political Change in the Young Nation,* 53; Albert Sidney Bolles, *The Financial History of the United States from 1789 to 1860,* 3rd ed. (New York: D. Appleton and Company, 1891), 103–26.

23. Paul, *Taxation in the United States,* 6.

24. Donald R. Hickey, *The War of 1812: A Forgotten Conflict* (Urbana: University of Illinois Press, 1990), 5–6.

25. Hickey, *War of 1812,* 6–7.

26. Forsythe, *Taxation and Political Change in the Young Nation,* 51–57.

27. Hickey, *War of 1812,* 12.

28. Hickey, *War of 1812,* 11.

29. Donald R. Hickey, "American Trade Restrictions during the War of 1812," *Journal of American History* 68, no. 3 (1981): 517.

30. Hickey, "American Trade Restrictions," 517–18; Hickey, *War of 1812,* 19–24.

31. Hickey, *War of 1812,* 26–28.

32. On Gallatin's criticism of Federalist economic policy, see, for instance, Albert Gallatin, "A sketch of the finances of the United States" (New York: William A. Davis, 1796). On Gallatin's rise to power and his relationship to Jefferson and other Republicans, see Alexander Balinky, *Albert Gallatin: Fiscal Theories and Policies* (New Brunswick, NJ: Rutgers University Press, 1958), 3–16.

33. Balinky, *Albert Gallatin*, 30–48.

34. Balinky, *Albert Gallatin*, 49–53. Gallatin hope to use a direct tax—levied on both land and slaves but not on commercial property—to bolster Republican electoral fortunes. For the convoluted politics of this strategy, see Einhorn, *American Taxation, American Slavery*, 189–90.

35. Balinky, *Albert Gallatin: Fiscal Theories and Policies*, 60–62.

36. On Gallatin's doubts about wholesale tax reduction, see Balinky, *Albert Gallatin*, 53–67.

37. For a similar critique of Republican tax policy, see Balinky, *Albert Gallatin*, 128–63.

38. Annual report of Secretary of Treasury on state of finances, November 7, 1807, 242–49; Alexander S. Balinky, "Gallatin's Theory of War Finance," *William and Mary Quarterly* 16, no. 1 (1959): 76 and passim.

39. Balinky, "Gallatin's Theory," 74.

40. Annual report of Secretary of Treasury on state of finances, December 16, 1808, 309.

41. Annual report of Secretary of Treasury on state of finances, December 8, 1809, 374

42. Annual report of Secretary of Treasury on state of finances, November 25, 1811, 497; Balinky, "Gallatin's Theory," 79.

43. Gallatin to Ezekiel Bacon, January 10, 1812, in ASP: Finance, 2: 524.

44. Gallatin to Ezekiel Bacon, January 10, 1812, in ASP: Finance, 2: 524; J. C. A. Stagg, *Mr. Madison's War: Politics, Diplomacy, and Warfare in the Early American Republic, 1783–1830* (Princeton, NJ: Princeton University Press, 1983), 151.

45. Hickey, *War of 1812*, 34–35; Stagg, *Mr. Madison's War*, 88–90; Bradford Perkins, *Prologue to War: England and the United States, 1805–1812* (Berkeley: University of California Press, 1961), 362–63.

46. Stagg, *Mr. Madison's War*, 90–91, 152; Hickey, *War of 1812*, 35; Perkins, *Prologue to War*, 364–66.

47. Hickey, *War of 1812*, 49–50.

48. Hickey, *War of 1812*, 50.

49. Hickey, *War of 1812*, 118–22.

50. Hickey, *War of 1812*, 120.

51. Hickey, *War of 1812*, 122; Stagg, *Mr. Madison's War*, 314–16.

52. Davis Rich Dewey, *Financial History of the United States*, 11th ed. (New York: Longmans, Green and Co., 1931), 139.

53. Hickey, *War of 1812*, 122–23.

54. Stagg, *Mr. Madison's War*, 375–79; Hickey, *War of 1812*, 165–66.

55. Stagg, *Mr. Madison's War*, 437; Hickey, *War of 1812*, 246–47.

56. Hickey, *War of 1812*, 247.

57. Dewey, *Financial History of the United States*, 139–40; Hickey, *War of 1812*, 248–49.

58. Hickey, *War of 1812*, 248.

59. Bolles, *Financial History of the United States*, 242.

60. Hickey, *War of 1812*, 2.

61. Brownlee, *Federal Taxation in America: A Short History*, 29.

CHAPTER 2

1. Robert Stanley, *Dimensions of Law in the Service of Order: Origins of the Federal Income Tax, 1861–1913* (New York: Oxford University Press, 1993), 25; Percy Ashley, *Modern Tariff History* (3rd ed., 1920) (New York: Howard Fertig, Inc., 1970), 150, 152–60.

2. Ashley, *Tariff History*, 167–70. For a modern perspective, see David E. Rosenbaum, "Tax Cuts and War Have Seldom Mixed," *New York Times*, March 9, 2003.

3. Act of March 3, 1857, 11 Stat. 192. See Harry Edwin Smith, *The United States Federal Internal Tax History from 1861 to 1871* (Boston: Houghton Mifflin Company, 1914): 2; Ashley, *Tariff History*, 176; J. Y. Mason, "Dialogues on Free Trade and Direct Taxation. No. II," *DeBow's Review and Industrial Resources, Statistics, etc. Devoted to Commerce* (September 1858): 352.

4. *New York Tribune*, Oct. 22, 1857, quoted in James M. McPherson, *Battle Cry of Freedom* (New York: Ballentine Books, 1988), 192. See Charles W. Calomiris and Larry Schweikart, "The Panic of 1857: Origins, Transmission, and Containment," *Journal of Economic History* 51 (1991): 807–9; George W. Van Vleck, *The Panic of 1857: An Analytic Study* (New York, 1943).

5. See Ashley, *Tariff History*, 177–78; Frederic C. Howe, *Taxation and Taxes in the United States under the Internal Revenue System, 1791–1895* (New York: Thomas Y. Crowell, 1896), 51; Smith, *Tax History*, 3; Robert T. Patterson, "Government Finance on the Eve of the Civil War," *Journal of Economic History* 12 (1952): 35, 37.

6. Prior to 1858, the last time the government ran a deficit was in 1849. U.S. Department of Commerce, "Historical Statistics of the United States, 1789–1945" (1949): 297, Series P 89–98.

7. Ashley, *Tariff History*, 179.

8. "Historical Statistics," at 297, Series P 89–98 (cumulative annual debt from 1858–61 amounting to $75,217,120); John F. Witte, *The Politics and Development of the Federal Income Tax* (Madison: The University of Wisconsin Press, 1985), 67. Others estimate the deficit at closer to $65 million. Patterson, "Government Finance," 37.

9. See Rose Razaghian, "Financing the Civil War: The Confederacy's Financial Strategy," Yale International Center for Finance Working Paper No. 04-45 (2005), http://ssrn.com/abstract=621761.

10. "The War Tax," *DeBow's Review and Industrial Resources, Statistics, etc. Devoted to Commerce* 6 (4 October/November 1861): 436.

11. *Journals of the Confederate Congress* 3(442) (December 8, 1863).

12. Richard Cecil Todd, *Confederate Finance* (Athens: The University of Georgia Press, 1954), 136 (citing a speech Stephens delivered on July 11, 1861).

13. J. C. Schwab, "The Finances of the Confederate States," *Political Science Quarterly* 7, no. 1 (March 1892): 38, 40; "A War Tax Is a Necessary Measure" *DeBow's Review and Industrial Resources, Statistics, etc. Devoted to Commerce* 6, no. 4 (October/November 1861): 436. The $3.5 million raised over the course of the war fell quite short of Confederate projections of $25 million in the first year of operation. Douglas B. Ball, *Financial Failure and Confederate Defeat* (Urbana: University of Illinois Press, 1991), 204–7.

14. Emory M. Thomas, *The Confederate Nation: 1861–1865* (New York: Harper, 1979), 137; James L. Sellers, "An Interpretation of Civil War Finance," *American Historical Review* 30, no. 2 (January 1925): 282; John Christopher Schwab, "Prices in the Confederate States, 1861–65," *Political Science Quarterly* 14, no. 2 (June 1899): 281, 286, 293–94; Peter Temin, "The Post-Bellum Recovery of the South and the Cost of the Civil War," *Journal of Economic History* 36, no. 4: 898–907; W. E. Woodward, *Meet General Grant* (New York: Horace Liveright, 1928), 235; R. Neil Fulghum, "Moneys for the Southern Cause," in *Documenting the American South: The Southern Homefront, 1861–1865,* http://docsouth.unc.edu/imls/currency/index.html.

15. Edwin R. A. Seligman, *The Income Tax* (New York: Macmillan, 1911), 482; "The Finances of the Confederated States," *New York Times,* March 16, 1861, 4 ("The weakness of the Confederated States in their finances, is shown by the fact that the proceeds of a special tax is mortgaged for the payment of their first loan. . . . If these States commence by mortgaging the best source of revenue for their *first* loan, what is to guarantee the *second,* that must speedily follow?") One reason the South lacked the ability to borrow is that some of the states had actually repudiated their own debts already.

16. Only South Carolina actually collected the direct tax itself in cash, although Mississippi collected taxes to make interest payments on bonds issued to fulfill their quota. Texas confiscated property located in the state but owned by Northerners, Alabama borrowed from state banks, and all other states issued securities to obtain the funds. Eugene M. Lerner, "The Monetary and Fiscal Programs of the Confederate Government, 1861–65," *Journal of Political Economy* 61, no. 6 (December 1954): 506, 509.

17. Seligman, *The Income Tax,* 482–83; Kossuth Kent Kennan, *Income Taxation: Methods and Results in Various Countries* (Milwaukee: Burdick and Allen, 1910), 269; Sidney Ratner, *Taxation and Democracy in America* (London: Octagon Books, 1980), 102–3.

18. See Richard Franklin Bensel, *Yankee Leviathan: The Origins of Central State Authority in America, 1859–1877* (Cambridge: Cambridge University Press, 1990), 167–68.

19. Seligman, *The Income Tax,* 483.

20. Razaghian, "Financing the Civil War," 4.

21. A. B. Moore to Gentlemen of the Senate and House of Representatives, October 28, 1861, quoted in Lerner, "Monetary and Fiscal Programs," 509.

22. Richard N. Current, "God and the Strongest Battalions," in *Why the North Won the Civil War* (Baton Rouge: Louisiana State University Press, 1960), 23.

23. *Report of the President, Directors, &c., of the Milledgeville R. Road Co. to the Stockholders,* Oct. 6, 1862, 6–7.

24. Georgia Lee Tatum, *Disloyalty in the Confederacy* (Chapel Hill: University of North Carolina Press, 1934), 19.

25. McPherson, *Battle Cry of Freedom*, 430.

26. Margaret Levi, *Consent, Dissent, and Patriotism* (Cambridge: Cambridge University Press, 1997), 96.

27. McPherson, *Battle Cry of Freedom*, 431–32; Levi, *Consent, Dissent*, 96.

28. R. P. Brooks, "Conscription in the Confederate States of America, 1862–1865," *Bulletin of the University of Georgia* 17, no. 4 (March 1917): 424–25.

29. McPherson, *Battle Cry of Freedom*, 431.

30. Albert Burton Moore, *Conscription and Conflict in the Confederacy* (New York: Macmillan Co., 1924), 70; Woodward, *Meet General Grant*, 230; The State, ex rel. Dawson, in re Strawbridge & Mays, 39 Ala. 367 (1864). For descriptions of the exemption more generally, see Peter Wallenstein, "Rich Man's War, Rich Man's Fight: Civil War and the Transformation of Public Finance in Georgia," *Journal of Southern History* 50, no. 1 (February 1984): 15, 16; Armistead L. Robinson, "In the Shadow of Old John Brown: Insurrection Anxiety and Confederate Mobilization, 1861–1863," *Journal of Negro History* 65, no. 4 (Autumn 1980): 279, 283.

31. Stephen V. Ash, "Poor Whites in the Occupied South, 1861–1865," *Journal of Southern History* 57, no. 1 (February 1991): 39, 51–52 (quoting anonymous letter to Aunt, April 8, 1864, in Civil War Collection, Tennessee State Library and Archives, Nashville). See Ella Lonn, *Desertion during the Civil War* (New York: The Century Co., 1928), 14–15.

32. Katherine A. Giuffre, "First in Flight: Desertion as Politics in the North Carolina Confederate Army," *Social Science History* 21, no. 2 (Summer 1997): 245, 249.

33. Lerner, "Monetary and Fiscal Programs," 509, n.22.

34. Randolph E. Paul, *Taxation in the United States* (Boston: Little, Brown & Co., 1954), 19; Ball, *Financial Failure*, 231. For more on Governor Brown, see Joseph H. Parks, "State Rights in a Crisis: Governor Joseph E. Brown Versus President Jefferson Davis," *Journal of Southern History* 32, no. 1 (February 1966): 3. Governor Brown was considered the only governor who was openly defiant of the Confederate government and especially the conscription acts. Tatum, *Disloyalty*, 15.

35. For unearned income, the lowest rate was 5 percent on incomes between $500 and $1,500 and the highest rate was 15 percent on incomes in excess of $10,000. For earned income, there was a 1 percent tax on incomes between $1,000 and $2,000 and a 2 percent rate on the amount in excess of $2,000. James M. Mathews, ed. *Public Laws of the Confederate States of America, Passed at the Third Session of the First Congress, 1863* (Richmond: R. M. Smith, 1863), Sec. 8(VI) (hereinafter *Confederate Statutes*); Ball, *Financial Failure*, 233. Corporations were required to reserve one-tenth of their annual earnings, set apart for dividends and reserves, and remit that to the collector. Any dividend subsequently paid would thus be exempt from further tax. Where the earnings exceeded 10 percent of the company's capital stock, the rate of tax increased from one-tenth to one-eighth, and where the earnings exceeded 20 percent of the company's capital stock, the rate of tax increased from one-eighth to one-sixth. *Confederate Statutes*, Sec. 8(VI); Steven A. Bank, "Entity Theory as Myth in the Origins of the Corporate Income Tax," *William & Mary Law Review* 43, no. 2 (December 2001): 447, 488–89.

36. Todd, *Confederate Finance*, 138 (quoting Memminger).

37. *Report of the Commissioner of Taxes Accompanying the Report of the Secretary of the Treasury* 1 (1863).

38. Bensel, *Yankee Leviathan*, 165, 183; Moore, *Conscription and Conflict*, 74.

39. Wallenstein, "Rich Man's War," 30.

40. Moore, *Conscription and Conflict*, 75–76.

41. Bensel, *Yankee Leviathan*, 166; Brooks, "Conscription in the Confederate States of America," 425.

42. *Confederate Statutes*, Secs. 1, 5, 11; Ball, *Financial Failure*, 233–35; Bensel, *Yankee Leviathan*, 169; Seligman, *The Income Tax*, 489; Tatum, *Disloyalty*, 19–20. Unlike the Provisional Constitution in effect when the 1861 direct taxes were enacted, the new constitution required apportionment, and the majority concluded that the lack of an adequate census made this task a practical impossibility (Ball, *Financial Failure*, 215–16, 234).

43. Thomas, *Confederate Nation*, 198; Seligman, *The Income Tax*, 489; Todd, *Confederate Finance*, 142.

44. The law exempted property up to a value of $500 for heads of household and $1,000 for soldiers and for families of deceased soldiers. "An Act to Levy Additional Taxes for the Common Defence and Support of the Government," February 17, 1864, Public Laws of the Confederate States of America, Sec. 5, 208, 210.

45. "The New Rebel Tax Law," *New York Times*, May 16, 1863 (reprinting an advertisement from the Richmond *Whig*).

46. "Affairs in Richmond," *New York Times*, April 26, 1863, 2 (reprinted from the *Richmond Enquirer*, April 16, 1863).

47. Woodward, *Meet General Grant*, 242–43.

48. David M. Potter, "Jefferson Davis and the Political Factors in Confederate Defeat," in *Why the North Won the Civil War* (Baton Rouge: Louisiana State University Press, 1960), 94.

49. Quoted in Seligman, *The Income Tax*, 492.

50. Ball, *Financial Failure*, 236; Bensel, *Yankee Leviathan*, 170. See Razaghian, "Financing the Civil War," 38 (table 8). By 1864, the war taxes raised almost 11 percent of the Confederacy's total revenues, a figure that compares favorably with the 15 percent raised by taxation in the North during the same period. Schwab, "Finances of the Confederate States," 41.

51. "An Act to Levy Additional Taxes for the Common Defence and Support of the Government," *Public Laws of the Confederate States of America, Passed at the Fourth Session of the First Congress, 1863–1864* (Richmond: R. M. Smith, 1864), 209; Seligman, *The Income Tax*, 490.

52. Seligman, *The Income Tax*, 491; Ratner, *Taxation and Democracy*, 107; Paul, *Taxation in the United States*, 22.

53. "Report of the Secretary of the Treasury," Senate Executive and Misc. Doc. No. 2, 1st Sess. 37th Cong. 7–8 (1861).

54. "Monetary Affairs," *New York Times*, July 18, 1861, 3. The *New York Tribune*, reporting the following day on the advances of the Union army in Virginia, wrote "it seems to be the universal and joyful conviction that this is the 'beginning of the end.' " Quoted in Smith, *Tax History*, 16.

55. The loan strategy began even before the hostilities started with the firing on Fort Sumter on April 12. On March 22, Chase opened bids on government securities totaling $8 million at a 6 percent rate. Smith, *Tax History*, 10. On July 17 and August 5, 1861, Congress passed loan acts that empowered the Secretary to borrow $250 million, using a combination of three-year Treasury notes at a rate of 7.3 percent or 20-year bonds with a rate not to exceed 7 percent. Ratner, *Taxation and Democracy*, 64; Witte, *Politics and Development*, 67.

56. McPherson, *Battle Cry of Freedom*, 345.

57. Cong. Globe, 37th Congress, 1st Session, 254 (July 25, 1861) (statement of Sen. Simmons, R-RI).

58. Quoted in McPherson, *Battle Cry of Freedom*, 348.

59. Cong. Globe, 37th Congress, 1st Session, 254 (July 25, 1861) (statement of Sen. Simmons, R-RI).

60. "The War Tax," *New York Times*, July 23, 1861, 4. The correspondent from the *London Times* concurred, noting that there are some in Europe "who will hesitate to trust in time of war, and for purposes of unproductive investment, a Federation of States, several of which in their individual capacity repudiated a debt in time of peace and prosperity." "Comments on the Budget of Secretary Chase," *London Times*, in *New York Times*, August 2, 1861, 3.

61. "Remarks on the Direct Tax Bill," *Scientific American* 5, no. 7 (August 17, 1861): 105.

62. Quoted in Ratner, *Taxation and Democracy*, 64.

63. "The New Tariff—The Direct Tax—The Income Tax—Virtual Repeal of Sub-Treasury Law," *New York Times*, August 3, 1861, 4.

64. Act of August 5, 1861, 12 Stat. 297. The House bill had proposed a 3 percent rate on all incomes over $600 and the Senate had proposed a 5 percent rate on all incomes over $1,000. In Conference, the houses settled on a 3 percent rate on income in excess of $800. Witte, *Politics and Development*, 68.

65. Bensel, *Yankee Leviathan*, 168. A primary difference was that while in the Confederacy most states paid their quota through issuances of state treasury notes, which compounded the inflation effect, in the Union at least nine of the states, plus the District of Columbia, chose to pay their quota by increasing their own general property tax. Only five states met their quotas through borrowing. Smith, *Tax History*, 38–39.

66. Ratner, *Taxation and Democracy*, 70; Smith, *Tax History*, 24–25.

67. "How the Expenses of the War Are to Be Met," *New York Times*, January 8, 1862, 1.

68. "The Delay of the Tax Bill," *New York Times*, February 13, 1862, 4.

69. Charles J. Bullock, "Financing the War," *Quarterly Journal of Economics* 31, no. 3 (May 1917): 357, 362.

70. "The Tax Bill," *Saturday Evening Post*, March 15, 1862, 3.

71. Howe, *Taxation and Taxes*, 65. Several popular journals made light of the breadth of the new internal excise taxes. The *Knickerbocker Magazine* proposed several humorous additions to the bill, including a $0.25 cent tax for speaking French or sneezing "with unusual noise." "Additions Proposed to the Tax Bill," *Saturday Evening Post*,

July 26, 1862, 6 (reprinted from *Knickerbocker Magazine*). *Scientific American* observed that the committee had thankfully omitted crinoline, a component for the production of "hooped skirts," from the tax list: "The fair portion of the community need not dread any retrenchment of their circumference; the gallantry of the Congressional committee has spared them this mortification." "The Tax Bill Amendment," *Scientific American* 8, no. 12 (March 21, 1863): 177.

72. It proposed a 3 percent tax on incomes in excess of $600 (which was the same as the House bill passed in 1861), compared with the 1861 Act's 3 percent rate on incomes in excess of $800. "The Tax Bill," *Saturday Evening Post,* March 15, 1862, 3; Stanley, *Dimensions of Law,* 29.

73. Under the proposal, the income tax would have had a 3 percent rate on incomes between $600 and $10,000, a 5 percent rate on incomes between $10,000 and $50,000, and a 7.5 percent rate on incomes in excess of $50,000. Cong. Globe, 37th Congress, 2d Session, 2486 (1862) (statement of Sen. Simmons).

74. Cong. Globe, 37th Congress, 2d Session, 2891 (1862).

75. Cong. Globe, 37th Congress, 2d Session, 2486 (1862).

76. Cong. Globe, 37th Congress, 2d Session, 2486 (1862).

77. Cong. Globe, 37th Congress, 2d Session, 2350 (1862).

78. Act of July 1, 1862, ch. 119, 12 Stat. 432, 473. See Joseph A. Hill, "The Civil War Income Tax," *Quarterly Journal of Economics* 8, no. 4 (July 1894): 426.

79. "The Tax Bill," *Saturday Evening Post,* March 22, 1862, 7. Customs duties were expected to raise $50 million and the excise tax on manufactured goods was expected to raise $30 million. The next largest item was the tax on spirits, which was expected to raise $15 million.

80. "The Tax Bill and the Manufacturers," *New York Times,* June 15, 1862, 3; Letter to the Editor ("A Reader of the Times and a Large Manufacturer"), "Instance of Triple and Quadruple Taxation," *New York Times,* June 28, 1862, 2.

81. Howe, *Taxation and Taxes,* 65.

82. Letter to the Editor, "Revision of the Tax Bill," *New York Times,* December 14, 1862, 3.

83. "Manufacturers Opposition to the Income Tax," *Merchants Magazine and Commercial Review* 49, no. 2 (August 1863): 152

84. "The Tax on Manufacturers," *Scientific American* 8, no. 25 (June 20, 1863): 393; "The Manufacturers and the Income Tax," *New York Times,* May 28, 1863, 4; Elmer Ellis, "Public Opinion and the Income Tax," *Mississippi Valley Historical Review* 27, no. 2 (September 1940): 225, 227. Part of manufacturers' concern surrounded the publicity feature with respect to their returns.

85. Letter from Edward McPherson, Treasury Department, Office of Internal Revenue, dated June 15, 1863, to Manufacturers Convention in "Manufacturers Opposition to the Income Tax," *Merchants Magazine and Commercial Review* 49, no. 2 (August 1863): 151 (quoting Edward McPherson, Treasury Department Office of Internal Revenue).

86. "The Tax on Manufacturers," 393.

87. E. B. Ward, "Manufacturers Opposition to the Income Tax," *Merchants Magazine and Commercial Review* 49, no. 2 (August 1863): 151, 152.

88. Howe, *Taxation and Taxes,* 58.

89. Quoted in Ratner, *Taxation and Democracy,* 90.

90. "Popular Fallacies Regarding Taxation," *New York Times,* April 8, 1864, 4.

91. Quoted in "Chapter on Taxation: Our Capacity for Taxation," *Advocate of Peace* 15 (January/February 1864): 24.

92. Howe, *Taxation and Taxes,* 62.

93. Act of June 30, 1864, ch. 173, 13 Stat. 223.

94. Act of July 4, 1864, 13 Stat. 417; Ratner, *Taxation and Democracy,* 89.

95. Cong. Globe, 38th Congress, 1st Session, 3527, 3528–29 (July 2, 1864).

96. Cong. Globe, 38th Congress, 1st Session, 1876 (April 26, 1864).

97. United States War Department, "Report of the Provost Marshall General" (1866) quoted in Levi,*Consent, Dissent,* 64.

98. Iver Bernstein, *The New York City Draft Riots: Their Significance for American Society and Politics in the Age of the Civil War* (New York: Oxford University Press, 1990), 5; McPherson, *Battle Cry of Freedom,* 609. On July 4, 1863, the same day Congress passed the emergency income tax act, Governor Seymour of New York issued the following warning to Republicans supporting emancipation and conscription: "Remember this— that the bloody and treasonable doctrine of public necessity can be proclaimed by a mob as well as by a government."

99. Ernest A. McKay, *The Civil War and New York City* (Syracuse: Syracuse University Press, 1990) (quoting Benjamin Wood).

100. McPherson, *Battle Cry of Freedom,* 601. Commutation was in part designed to avoid the unsavory tactics of "substitute brokers" by allowing the government to find a substitute for a fee far below that charged by most brokers. "General Intelligence," *Christian Advocate and Journal,* July 23, 1863, 30; "The Alleviations of the Draft," *The Independent—Devoted to the Consideration of Politics, Social, and Economic Tendencies, History, Literature, and the Arts,* July 23, 1863, 764. Nevertheless, commutation was demonized by its opponents and was eventually repealed for all but conscientious objectors in the middle of 1864. McPherson, *Battle Cry of Freedom,* 601.

101. McKay, *The Civil War,* 214.

102. McPherson, *Battle Cry of Freedom,* 601.

103. Cong. Globe, 38th Congress, 1st Session, 1876–77 (April 26, 1864).

104. Cong. Globe, 38th Congress, 1st Session, 2515 (May 27, 1864).

105. Cong. Globe, 38th Congress, 1st Session, 2760 (May 27, 1864).

106. Ratner, *Taxation and Democracy,* 96.

107. Hill, "The Civil War Income Tax," 436.

108. Carl Benson, Letter to the Editor, "Income Tax Returns," *New York Times,* February 5, 1865, 2; Ratner, *Taxation and Democracy,* 97. Under Morrill's proposal, the top rate would increase from 7.5 to 10 percent on incomes over $3,000. The House eventually settled on a more modest increase to a tax of 10 percent on incomes over $5,000.

109. Howe, *Taxation and Taxes,* 68.

110. Act of March 3, 1865, ch. 78, 13 Stat. 469. The 1865 Act's income tax feature was later subject to constitutional challenge as an unapportioned direct tax. The Court upheld the tax on the grounds that it was more similar to a duty or excise than to a direct tax. *Springer v. United States,* 102 U.S. 586 (1880).

111. "Historical Statistics," 297, 300 Series P 89–98, 99–108.

112. See "Historical Statistics," 301, Series P 99–108; William H. Glasson, *Federal Military Pensions in the United States* (New York: Oxford University Press, 1918), 124.

113. Cong. Globe, 39th Congress, 1st Session, 2783 (1866).

114. "Taxes on Manufacturers," *New York Times,* August 27, 1865, 4.

115. "The Income Tax," *Arthur's Home Magazine* 27, no. 1 (January 1866): 80.

116. The excise tax on cotton was particularly controversial, in part because there were calls to increase its rate as the southern states rejoined the Union. See, for example, "Tax on Cotton," *New York Times,* January 13, 1866, 4; Letter to the Editor, "The Excise Tax on Cotton," *New York Times,* April 28, 1866, 2; "Hon. Reverdy Johnson on the Cotton Tax," Selma (AL) Messenger, in *New York Times,* October 18, 1866, 5; "The Southern Cotton Trade and the Excise Laws," *DeBow's Review, Devoted to the Restoration of the Southern States* 2, no. 5 (November 1866): 527; "The Cotton Tax and the Industries of the North," *Merchants Magazine and Commercial Review* 55, no. 6 (December 1866): 409.

Cotton growers were not the only ones to voice their displeasure. There were protests by shipbuilders, publishers, and manufacturers of wool, among many others. See, for example, "The Worsted Manufacture and the Tax on Wool," *New York Times,* January 17, 1867, 4; "Convention of Shipbuilders in Maine," *New York Times,* January 31, 1867, 5; "The Tax on Advertisements," *Chicago Tribune,* February 3, 1867, reprinted in *New York Times,* February 16, 1867, 5.

117. See Act of July 13, 1866, 14 Stat. 138 (applying the 10 percent rate on incomes above $5,000 to formerly exempt government officials).

118. Wells had served on an advisory body to Treasury Secretary Hugh McCulloch before his appointment. See Stanley, *Dimensions of Law,* 44; Smith, *Tax History,* 235 (describing the recommendations of the special reports of the commission); Howe, *Taxation and Taxes,* 72. The wholesale price index, which had stood at 89 in 1861, was still at 174 by 1866 after a wartime peak of 193 in 1864. "Historical Statistics," 232, Series L 1–14. More alarmingly, under the Federal Reserve Board of New York, the cost-of-living index in 1866 was at an all-time high of 103, after being at 63 in 1861. It was not until 1912 that the index even approached that high again. "Historical Statistics," 235, Series L 36–39.

119. See Smith, *Tax History,* 238.

120. Act of July 13, 1866, 14 Stat. 138.

121. Act of March 2, 1867, 14 Stat. 478.

122. Stanley, *Dimensions of Law,* 40 (table 1-5).

123. Howe, *Taxation and Taxes,* 78; Smith, *Tax History,* 241–42; "Repeal of the Cotton Tax," *Merchants Magazine and Commercial Review* 58, no. 1 (January 1868): 31; "Cotton and the Cotton Trade," *DeBow's Review* 5, no. 1 (January 1868): 74.

124. "The Income Tax," *New York Times,* January 19, 1871, 4.

125. See "The Odious Tax—Circular of the Anti-Income Tax Association," *New York Times,* April 2, 1871, 8; "The East—An Anti-Income Tax Association in Boston," *New York Times,* April 16, 1871, 1; "The Anti-Income Tax Association," *New York Times,* June 20, 1871, 8 (describing a motion to enjoin a collector in Brooklyn).

126. Cong. Globe, 42d Congress, 2d Session, 1734 (1872).

127. See "Historical Statistics," 233, Series L 15–25; "Historical Statistics," 297, Series P 89–98.

128. See Roy Blough, "The Evolution of the Federal Tax System," *Law and Contemporary Problems* 7, no. 2 (Spring 1940): 163.

129. Ratner, *Taxation and Democracy,* 128, 135; "The New Tax Law," *New York Times,* June 6, 1872, 12.

130. Ellis, "Public Opinion," 235.

CHAPTER 3

1. See, for example, "Washington Notes: A New Era in National Finance," *Journal of Political Economy* 23, no. 10 (December 1915): 993, 1001.

2. "$3,672,000,000 Paid in Internal Taxes," *New York Times,* July 2, 1918, at 19.

3. Elmer Ellis, "Public Opinion and the Income Tax," *Mississippi Valley Historical Review* 27, no. 2 (September 1940): 225, 231, 235.

4. *Pollock v. Farmers' Loan & Trust Co.,* 157 U.S. 429 (1895).

5. *Pollock v. Farmers' Loan & Trust Co.,* 158 U.S. 601, 637 (rehearing).

6. 31 Cong. Rec. 5090 (1898) (statement of Sen. Chilton, D-TX).

7. Act of June 13, 1898, ch. 448, § 27, 29, 30 Stat. 448, 464. See "Taxes to Wage a War," *Washington Post,* May 17, 1898, 4A.

8. U.S. Department of Commerce, *Historical Statistics of the United States: Colonial Times to 1970,* pt. 1, 212 (Series E 183–186) (1975); John D. Buenker, *The Income Tax and the Progressive Era* (New York: Garland Publishers, 1985), 34.

9. Buenker, *The Income Tax,* 35 (quoting the Senate Select Committee on Wages and Prices, chaired by Senator Henry Cabot Lodge).

10. Robert Stanley, *Dimensions of Law in the Service of Order: Origins of the Federal Income Tax, 1861–1913* (New York: Oxford University Press, 1993), 122 (quoting from the *Atlanta Constitution* in June 1893); Sidney Ratner, James H. Soltow, and Richard Sylla, *The Evolution of the American Economy* (New York: Basic Books, 1979): 516, 518.

11. See, for example, "National Finances in Shape for War," *New York Times,* May 3, 1914 (comparing the fiscal situation in the U.S. with Mexico); "War Bonds Unlikely," *New York Times,* April 23, 1914, 4. ("The Administration is so hopeful that there will be nothing like a general war with Mexico that estimates have not been made of the money Congress will be asked to vote. . . . For the present the campaign will be paid for out of current funds.")

12. Randolph E. Paul, *Taxation for Prosperity* (New York: Bobbs-Merrill Co., 1947), 23.

13. "Plan for War Tax to Restore Revenue," *New York Times,* August 8, 1914, 5.

14. "The Proposed War Tax," *Outlook,* September 6, 1914, 113; "What We Pay to See Europe at War," *Literary Digest* 49 (1914): 491; "Taxing Us for Europe's War," *Literary Digest* 49 (1914): 874; "New Revenue Taxes," *New York Times,* September 5, 1914, 6.

15. "A Warning to Ourselves," *Wall Street Journal,* September 10, 1914, 1.

16. "Congress May Take a Rest," *Wall Street Journal,* March 4, 1915, 8. ("If current but unpublished reports from England are correct, the war will be ended before next December, and the country will then also have a chance to at least partially adjust itself to the new conditions before Congress again takes charge of the business affairs of the nation.")

17. "Predicts a Deficit of Many Millions," *New York Times,* March 15, 1915, 14.

18. Randolph E. Paul, *Taxation in the United States* (Boston: Little, Brown & Co., 1954), 104–5.

19. "President to War on Foes within as Nation's Peril," *New York Times,* November 30, 1915, 1.

20. Paul, *Taxation in the United States,* 108; "Federal Tax Bill to Meet Preparedness," *Wall Street Journal,* June 22, 1916, 8; "Mr. McAdoo's Taxation Proposals," *Outlook* (December 8, 1915): 819; "Find Many Puzzles in Inheritance Tax," *New York Times,* September 9, 1916, 5.

21. U.S. Congress, House. Committee on Ways and Means. *To Increase the Revenue, and for Other Purposes.* 64th Congress, 1st Session, 1916, 1916 H. Rept. 922, 3.

22. W. Elliot Brownlee, *Federal Taxation in America: A Short History, New Edition* (Cambridge: Cambridge University Press, 2004), 60.

23. W. Elliot Brownlee, "Wilson and Financing the Modern State: The Revenue Act of 1916," *Proceedings of the American Philosophical Society* 129, no. 2 (June 1985): 173, 177; W. Elliot Brownlee, "Social Investigation and Political Learning in the Financing of World War I," in *The State and Social Investigation in Britain and the United States,* edited by Michael J. Lacey and Mary O. Furner (Cambridge: Cambridge University Press, 1993), 328; "Washington Notes," *Journal of Political Economy* 23 (1915): 993, 1001.

24. "Incomplete Preparedness," *New Republic,* February 26, 1916, 94.

25. "Calls New Tax Fairer," *New York Times,* July 17, 1916, 12 (quoting James J. Hopper, President of the Association for an Equitable Federal Income Tax); "Penrose Predicts World Trade War," *New York Times,* August 24, 1916, 17.

26. Brownlee, "Wilson and Financing the Modern State," 195–96.

27. "Powder Makers Oppose Tax on Munitions," *Wall Street Journal,* July 20, 1916, 6; "Protest Munitions Tax and British Boycott," *Los Angeles Times,* July 22, 1916, II1; "Powder Co. Protests against Munitions Tax," *Wall Street Journal,* July 25, 1916, 6. See also Brownlee, "Wilson and Financing the Modern State," 198 (citing a memorial of protest from Westinghouse Electric, Midvale Steel and Ordnance Co., and Butterworth Judson Corporation). Part of the outrage among powder manufacturers was that the bill originally proposed a higher rate on them than manufacturers of other munitions items.

28. "Powder Makers," 6 (Wilmington Chamber of Commerce); "Protest Munitions Tax," II1 (Los Angeles Chamber of Commerce).

29. "Propose Munitions Tax," *Wall Street Journal,* June 27, 1916, 1.

30. "Large Amounts for Drawbacks," *New York Times*, November 3, 1915, 17; "Steel at New Record High," *Wall Street Journal*, September 12, 1916, 4.

31. "Inequitable Taxation," *New York Times*, July 24, 1916, 8.

32. Brownlee, "Social Investigation," 328.

33. See, for example, "Germans Using Caution," *New York Times*, February 5, 1917, 1. ("It is only a question of time, in the opinion of officials, when Germany will commit an overt act, and President Wilson will feel compelled to go before Congress and ask for authority to use the land and naval forces of the United States to uphold the honor of the Government.")

34. Paul, *Taxation in the United States*, 110.

35. "Fears Tax Levies to Get $500,000,000," *New York Times*, December 20, 1916, 12.

36. Paul, *Taxation in the United States*, 110.

37. "To Tax 'Excess Profits' " *Literary Digest* 54 (1917): 175; "Merchants Fight New Tax," *New York Times*, February 1, 1917, 13; "Excess Profits Tax," *New York Times*, February 10, 1917, 11; "Unfair Supertaxation," *Los Angeles Times*, February 13, 1917, II4.

38. "Caucus Agrees to Tax Profits and Issue Bonds," *New York Times*, January 27, 1917, 1; "House in Debate on Revenue Bill," *New York Times*, January 28, 1917, 1. See also "Making Taxation Odious," *The Bellman* 22 (1917): 173, 174. ("To cap the climax of sectional taxation, designed to punish American business men in the North, while avoiding, for purely political reasons, assessment upon the same class in the South, comes the proposed excess profits tax.")

39. Cong. Rec. 64th Congress, 2d Session, 2267 (1917) (statement of Rep. Kitchin).

40. "Revenue Bill Fight Over Sectionalism," *New York Times*, February 1, 1917, 13.

41. Cong. Rec., 65th Congress, 1st Session, April 2, 1917. See, for example, "Government Acts Swiftly," *New York Times*, April 7, 1917, 1. ("It seemed likely tonight that a heavy percentage of the war bill would be raised by increased taxation, and that whatever bond issues were necessary would be placed through the Federal Reserve Board or raised by popular subscription or by both methods, and that there would be no appeal to the big private baking interests of the country to underwrite any part of the issue.") This followed from assumptions about financing war preparedness. See O. M. W. Sprague, "The Conscription of Income," *New Republic*, February 24, 1917, 93. ("All the funds required for the war, colossal in amount as they are certain to be, can and should be secured from taxation levied during the conflict and not by means of loans.")

42. T. S. Adams, "Customary War Finance," *New Republic*, April 7, 1917, 292 (quoting Simmons).

43. Alternatively, Columbia economist Edwin Seligman argued that even if this generation's taxpayers should bear the cost, it should be borne over a decade rather than in one or two years. Edwin R. A. Seligman, "The House Revenue Bill," *New York Times*, May 31, 1917, 10. But see E. Dana Durant, "Taxation Versus Bond Issues for Financing the War," *Journal of Political Economy* 25 (1917): 888, 892 (arguing that it was a fallacy that borrowing would push the costs of war off to future generations).

44. Brownlee, "Social Investigation," 337.

45. "Congress to Meet at Noon," *New York Times*, April 2, 1917, 1.

46. David M. Kennedy, *Over Here: The First World War and American Society* (Oxford: Oxford University Press, 2004), 100. On the other hand, there were reports of substantial business interest in bonds and corresponding concern about relying too heavily on taxation. See "Wall Street Feels Gravity of the War," *New York Times*, April 7, 1917, 14; "Bond Issue Hailed by City's Bankers," *New York Times*, April 9, 1917, 2; "Bankers Confer Over Bonds," *New York Times*, April 10, 1917, 2; "Taxation for War," *Wall Street Journal*, April 12, 1917, 1.

47. Brownlee, "Social Investigation," 340.

48. "Calls Bond Issue 1917 Liberty Loan," *New York Times*, April 29, 1917, 4.

49. William G. McAdoo, *Crowded Years* (Boston: Houghton Mifflin, 1931), 378–79.

50. McAdoo, *Crowded Years*, 378–79; "Popular Loan to Aid Allies," *New York Times*, April 8, 1917, 1.

51. Even before Congress authorized the bond issuance, there was substantial indication of interest among the public. See "Many Ask about Bonds," *New York Times*, April 13, 1917, 3 ("The communications received indicate the intense interest that the public is displaying in the bond issue and convince bankers that it will be an easy matter for the Government to dispose of the bonds."); "Nation Opens Its Purse," *New York Times*, April 9, 1917, 1 ("Officials in charge of the financial program found themselves today the centre of a country-wide bombardment of telegrams and letters of approval. From every part of the country came assurances of support. . . . Officials were stirred by the unanimity of the approval and the unmistakable note of patriotic support in the great volume of communications received."); Prominent businessmen, such as George Eastman of Kodak, announced their interest in personally subscribing to $2.5 million in bonds, and there were numerous reports of wealthy investors seeking to acquire $1 million or more in bonds. "Big Bond Buyers Ready," *New York Times*, April 15, 1917, 1. No less an authority than J. P. Morgan predicted that the bond offering would be widely subscribed. "Morgan Predicts Success of Bonds," *New York Times*, April 10, 1917, 2.

52. "Popular Loan to Aid Allies," *New York Times*, April 8, 1917, 1. ("The issue of the bonds will be expedited by every agency in the command of the Government. Fiscal agents in every part of the country will be authorized to explain the character of the loan and facilitate subscriptions.")

53. Kennedy, *Over Here*, 105; Ronald Schaffer, *America in the Great War: The Rise of the War Welfare State* (Oxford: Oxford University Press, 1991): 11–12; Brownlee, *Federal Taxation*, 68; McAdoo, *Crowded Years*, 385–86.

54. Kennedy, *Over Here*, 106.

55. McAdoo, *Crowded Years*, 391; Luigi Griscuolo, "Taxation and the Bond Market," *The Independent* 91 (1917): 36, 37; Brownlee, "Social Investigation," 345.

56. "Paying the Bills," *The Bellman* 23 (1917): 453.

57. "Most Bankers Favor Tax Free War Bonds," *New York Times*, April 17, 1917, 3. See Marshall A. Robinson, "Federal Debt Management: Civil War, World War I, and World War II," *American Economic Review* 45 (1955): 388, 391, 400. T. S. Adams also made an equitable argument, but did not concede that tax-exemption was critical for sales of the bonds. Adams, "Customary War Finance," 294. ("It gives the rich an exemption of ten, twelve or fifteen per cent, while it yields the poorer investor two per cent or nothing at all. And if, as is not unlikely, war conditions force the income tax up, with a

higher spread between the lower and upper rates, the leakage here described will be even more serious.") See also "War Taxation in Great Britain," *New Republic*, May 12, 1917, 44. ("To those with small incomes the exemption is of little or no value. It is a most undemocratic arrangement, which will surely tend toward an undesirable concentration of ownership of the bonds.")

58. Robinson, "Federal Debt Management," 391.

59. Edwin R. A. Seligman, "The House Revenue Bill: A Constructive Criticism. How Much Should Be Raised by Taxation?" *New York Times*, May 31, 1917, 10.

60. "Taxes and Taxpayers," *The Nation* 104 (1917): 520.

61. Schaffer, *America in the Great War*, 32–33. Some of the increase in prices was popularly attributed to the tax changes enacted in 1916, although commentators sought to discount this possibility. "Tax Increase a Small Element of the High Cost of Living," *The American Century* 16 (1917): 152.

62. Paul, *Taxation for Prosperity*, 25; Kennedy, *Over Here*, 118, 185. Just in case the prohibition bills failed in the Lever bill, temperance supporters also attached prohibition provisions in the war revenue bill. "Prohibition Bills Before Congress," *The Survey*, June 23, 1917, 274.

63. David Stevenson, *Cataclysm: The First World War as Political Tragedy* (New York: Basic Books, 2004), 301; Kennedy, *Over Here*, 169.

64. Schaffer, *America in the Great War*, 176.

65. Oliver M. W. Sprague, "Conscription of Income Once More," *New Republic*, July 14, 1917, 300, 301. This was not merely a clever use of the conscription metaphor to push for progressive taxation; rather, it was part of a campaign to rely heavily on taxation rather than borrowing. In its most extreme version, the thought was that all income above a certain threshold could simply be taken at a 100 percent rate.

66. Cong. Rec., 64th Congress, 2d Session, 2149 (May 11, 1917).

67. Cong. Rec., 64th Congress, 2d Session, 2149–50 (May 11, 1917).

68. Cong. Rec., 64th Congress, 2d Session, 2151, 2294 (May 11, 14, 1917).

69. Sprague, "Conscription of Income Once More," 301.

70. Sprague, "Conscription of Income Once More," 301.

71. Samuel McCune Lindsey, "Social Aspects of War Taxes," *The Survey* 38 (July 28, 1917): 365; "Business Pledges Its All to Nation," *New York Times*, September 22, 1917, 1.

72. "Paying the Bills," *The Bellman* 23 (October 27, 1917): 453.

73. "Taxation, Sounds and Unsound," *The Independent*, June 16, 1917; Cong. Rec. 64th Congress, 2d Session, 2141 (May 11, 1917) (statement of Rep. Knutsen, R-MN); "A Constructive Suggestion for Certain Amendments in the Revenue Bill," *Overland Monthly and Out West Magazine* 70(1) (July 1917): 94; "Your Money or Your Life," *The New Republic*, October 13, 1917, 296–97.

74. Cong. Rec., 64th Congress, 2d Session, 2125, 2149 (May 11, 1917).

75. See "Drafting Every Pocketbook," *Literary Digest* 55 (October 13, 1917): 14; Charles F. Speare, "Uncle Sam's War Revenues," *Review of Reviews* 6 (September 1917): 293; "The Financial Situation in America and Europe," *New York Times*, October 8, 1917, 13; John W. Weeks, "Killing the Golden Goose," *The Independent*, September 8, 1917.

76. Kennedy, *Over Here,* 108 (quoting Hiram Johnson in letter to Theodore Roosevelt, September 8, 1917).

77. John R. Hicks, Ursula K. Hicks, and L. Rostas, *The Taxation of War Wealth* (Oxford: Clarendon Press, 1941), 120; "President Urges Senate to Speed," *New York Times,* June 5, 1917, 2; "House May Redraft the Revenue Bill," *New York Times,* August 2, 1917, 11.

78. "The Liberty Tax," *New York Times,* November 25, 1917, M1; Edwin R. A. Seligman, "The War Revenue Act," *Political Science Quarterly* 33(1) (March 1918): 1.

79. Roy G. Blakey, "The War Revenue Act of 1917," *American Economic Review* 7(4) (December 1917): 791, 794–96.

80. T. S. Adams, "Principles of Excess Profits Taxation," *Annals of the American Academy of Political and Social Science* 75 (January 1918): 147, 153.

81. Blakey, "The War Revenue Act of 1917," 806–8; F. W. Taussig, "The War Tax Act of 1917," *Quarterly Journal of Economics* 32(1) (November 1917): 1, 5–6; Seligman, "The War Revenue Act," 15–16.

82. Kennedy, *Over Here,* 169.

83. "Revising the Tax Laws," *Outlook,* January 16, 1918, 83.

84. C. W. Barron, "War Finance," *Wall Street Journal,* February 2, 1918, 1.

85. "Business Pledges Full Limit for War," *New York Times,* April 13, 1918, 13.

86. F. H. Hankins, "Excess Profits Taxation, the War Finance Corporation and Reconstruction after the War," *The Public* 21 (April 13, 1918): 461, 462.

87. J. F. Zoller, "A Criticism of the War Revenue Act of 1917," *Annals of the American Academy of Political and Social Science* 75 (January 1918): 182, 188–90.

88. Seligman, "The War Revenue Act," 28; Charles W. McKay, "Intangible Values and War Tax," *Industrial Management* 55 (February 1918): 129; "War Taxes Burden Railroad Income," *Wall Street Journal,* January 30, 1918, 2.

89. Brownlee, "Social Investigation and Political Learning," 355.

90. "Shall the Revenue Law Be Revised?" *The Nation* 105 (December 27, 1917): 710; Brownlee, "Social Investigation and Political Learning," 349; "New Tax Primer: Excess Profits," *New York Times,* March 14, 1918, 5.

91. Brownlee, "Social Investigation and Political Learning," 358.

92. "Senate Leaders Favor Repeal of War Tax Law," *New York Times,* December 10, 1917, 1; "Shall the Revenue Law Be Revised?" *The Nation* 105 (December 27, 1917): 710, 711.

93. "Smoot Bill in to Clarify Taxes," *New York Times,* January 6, 1918, 6.

94. " 'Four-Minute Men' in Income Tax Drive," *New York Times,* March 12, 1918, 12; Schaffer, *America in the Great War,* 6.

95. " 'Four-Minute Men,' " 12.

96. "Tinkering the Revenue Bill," *The Nation,* September 6, 1917, 239.

97. "Asks New Tax Bill at Present Session," *New York Times,* May 10, 1918, 5.

98. Brownlee, "Social Investigation," 356, n.69 (quoting letter from Rainey to McAdoo, May 21, 1918).

99. "Asks New Tax Bill," 5.

100. "Our War Expenditure to Date," *The Nation,* April 11, 1918, 441.

101. Indeed, many members of Congress suspected that McAdoo had been able to remain so resolute in favor of a bill because he was doing Wilson's bidding all along. "Wilson to Say if New Revenue Act Is Necessary," *New York Times,* May 21, 1918, 1.

102. "Full Text of President Wilson's Address to the Houses of Congress in Joint Session," *New York Times,* May 28, 1918, 6. See Seward W. Livermore, *Politics Is Adjourned: Woodrow Wilson and the War Congress, 1916–1918* (Middletown, CT: Wesleyan University Press, 1966).

103. "The Law and the Profits," *The Literary Digest* 57 (June 15, 1918): 14; "Funds for the War, and Hope for Business," *New York Times,* May 28, 1918, 12.

104. McAdoo, *Crowded Years,* 411; "M'Adoo Advises Doubling War Tax," *New York Times,* June 7, 1918, 1; "Funds for the War, and Hope for Business," *New York Times,* May 28, 1918, 12–13.

105. McAdoo, *Crowded Years,* 411.

106. "Estimated War Tax Hits the Rich Hard," *New York Times,* March 13, 1918, 11.

107. "Oscar W. Underwood on War Taxes," *New York Times,* June 2, 1918, 76.

108. "Duty First—Politics Later," *The Bellman* 24 (June 1, 1918): 593.

109. "War Debts and Taxation," *The American Review of Reviews,* September 1918, 222, 224. ("One of the quickest and most effective ways to bring a country to a sense of what war means and the sacrifices and denials it imposes is through taxation that does not infringe on capital saved, but pares the family budget down to the strict essentials.") "Taxes That Will Make Us Save Money," *The Literary Digest,* September 14, 1918, 14.

110. "A New Revenue Bill," *The Public* 21 (May 18, 1918): 623.

111. "Daniels Tells of U-Boats," *New York Times,* July 5, 1918, 8.

112. "Hoover Favors Tax to Curb Profiteers," *New York Times,* July 11, 1918, 7.

113. Paul, *Taxation for Prosperity,* 27.

114. "Wants Regarding of Excess Profits," *New York Times,* June 15, 1918, 15; Claude Kitchin, "Who Will Pay the New Taxes," *Forum* (August 1918): 149. Kitchin's claims were later disputed, at least with respect to United States Steel. "Tax on War Profits Favored by Business," *Wall Street Journal,* August 2, 1918, 9.

115. U.S. Congress, House of Representatives, *Hearings before the Committee on Ways and Means on the Proposed Revenue Act of 1918* (Washington, DC: U.S. Government Printing Office, 1918); "Suggest New Basis for War Profit Tax," *New York Times,* June 27, 1918, 7.

116. "Tax Exemption Pleas Nettle Congressmen," *New York Times,* June 13, 1918, 14; "Wants Regrading of Excess Profits," *New York Times,* June 15, 1918, 15; "The Stock Market: Changes in Tax Law Proposed," *Wall St. Journal,* June 26, 1918, 4; "Suggest New Basis for War Profit Tax," *New York Times,* June 27, 1918, 7; "War Tax Simplification Urged by W. B. Dickson," *Wall Street Journal,* July 1, 1918, 5; "Heavier War Taxes Urged by Committee," *New York Times,* July 15, 1918, 9; "Higher Taxes Urged by Leading Business Men," *Wall Street Journal,* July 17, 1918, 7; "Tax on War Profits Favored by Business," *Wall Street Journal,* August 2, 1918, 9.

117. "War-Profits and Excess Profits," *The Literary Digest* 58 (August 31, 1918): 13.

118. "McAdoo for 80% Tax on All War Profits," *New York Times,* August 8, 1918, 17.

119. "Higher Profits Tax Gaining Adherents," *New York Times,* August 5, 1918, 11.

120. "The Profits Tax Compromise," *New York Times,* August 17, 1918, 6.

121. U.S. Congress, House. Committee on Ways and Means. *Revenue Bill of 1918.* 65th Congress, 2d Session, 1918. H. Rept. 767 at 16. To address this same point, the House bill included a provision subjecting undistributed profits to a normal tax of 18 percent, while distributed profits would be subject to the lower rate of 12 percent.

122. "M'Adoo Rejects Tax Revision," *New York Times,* August 20, 1918, 6.

123. "Congress May Put 75 Per Cent. Tax on War Profits," *New York Times,* June 3, 1918, 1.

124. "Protecting Profits," *The Public* 21 (October 19, 1918): 1303.

125. "Senators Ready for Long Fight on Revenue Bill," *New York Times,* September 5, 1918, 1; "The Revenue Bill," *The Public,* September 14, 1918, 1167; "Sniping at the New Tax Bill," *The Literary Digest* 58 (September 21, 1918): 15.

126. "Taxes That Will Make Us Save Money," *Literary Digest* 58 (September 14, 1918): 14.

127. Mary Sargent Potter, "The Proposed Tax on Servants," *North American Review* 208 (November 1918): 745.

128. "Artists and the Luxury Tax," *The Public* 21 (July 20, 1918): 928.

129. "The Revenue Bill," *The Public* 21 (September 14, 1918): 1168.

130. "The Revenue Bill," *New Republic,* September 14, 1918, 184–85.

131. "Extend Profits Tax to Partnerships," *New York Times,* October 30, 1918, 15.

132. "Sniping at the New Tax Bill," *The Literary Digest* 58 (September 21, 1918): 15.

133. McAdoo, *Crowded Years,* 412.

134. "Thousands Protest Against Luxury Tax," *New York Times,* January 31, 1919, 17.

135. Roy G. Blakey and Gladys C. Blakey, "The Revenue Act of 1918," *American Economic Review* 9 (June 1919): 213, 214.

136. Paul, *Taxation for Prosperity,* 27.

137. Robert Murray Haig, "The Revenue Act of 1918," *Political Science Quarterly* 34 (September 1919): 369, 379.

138. Blakey and Blakey, "The Revenue Act of 1918," 226–28.

139. "Excess Profits Taxes Inequitable and Unjust," *Wall Street Journal,* December 18, 1918, 9; "Sees Inequalities in Income Tax Bill," *New York Times,* January 4, 1919, 14. "Watered" stock was stock that was issued for less than the stated par value.

140. "Prohibition Becomes Part of Federal Constitution," *Wall Street Journal,* January 17, 1919, 2.

141. "War-Taxes for Peace Years," *Literary Digest* 59 (December 21, 1918): 8.

142. *Historical Statistics,* 295–96 (Series P 89–98).

143. Paul, *Taxation in the United States,* 121.

144. Charles E. Lord, "Address," in *Proceedings of the National Industrial Tax Conference, Special Committee,* No. 9 45, 49 (1920).

145. 61 Cong. Rec. 151 (1921) (statement of Sen. Smoot). A companion bill authored by Representative Isaac Bacharach of New Jersey was introduced in the House. See "Prepare to Press for Tax on Sales," *New York Times,* April 11, 1921, 1.

146. Internal-Revenue Hearings on the Proposed Revenue Act of 1921 before the Sen. Fin. Committee, 67th Congress, 1st Session, 30 (1921).

147. Hearings on Internal-Revenue Revision, House Ways & Means Committee, 67th Congress, 1st Session, 144 (1921).

148. 61 Cong. Rec. 5232 (1921).

CHAPTER 4

1. On the importance of "sacrifice" to wartime politics, see Mark Hugh Leff, "The Politics of Sacrifice on the American Home Front in World War II," *Journal of American History* 77, no. 4 (1991).

2. Gallup Poll, Feb. 1944 (cited in *Public Opinion on Taxes, AEI Studies in Public Opinion*).

3. Jack Beatty, "Politics as Usual," *Atlantic Monthly* (October 3, 2001).

4. On the number of taxpayers, see U.S. Department of the Treasury, "Statistics of Income for 1947," (Washington, DC: United States Treasury Department, 1950), Part 1, 55–60. On tax return filing, see W. Elliot Brownlee, *Federal Taxation in America: A Short History,* 2nd ed., Woodrow Wilson Center Series (Washington, DC, and New York: Woodrow Wilson Center Press and Cambridge University Press, 2004). On rates, see United States Department of the Treasury and Internal Revenue Service, "Personal Exemptions and Individual Income Tax Rates, 1913–2002," *Statistics of Income Bulletin* (2002). On the composition of total revenue, see Office of Management and Budget, *Historical Tables, Budget of the United States Government for Fiscal Year 2005* (Washington, DC: Executive Office of the President, Office of Management and Budget, 2004), 31.

5. For fiscal year 1929, there were 2,458,049 federal income tax returns filed on which tax was owed (Department of Commerce, Bureau of the Census, *Historical Statistics of the United States, Colonial Times to 1970* [Washington, DC: Government Printing Office, 1975], 1110). The total resident population of persons age 21 and over for 1929 was 71,897,000 (Department of Commerce, Bureau of the Census, *Historical Statistics of the United States, Colonial Times to 1970* [Washington, DC: Government Printing Office, 1975], 10).

6. For more detailed treatments of New Deal taxation, see Joseph J. Thorndike, "The Price of Civilization: Taxation in Depression and War, 1932–1945" (University of Virginia, 2005); Mark Hugh Leff, *The Limits of Symbolic Reform: The New Deal and Taxation, 1933–1939* (New York: Cambridge University Press, 1984). On the importance of New Deal tax debates to the wartime fiscal watershed, see Brownlee, *Federal Taxation in America,* 112.

7. Stephen Daggett and Nina M. Serafino, Foreign Affairs and National Defense Division, Congressional Research Service, *Costs of Major U.S. Wars and Recent U.S. Overseas Military Operations* (October 2001).

8. *The Budget for Fiscal Year 2007*, Historical Tables, Table 1.2.

9. Hugh Rockoff, "The United States: From Ploughshares to Swords," in *The Economics of World War II: Six Great Powers in International Comparison*, edited by Mark Harrison (Cambridge: Cambridge University Press, 1998): 107–111.

10. Randolph E. Paul, *Taxation for Prosperity* (Indianapolis: Bobbs-Merrill Co., 1947): 70.

11. Committee on Ways and Means, *The Revenue Bill of 1940*, 76th Congress, 3rd Session, 10 June 1940, 7; Committee on Finance, *Revenue Act of 1940*, 77th Congress, 1st Session, 12–14 June 1940, 33.

12. *Revenue Act of 1940*, 32. Only $14 million of the new revenue would come from the new taxpayers; the other $61 million would result from existing income taxpayers, who would see their liability rise as the exemption fell. In addition, the Treasury believed that better compliance among existing taxpayers would raise perhaps $25 million.

13. *Revenue Act of 1940*, 35.

14. Jerry Tempalski, U.S. Dept. of Treasury, *Revenue Effects of Major Tax Bills*, OTA Working Paper 81 at p. 17 (July 2003).

15. Franklin D. Roosevelt, "Message to Congress on a Steeply Graduated Excess Profits Tax," 1 July 1940; available from http://www.presidency.ucsb.edu/ws/index.php?pid=15974&st=&st1=.

16. George Douglas, "Excess Profits Taxation and the Taxpayer," *Law and Contemporary Problems* 10, no. 1 (1943): 140, 143.

17. Paul, *Taxation for Prosperity*, 72.

18. See, for example, John Richard Hicks, Ursula Kathleen Webb Hicks, and L. Rostás, *The Taxation of War Wealth*, 2nd ed. (Oxford: Clarendon Press, 1942).

19. George E. Lent, "Excess Profits Taxation in the United States," *Journal of Political Economy* 59, no. 6 (1951): 481, 484.

20. Douglas, "Excess Profits Taxation," 144.

21. "Airlines Request War Tax Waiver," *New York Times*, August 13, 1940, page 12.

22. Frank L. Kluckhorn, "Clash on Draft," *New York Times*, August 7, 1940, page 1.

23. Harold M. Groves, "An Appraisal of the Excess Profits Tax from a Fiscal Standpoint," *Law and Contemporary Problems* 10, no. 1 (1943).

24. The Second Revenue Act of 1940 raised the normal income tax rate for corporations to 24 percent for all companies earning more than $25,000 in net income. Excess profits were taxed at rates ranging from 25 to 50 percent, depending on income. In computing the new tax, companies were granted a flat $5,000 exemption, plus a credit computed by one of the two methods described above. The bill also retained the accelerated amortization first proposed by the White House, although it notably deprived the government of any role in the postwar disposition of these facilities. See Roy G. Blakey and Gladys Blakey, "The Two Federal Revenue Acts of 1940," *American Economic Review* 30, no. 4 (1940): 733.

25. Quoted in Randolph E. Paul, *Taxation in the United States* (Boston: Little Brown, 1954), 265.

26. Paul, *Taxation in the United States*, 735.

27. Franklin D. Roosevelt, "Annual Message to Congress, January 6th, 1941," http://www.presidency.ucsb.edu/ws/index.php?pid=16092&st=&st1=; "Tax Prospects: Sharply Increased Rates Likely on Corporation and Individual Incomes," *Wall Street Journal,* 7 January 1941.

28. Paul, *Taxation for Prosperity,* 75.

29. Paul, *Taxation for Prosperity,* 75–76.

30. Paul, *Taxation for Prosperity,* 76.

31. Most significantly, the Senate rejected a House proposal to impose an additional 10 percent tax on companies using the invested capital base for the excess profits tax.

32. Roy G. Blakey and Gladys Blakey, "The Revenue Act of 1941," *American Economic Review* 31, no. 4 (1941): 816; Roy G. Blakey and Gladys Blakey, "Federal Revenue Legislation, 1943–1944," *American Political Science Review* 38, no. 2 (1944): 329.

33. Effectively, rates topped out at 24 percent for large companies, while those with smaller incomes paid 15 to 19 percent. In 1942, rates went higher still. The revenue from this tax was substantial, ranging from $3.7 billion in fiscal year 1941 to $4.5 billion in 1943. But the tax raised far less than the levy on excess profits, which ranged from a $3.4 billion in 1941 to $11.4 billion in 1943. For data on the corporate income tax, see United States Bureau of the Census, *Historical Statistics of the United States, Colonial Times to 1970,* Bicentennial ed. (Washington, DC: U.S. Government Printing Office, 1975), 1109.

34. Blakey and Blakey, "The Revenue Act of 1941," 817.

35. Committee on Ways and Means, *Revenue Revision of 1941,* 77th Congress, 1st Session, 24, 28–30 April, 1–2, 5–9 May 1941, 48, 56.

36. "Roosevelt and Doughton Letters and Morgenthau's Note," *New York Times,* 3 August 1941.

37. Blakey and Blakey, "The Revenue Act of 1941," 817.

38. "The Limits of Taxation," *New York Times,* December 5, 1941, page 22.

39. Robert Murray Haig, *Financing Total War* 4 (New York: Columbia University Press, 1942). In lectures delivered at Columbia in February 1941, Haig explained that "total war implies . . . not only a willingness on the part of everyone to fight and to work; it implies also a willingness to sacrifice, a willingness to do without almost everything for the period of the war."

40. "Conference Fixed on War Tax Plans," *New York Times* December 11, 1941, page 33.

41. Committee on Ways and Means, *Revenue Revision of 1942,* 77th Congress, 2nd Session, 3, 5, 9–13, 16–20, 23–24 March 1942, 274, 510–11; Felix Cotten, "Fix 8% Sales Tax, Nam Urges House," *Washington Post* March 13, 1942; "48-Hour Week Asked by Small Business; Sales Tax Also Favored in National Poll," *New York Times,* March 17, 1942; Henry N. Dorris, "$3,680,000,000 Yield Seen in Sales Tax," *New York Times,* March 17, 1942; Henry N. Dorris, "Retailers Line up for 5% Sales Tax," *New York Times,* April 1, 1942; "Retailers Propose 5% Sales Tax to Raise $3 Billion," *Wall Street Journal,* April 1, 1942.

42. "Sales Tax Gains Favor with House Committee," *Washington Post,* January 9, 1942; "Sentiment Grows for the Sales Tax," *New York Times,* January 11, 1942; Donald A. Young, "General Sales Tax Considered Reluctantly by House Group," *Washington Post,* January 11, 1942; Felix Cotten, "House Leaders Lean Strongly to Sales Tax," *Washington Post,* May 3, 1942. "A Tax for Everyone," *Time,* May 11, 1942.

43. Roy Blough, "Evils of the Sales Tax," in *Box 44; Papers of Roy Blough*, Harry S. Truman Presidential Library, Independence, MO (1942).

44. Paul, *Taxation in the United States*, 325.

45. *Revenue Revision of 1942*, 913.

46. Robert De Vore, "Treadway Predicts Sales Tax Adoption," *Washington Post* April 7, 1942; Cotten, "House Leaders Lean Strongly to Sales Tax"; "General Sales Tax Is Advocated by Robertson of Ways and Means Group; AFL Hits Wider Income Base," *Wall Street Journal*, May 18, 1942; Robert W. Langbaum, "General Sales Tax Urged," *New York Times*, June 20, 1942; "Majority Backs Levy on Sales, George Says," *The Washington Post*, September 8, 1942.

47. Paul, *Taxation in the United States*, 323.

48. Office of Management and Budget, *Historical Tables, Budget of the United States Government for Fiscal Year 2005*, 29, 31.

49. Paul, *Taxation in the United States*, 271; Franklin D. Roosevelt, *The Public Papers and Addresses of Franklin D. Roosevelt*, edited by Samuel Irving Rosenman, vol. 11 (New York: Random House, 1938), 15.

50. George Douglas, "Excess Profits Taxation and the Taxpayer," *Law and Contemporary Problems* 10, no. 1 (1943); Cotten, "Fix 8% Sales Tax, Nam Urges House."

51. *Revenue Revision of 1942*, 297–300.

52. *Revenue Revision of 1942*, 297–300; Paul, *Taxation in the United States*.

53. Paul, *Taxation in the United States*, 300.

54. Arthur Krock, "Spiritual Values Rise with War's Sacrifices," *New York Times*, May 10, 1942, E3.

55. Haig, *Financing Total War*, 30.

56. Franklin D. Roosevelt, "Message to Congress on an Economic Stabilization Program," April 27, 1942, in *The American Presidency Project*, edited by John Woolley and Gerhard Peters. Santa Barbara, CA: University of California (hosted), Gerhard Peters (database). http://www.presidency.ucsb.edu/ws/?pid=16251.

57. Paul, *Taxation in the United States*, 301–2; "A Supertax on Individual Incomes above $25,000," in *Box 54; Super Taxes; Records of the Office of Tax Analysis/Division of Tax Research; General Records of the Department of the Treasury, Record Group 56; National Archives*, College Park, MD (1942).

58. Roy G. Blakey and Gladys Blakey, "The Federal Revenue Act of 1942," *American Political Science Review* 36, no. 6 (1942): 1071–72.

59. Carolyn Jones, "Mass-Based Income Taxation: Creating a Taxpaying Culture, 1940–1952," in *Funding the Modern American State, 1941–1995: The Rise and Fall of the Era of Easy Finance*, edited by W. Elliot Brownlee (Washington and New York: Woodrow Wilson Center Press and Cambridge University Press, 1996), 107–8. Jones provides an excellent portrait of the wartime public relations campaign around tax responsibilities.

60. Quoted in Jones, "Mass-Based Income Taxation."

61. Quoted in Jones, "Mass-Based Income Taxation."

62. For an excellent account of the victory tax, see Dennis J. Ventry, "The Victory Tax of 1942," *Tax Notes* 75 (1997).

63. Paul, *Taxation in the United States*, 319.

64. W. Elliot Brownlee, "Tax Regimes, National Crisis, and State-Building in America," in *Funding the Modern American State, 1941–1995: The Rise and Fall of the Era of Easy Finance*, edited by W. Elliot Brownlee (Washington and New York: Woodrow Wilson Center Press and Cambridge University Press, 1996), 92.

65. Randolph E. Paul, "Statement before the House Ways and Means Committee," in *Box 54; Collection and Payment;* Records of the Office of Tax Analysis/Division of Tax Research; General Records of the Department of the Treasury, Record Group 56; National Archives, College Park, MD (1943).

66. Paul, *Taxation in the United States*, 329.

67. Brownlee, *Federal Taxation in America*, 92, 116.

68. Paul, *Taxation in the United States*, 335.

69. Franklin D. Roosevelt, "Letter to Congress on Tax Bills," May 17, 1943, in *The American Presidency Project*, edited by John Woolley and Gerhard Peters. Santa Barbara, CA: University of California (hosted), Gerhard Peters (database). http://www.presidency. ucsb.edu/ws/?pid=16400.

70. "Not Current but Eminently Quotable," *Tax Notes* 70 (1996).

71. Jones, "Mass-Based Income Taxation."

72. Committee on Ways and Means, *Revenue Revision of 1943*, 78th Congress, 1st Session, 4–8, 11–16, 18–20, 1943, 4.

73. Paul, *Taxation in the United States*, 356; "The High Cost of Morgenthau," *Time*, October 18, 1943.

74. Paul, *Taxation in the United States*, 358.

75. Committee on Ways and Means, "The Revenue Bill of 1943" (Washington, DC: Government Printing Office, 1943), 2.

76. Committee on Ways and Means, "The Revenue Bill of 1943," 5; Committee on Ways and Means, "The Revenue Bill of 1943: Supplemental Views" (Washington, DC: Government Printing Office, 1943), 2.

77. "The Nation," *New York Times*, December 5, 1943, E2.

78. Franklin D. Roosevelt, "Veto of a Revenue Bill," February 22, 1944, in *The Public Papers and Addresses of Franklin D. Roosevelt*, edited by Samuel Irving Rosenman, vol. 13 (New York: Random House, 1950), 72–75.

79. Franklin D. Roosevelt, "Veto of a Revenue Bill."

80. Paul, *Taxation in the United States*, 373.

81. Among its various major provisions, the Revenue Act of 1943 left individual income tax rates, as well as exemptions, unchanged; left estate tax rates and exemption unchanged; cut the Victory Tax rate from 5 to 3 percent, but repealed credits allowed under the levy; raised the excess profits rate from 90 to 95 percent but also raised the exemption from $5,000 to $10,000; and raised a range of excise taxes, totaling more than $1 billion in new revenue. For a summary, see Paul, *Taxation in the United States*, 375–78.

82. Sidney Ratner, *Taxation and Democracy in America* (New York: John Wiley and Sons, 1967), 519.

83. Office of Management and Budget, "The Budget for Fiscal Year 2007, Historical Tables" (Washington, DC: Executive Office of the President, 2006), 31.

84. "The Budget for Fiscal Year 2007."

CHAPTER 5

1. The dates used here are those used by the U.S. Department of Veteran Affairs. See U.S. Department of Veteran Affairs, *America's Wars*, November 2004, http://www1.va.gov/opa/fact.

2. Revenue Act of 1945 (Ch. 200, 59 Stat. 264; Ch. 210 and 211, 59 Stat 294; Ch. 453, 59 Stat. 556); Revenue Act of 1948 (Ch. 168, 62 Stat. 110).

3. Revenue Act of 1962 (P.L. 87-834, 76 Stat. 960); Revenue Act of 1964 (P.L. 88-272, 78 Stat. 19).

4. Indeed, the term "McCarthyism" originated just four months before the North Korean invasion in a February 1950 *Washington Post* editorial cartoon by Herbert Block.

5. The division of Korea into North and South has its origins in World War II and the Japanese occupation of the Korean peninsula from 1910 to 1945. Two days after the bombing of Hiroshima on August 6, 1945, Soviet troops entered the Korean peninsula from the North. In September, U.S. troops entered the peninsula from the South. On September 6, 1945, the United States and the Soviet Union agreed that the country should be divided along the 38th parallel. Although there were efforts in the ensuing three years to unify the peninsula, by mid-1948, it had become apparent that this would not occur. In August 1948, the Republic of Korea (South) was established. In September of that year, the People's Republic of Korea (North) was established.

6. James T. Patterson, *Grand Expectations: The United States, 1945–1974*, (Oxford, UK: Oxford University Press, 1996) (overview of U.S. involvement in the Korean War).

7. John D. Morris, *Tax Cuts in Peril over Korea Crisis, New York Times* June 28, 1950, 25.

8. Harry S. Truman, "Special Message to the Congress on Tax Policy," January 23, 1950.

9. Congressional Quarterly, *Congress and the Nation: 1945–1964*, (Washington, DC: Congressional Quarterly, 1998), 408–9.

10. "Fiscal Unpreparedness," *New York Times*, July 5, 1950.

11. "May Alter Excise Tax Cuts: Senate Group Will Try to Keep Basic House Plan, Says George," *New York Times*, July 5, 1950, 46.

12. "Realism on Taxes," *New York Times*, July 14, 1950.

13. John F. Witte, *The Politics and Development of the Federal Income Tax* (Madison: University of Wisconsin Press, 1985).

14. "Text of President's Broadcast on the Korean Crisis," *New York Times*, July 20, 1950, 15.

15. "To Pay-As-We-Go?" *New York Times*, July 26, 1950, 24.

16. "Tax Action Delay Urged on Senate," *New York Times,* July 10, 1950, 29.

17. "War Footing," *New York Times,* July 23, 1950, E1; "Public Favors Tax for War, Survey Finds," *Los Angeles Times,* August 24, 1950, 13.

18. Dulles was closely associated with Republican Governor of New York Thomas Dewey, the unsuccessful GOP candidate for the presidency in 1944 and 1948. In 1949, Dewey appointed Dulles to the U.S. Senate to fill a vacancy caused by the resignation of Democrat Robert F. Wagner. Dulles later served as secretary of state under Dwight Eisenhower.

19. John Foster Dulles, "To Save Humanity from the Deep Abyss," *New York Times,* July 30, 1950, SM3; "Dulles Warns U.S. It Faces Sacrifice," *New York Times,* July 5, 1950, 14.

20. "Nixon Urges Plan for Lasting Peace: GOP Senatorial Nominee Wars Defeat in Korea Means War," *Los Angeles Times,* August 31, 1950, 6.

21. "Confusion on Taxes," *New York Times,* September 16, 1950, 13.

22. "President Pleads for Tax-Bill Speed," *New York Times,* August 31, 1950, 18.

23. "Rayburn Charges Delaying of Taxes," *New York Times,* September 11, 1950, 18.

24. Witte describes this provision as one that "bound the revenue committees of Congress to report a bill establishing a retroactive excess profits tax at the earliest possible opportunity in the next Congress" (Witte, *Politics and Development,* 138).

25. John E. Mueller, "Trends in Popular Support for the Wars in Korea and Vietnam," *American Political Science Review* 65, no. 2 (1970), 358:

26. Less than a year before the North Korean invasion, China had "fallen" to the communists with Mao Zedong's proclamation of the People's Republic of China on October 1, 1949. Republican critics of the administration (joined by some Democrats, including John Kennedy, then a young member of the House of Representatives from Massachusetts's 11th congressional district) charged Truman with having "lost China." During the first half of 1950, headlines featured a number of figures that today we associate with the Red Scare of the McCarthy era—Alger Hiss, Klaus Fuchs, and Julius and Ethel Rosenberg (James T. Patterson, *Grand Expectations* 165–205).

27. "Mrs. Douglas' View on Reds Challenged," *Los Angeles Times,* August 30, 1950, 8.

28. Michael Hogan, *A Cross of Iron: Harry S. Truman and the Origins of the National Security State, 1945–1954* (Cambridge, UK: Cambridge University Press, 1998).

29. Walter W. Ruch, "Pay-As-You-Go Aim Proposed by Taft," *New York Times,* September 1, 1950, 35; Joseph A. Loftus, "Senators to Check Charitable Funds," *New York Times,* August 10, 1950, 13.

30. Patterson, *Grand Expectations,* 215–16.

31. Patterson, *Grand Expectations,* 219.

32. Patterson, *Grand Expectations,* 220.

33. "Oral History Interview with John W. Snyder, Secretary of the Treasury in the Truman Administration, 1946–1953" July 2, 1969 (available in the Truman Presidential Museum and Library).

34. "Text of Truman Letter Asking Profits Tax," *New York Times,* November 15, 1950, A20.

35. John D. Morris, "Snyder Advocates a 75 Per Cent Tax on Excess Profits," *New York Times,* November 16, 1950, 1.

36. Patterson, *Grand Expectations,* 221.

37. Patterson, *Grand Expectations,* 221.

38. Patterson, *Grand Expectations,* 222.

39. "Text of President's Address on 'Great Danger' Facing the Nation," *New York Times,* December 16, 1950, 4.

40. "Congress to Speed New Arms Billions; Profit Tax is 'Sure,' " *New York Times,* December 3, 1950, 1.

41. "Great Austerity Period Predicted by Byrd in U.S. Rearmament Efforts," *New York Times,* December 17, 1950, 10.

42. Patterson, *Grand Expectations,* 221.

43. "President Is Blunt: Says We Must Work and Sacrifice to Build an Arsenal of Freedom," *New York Times,* December 16, 1950, 1.

44. "The Front Line of Taxation," *New York Times,* December 4, 1950.

45. William S. White, "Taft Offers to Aid Truman in Shaping U.S. Foreign Policy," *New York Times,* January 10, 1951.

46. "Excess Profits Tax on Corporations," Hearings before the Committee on Finance, U.S. Senate (81st Congress, 2nd Session) on H.R. 9827, December 4–8, 1950, 113.

47. S. Rep. 81-2679, P.L. 81-909, "Excess Profits Tax Act of 1950," December 18, 1950.

48. Democrats had held a 12 seat majority in the Senate and a 92 seat majority in the House. Following the November elections, Democrats held a 2 seat majority in the Senate and a 35 seat majority in the House (Patterson, *Grand Expectations,* 223).

49. John D. Morris, "Korean War Opens New Fiscal Era of Rising Costs, Taxes and Debt," *New York Times* January 2, 1951, 34.

50. Mueller, "Trends in Popular Support," 361.

51. A. E. Holmans, *United States Fiscal Policy: 1945–1959* (London: Oxford University Press, 1961), 165–66.

52. "Revenue Revision of 1951, Hearings Before the Committee on Ways and Means, House of Representatives, Eighty-Second Congress, First Session on Revenue Revision of 1951," part 3, 2102–7, 2321–24.

53. Fiscal year 1951 outlays exceeded projections by roughly $2.4 billion, with the result that the additional $11 billion in revenue converted the projected deficit from $5.1 billion to a surplus of $3.5 billion.

54. "Size of Budget Surplus Due Today; News Likely to Strengthen Senate Opposition to Truman Tax Requests," *Wall Street Journal,* July 2, 1951, 3.

55. "Revenue Act of 1951, Hearings Before the Committee on Finance, United States Senate, Eighty-Second Congress, First Session on H.R. 4473," part 1, 57–58.

See also C. P. Trussell, "10 Billion Tax Rise Urged by Johnston," *New York Times,* July 3, 1951, 2. (Economic Stabilization Administrator Eric Johnston urged the committee "not to take too much comfort from the present $3,000,000,000 surplus.")

56. Senate Hearings, part I, 67.

57. C. P. Trussell, "Tax Increase Held Unnecessary Now," *New York Times,* July 17, 1951, 30.

58. "Revenue Act of 1951, First Session on H.R. 4473," 54.

59. *Congress and the Nation,* 412.

60. "House Rejects Tax Rise Bill in Surprise Move, 203 to 157; Delay until 1952 Possible," *New York Times,* October 17, 1951, 1.

61. John D. Morris, "Vote Is 185 to 160: Earlier Defeat Reversed as 26 Heed Appeal by White House, Rayburn Voices Warning," *New York Times* October 20, 1951, 1.

62. *Congress and the Nation,* 412.

63. "Taft Renews Call for Korean Truce," *New York Times,* November 18, 1951, 62 (quoting Senator Taft).

64. Lee E. Ohanian, "The Macroeconomic Effects of War Finance in the United States: World War II and the Korean War," *American Economic Review* 87(1997): 23.

65. Jerry Tempalski, "Revenue Effects of Major Tax Bills," Working Paper 81 (Washington, DC: Office of Tax Analysis, 2003).

66. During the 81st Congress (1949–1951), Democrats enjoyed a 263 to 171 majority in the House and a 54 to 42 majority in the Senate. During the 89th Congress (1965–1967), Democrats enjoyed a 295 to 140 majority in the House and a 68 to 32 majority in the Senate.

67. Geoffrey Warner, "Lyndon Johnson's War, Part I: Escalation," International Affairs 79 (2003): 829–53 (describing the period from January 1964 to July 1965 when the United States began bombing North Vietnam and significantly increased the troop presence for ground operations in South Vietnam).

68. George C. Herring, *America's Longest War: The United States and Vietnam: 1950–1975* (1979); Stanley Karnow, *Vietnam: A History* (1983).

69. Patterson, *Grand Expectations,* 595.

70. Robert Mann, *The Walls of Jericho: Lyndon Johnson, Hubert Humphrey, Richard Russell, and the Struggle for Civil Rights* (New York: Harcourt, Brace, and Company, 1996), 459–77 (discussing the politics of the Voting Rights Act of 1965). Eric Patashnik and Julian Zelizer, "Paying for Medicare: Benefits, Budgets, and Wilbur Mills's Policy Legacy," *Journal of Health Policy, Politics, and Law* 26(2001): 7.

71. Joint Resolution of Congress, H.J. Res. 1145 (August 7, 1964). The Tonkin Resolution was quite broad, prompting Johnson to quip, "It's like Grandma's nightshirt— it covers everything" (Robert Dallek, *Lyndon B. Johnson: Portrait of a President* [New York: Oxford University Press, 2004], 179.

72. Karnow, *Vietnam,* 441.

73. "Johnson Repeats Hope for Tax Cut," *New York Times,* August 12, 1964, 16; "Transcript of President Johnson's News Conference," *New York Times,* September 10, 1964, 18 (describing a "study on the extent of further [tax] cuts that would be desirable and effective").

74. John D. Pomfret, "President Vows Further Tax Cuts to Help the Poor," *New York Times,* June 22, 1965, 1.

75. Edwin L. Dale, "Treasury Doubts Vietnam War Will Raise Taxes," *New York Times*, 3 (describing testimony of Under Secretary of the Treasury Joseph W. Barr before a subcommittee of the Joint Economic Committee).

76. Jack Raymond, "U.S. to Increase Military Forces by 330,000 Men," *New York Times*, July 30, 1965, 1.

77. Tom Wicker, " 'Guns or Butter' Republicans Pressing the Issue," *New York Times*, August 15, 1965, E9; Edwin L. Dale, Jr., "National Affairs: No 'Guns or Butter,' " *New York Times*, August 29, 1965.

78. Donald F. Kettl, "The Economic Education of Lyndon Johnson: Guns, Butter, and Taxes," in The Johnson Years, vol. 2, edited by Robert Devine (Lawrence, KS: , 1987); David Halberstam, "How the Economy Went Haywire," *Atlantic Monthly*, September 1972, 56–60; Ronald King, "The President and Fiscal Policy in 1996: The Year Taxes Were Not Raised," *Polity* 17, no. 4 (Summer 1985): 685–714; John W. Sloan, "President Johnson, the Council of Economic Advisors, and the Failure to Raise Taxes in 1966 and 1967," Presidential Studies Quarterly 15(1985): 89–98.

79. Lyndon B. Johnson, "Annual Message to the Congress on the State of the Union," January 12, 1966.

80. David Halberstam, "How the Economy Went Haywire," *Atlantic Monthly* 1972: 56–60. Halberstam's *Atlantic Monthly* essay was later published as the final chapter in a revised edition of his best-selling book on Vietnam, *The Best and the Brightest* (1992).

81. Halberstam, "How the Economy Went Haywire," 58.

82. The bill also temporarily suspended certain excise tax reductions enacted in 1965.

83. "Milk Toast with Sugar," *New York Times*, March 12, 1966, 26.

84. George Lardner, Jr., "The Day Congress Played Santa: A Look at the Christmas Tree Bill," *Washington Post*, December 25, 1966, A1, A10.

85. "American Military Death Toll in Vietnam Passes 5,000 Mark," *New York Times*, September 16, 1966, 2.

86. "Johnson Signs 8 Bills Supporting Great Society," *New York Times*, November 4, 1966, 20. The Great Society legislation that Johnson signed into law on November 3 included the Comprehensive Health Planning and Public Health Services Act (P.L. 89-749), the Elementary and Secondary Education Amendments of 1966 (P.L. 89-750), the Allied Health Professions Personnel Training Act of 1966 (P.L. 89-751), the Higher Education Amendments of 1966 (P.L. 89-752), the Clean Water Restoration Act of 1966 (P.L. 89-753) the Demonstration Cities and Metropolitan Development Act of 1966 (P.L. 89-754) the Fair Packaging and Labeling Act of 1966 (P.L. 89-755); and the Child Protection Act (P.L. 89-756).

87. John W. Sloan, "President Johnson," 89, 97.

88. Lyndon B. Johnson, "Annual Message to the Congress on the State of the Union," January 10, 1967.

89. Johnson, "State of the Union," 1967.

90. Norman C. Miller, "Legislators Seem Likely to Back Johnson's Plan for 6% Income Tax Rise," *Wall Street Journal*, January 12, 1967, 1.

91. Miller, "Legislators Seem Likely," 1.

92. "Long Doubts Need for Tax Increase," *New York Times,* January 19, 1967, 18.

93. Patterson, *Grand Expectations,* 598 (citing Doris Kearns Goodwin, to whom Johnson made these remarks).

94. John Herbers, "Mills Feud with Johnson Creates Crisis in House," *New York Times,* October 15, 1967, 45.

95. Irwin Unger and Debi Unger, *America in the 1960s,"* 45.

96. Jerry Tempalski, "Revenue Effects of Major Tax Bills," Working Paper 81 (Washington, DC: Office of Tax Analysis, 2003).

97. Newsweek, March 11, 1968.

98. Witte, *Politics and Development,* 166.

99. "Treasury Secretary Warns of Taxpayers' Revolt," *New York Times,* January 18, 1969, 15.

100. "Tax Reform," *Congressional Quarterly Weekly Report,* May 16, 1969, 736 (noting that signers of the letter were all members of the liberal "Democratic Study Group").

101. "Tax Reform," 736.

102. Eileen Shanahan, "Kennedy Couples Surtax to Reform," *New York Times,* April 9, 1969.

103. "Administration, House Leaders Compromise on Surtax," *Congressional Quarterly Weekly Report,* June 13, 1969, 1013.

104. "Surtax Extension," *Congressional Quarterly Weekly Report,* July 18, 1969, 1290 ("Mansfield in a July 14 statement on the Senate floor said the surtax bill would probably be defeated on the Senate floor if major tax reforms were not tied to it"); "Oil Depletion, Bank and Utility Tax Advantages Cut," *Congressional Quarterly Weekly Report* July 25, 1969, 1315 ("Maj. Leader Mike Mansfield (D. Mont.) had said he would not schedule a vote on extension of the surtax until the House tax reform bill was ready for Senate floor action"); "Surtax Extension," *Congressional Quarterly Weekly Report,* July 25, 1969, 1316 (Mansfield "remained firm in his resolve to tie tax reform to the surtax even after a July 22 meeting with President Nixon who had been equally firm in his desire to get the surtax extended"); "House Votes Overwhelmingly for Landmark Tax Reform," *Congressional Quarterly Weekly Report* August 8, 1969, 1424, 1428 ("Committee added on to the tax reform bill the rest of the surtax extension package"); "House Accepts Senate Compromise on Surtax Extension," *Congressional Quarterly Weekly Report,* August 8, 1969, 1013.

105. More precisely, the Treasury Department estimated that in the long run the law's "tax reform" provisions would produce an annual net revenue gain of $3.32 billion, while repeal of the investment tax credit would produce an annual revenue gain of $3.3 billion—for a combined revenue gain of $6.62 billion per year. The law's "tax relief" provisions would result in an annual revenue loss of $9.134 billion over the long run. Thus, on balance, the Treasury estimated that the Tax Reform Act of 1969 would reduce federal revenues in the long run by $2.514 billion per year. Joint Committee on Taxation, General Explanation of the Tax Reform Act of 1969 (H.R. 13270, 91st Congress, Public Law 91-272), December 3, 1970.

106. Combat Area Casualties Current File, Combat Deaths between January 1, 1969, and December 31, 1969 (U.S. Archives), http://www.archives.gov/research/vietnam-war/casualty-statistics.html#year.

107. Ronald Brownstein, "Bush Breaks with 140 Years of History in Plan for Wartime Tax Cut," *Los Angeles Times,* January 13, 2003.

108. Combat Area Casualties Current File, Combat Deaths for Years 1970 and 1971 (U.S. Archives), http://www.archives.gov/research/vietnam-war/casualty-statistics.html#year.

109. "13 Democrats Urge Nixon to Seek Tax Cut," *New York Times,* July 13, 1971, 37.

110. Warren Weaver, Jr., "Leading Democrats Call Nixon's Economic Policy Inadequate and Ill-Timed," *New York Times,* August 17, 1971, 17. The August 15th speech is also when Nixon announced wage-price controls as well as the policy that the United States would no longer redeem currency for gold.

111. "Miscalculations Almost Killed Tax Surcharge," *Congressional Quarterly Weekly Report,* July 26, 1968.

112. Melvin Small, "The Domestic Course of the War," in *The Oxford Companion to American Military History,* edited by John Whiteclay (Oxford, U.K.: Oxford University Press, 1999).

113. Patterson, *Grand Expectations,* 608 (citing George Herring, "People Quite Apart: Americans, South Vietnamese, and the War in Vietnam," *Diplomatic History* 9(1990): 39–40; and Kearns, *Lyndon Johnson,* 324–27).

114. "Action in Tonkin Gulf," *Time,* August 14, 1964 (quoting U.N. Ambassador Adlai Stevenson).

CHAPTER 6

1. Text of Republican Contract with America, http://www.house.gov/house/Contract/CONTRACT.html.

2. Barbara Kirchheimer, "Republicans Eager to Push Their Tax Agenda in New Congress," *Tax Notes* 65 (November 14, 1994): 799; Barbara Kirchheimer, "The Contract: What's In It?" *Tax Notes* 65 (November 21, 1994): 935.

3. William J. Clinton, "Remarks on Vetoing Budget Reconciliation Legislation and an Exchange with Reporters," *The American Presidency Project* (December 6, 1995). Todd S. Purdum, "As Long Promised, President Vetoes the G.O.P. Budget," *New York Times,* December 7, 1995, A1.

4. William J. Clinton, "Remarks on Returning without Approval to the House of Representatives the 'Taxpayer Refund and Relief Act of 1999,' " *The American Presidency Project* (September 23, 1999). Richard Stevenson, "Clinton Vetoes Tax Cut but Seeks Accord," *New York Times* September 24, 1999, A20.

5. "Table 1.2, Summary of Receipts, Outlays, and Surpluses or Deficits as Percentages of GDP: 1930–2011," *Historical Tables, Budget of the United States Government,* Fiscal Year 2007.

6. Lawrence B. Lindsey, "What to Do with $1 Trillion More in Taxes," AEI Online, January 1, 2000.

7. Richard L. Berke, "In a Fierce Debate, Bush Promises to Cut Taxes, Calling to Mind His Father," *New York Times,* January 7, 2000, A15.

8. Alison Mitchell, "Spate of Numerical Sparring Highlights the Fiscal Focus of the Presidential Race," *The New York Times,* May 3, 2000, A25.

9. Citizens for Tax Justice, "Summary and Analysis of George W. Bush's Tax Plan: Updated August 2000," http://www.ctj.org/pdf/bush0800.pdf.

10. Richard W. Stevenson, "Republicans Can't Match Bush's Plan for Tax Cuts," *New York Times,* March 1, 2000, A18.

11. Bob Woodward, *Plan of Attack* (London: Simon & Schuster, 2004), 28.

12. Richard W. Stevenson, "Bush's Proposal to Cut Taxes Is Swiftly Introduced in Senate," *New York Times,* January 23, 2001, A15; Lizette Alvarez, "Head of House Panel Backs Swift Action on Tax Rates," *New York Times,* January 27, 2001, A11; Richard W. Stevenson, "Bush Wants Tax Cut Sooner to Aid Economy This Year," *New York Times,* February 5, 2001, A12; Alison Mitchell, "Congressional Republicans See Bush's Big Tax Cut and Think Bigger," *New York Times,* February 7, 2001, A13; David E. Sanger, "Bush Tax Plan Sent to Congress, Starting the Jostling for Position," *New York Times,* February 9, 2001, A1.

13. Bush Budget Submission, February 2001.

14. Alison Mitchell, "Two Moderate Republicans Oppose Bush Tax Plan as Democrats Offer Their Own," *New York Times,* February 16, 2001, A16.

15. Lizette Alvarez, "Head of House Panel Backs Swift Action on Tax Rates," *New York Times,* January 27, 2001, A11.

16. Jack Kemp, "We Can Afford a Much Bigger Tax Cut," *New York Times,* February 21, 2001, A19.

17. David E. Rosenbaum, "Republicans, in New Tactic, Offer Increase in Tax Breaks," *New York Times,* March 15, 2001, A22.

18. Richard W. Stevenson, "Happily in the Middle: As Debate Rages about Tax Cuts, Bush Plan Takes on Mainstream Air," *New York Times,* February 9, 2001, A20. See also Daniel J. Parks and Andrew Taylor, "The Republican Challenge: Roping the Fiscal Strays," *Congressional Quarterly,* February 10, 2001, 314–17.

19. Stevenson, "Happily in the Middle."

20. Lori Nitschke, "Tax Plan Destined for Revision," *Congressional Quarterly Weekly,* February 10, 2001, 318–20.

21. David E. Sanger, "President's Signature Turns Broad Tax Cut, and a Campaign Promise, into Law," *New York Times,* June 8, 2001, A22.

22. Alison Mitchell, "G.O.P. Senator Plans Shift, Giving Democrats Control in Setback for White House," *New York Times,* May 24, 2001, A1; "If Mr. Jeffords Jumps," *New York Times,* May 24, 2001, A28; David Rapp, "What Jeffords Has Wrought," *Congressional Quarterly Weekly,* May 26, 2001, 1200.

23. Elaine Sciolino, "Long Battle Seen," *New York Times,* September 16, 2001, 1.

24. "War without Illusions," *New York Times,* September 15, 2001, A22.

25. Thomas Friedman, "World War III," *New York Times,* September 13, 2001, A27; Jim Rutenberg, "From Pundits and Polls, Talk of War Fills the Air," *New York Times,* September 14, 2001, A24.

26. Eric V. Larson and Bogdan Savych, *American Public Support for U.S. Military Operations from Mogadishu to Baghdad* (Santa Monica, CA: RAND Corporation, 2005).

27. Larson and Savych, *American Public Support,* 94.

28. Larson and Savych, *American Public Support*, 98.

29. Larson and Savych, *American Public Support*, 98.

30. Laura D. Tyson, "Financing the Fight against Terrorism," *New York Times,* October 8, 2001, A17.

31. Citizens for Tax Justice, "Freeze the Tax Cuts," September 18, 2001.

32. Richard W. Stevenson, "The Prospect of a War without a Wartime Boom," *New York Times,* September 23, 2001, WK4. For the dating of the recession to March 2001, see Business Cycle Dating Committee, National Bureau of Economic Research, "The Business-Cycle Peak of March 2001," November 26, 2001.

33. Frank Rich, "War Is Heck," *New York Times,* November 10, 2001, A23.

34. Alison Mitchell and Richard W. Stevenson, "Bush and Leaders Confer on Way to Bolster Weakened Economy," *New York Times,* September 20, 2001, B1; Richard W. Stevenson, "Many Stimulus Options Weighed," *New York Times,* September 27, 2001, B6.

35. Richard W. Stevenson, "House G.O.P. Tax-Cut Plans Jeopardize Chance of a Deal," *New York Times,* October 11, 2001, B10.

36. Julie Hirschfeld Davis, "Stimulus Bill Succumbs, Taking Tax Issues with It," *Congressional Quarterly,* December 22, 2001, 3073.

37. H.J. Res. 114 (October 10, 2002).

38. Ron Suskind, *The Price of Loyalty: George W. Bush, the White House, and the Education of Paul O'Neill* (New York: Simon & Schuster, 2004), 305.

39. George W. Bush, "Address to the Nation on Iraq," March 19, 2003.

40. David E. Rosenbaum, "Votes in Two Chambers Back Bush Tax Cuts," *New York Times,* March 22, 2003, A8.

41. Democratic Staff, Senate Budget Committee, "A Review of Newspaper Editorials Opposing Bush Tax Cut Proposal," May 7, 2003 (providing excerpts from 85 editorials opposing 2003 Bush tax cuts).

42. "Troops Fight the War, Their Kids Will Pay for It," *The Virginian-Pilot,* March 27, 2003.

43. Leonard E. Burman and David Gunter, "17 Percent of Families Have Stock Dividends," *Tax Notes 1261,* May 26, 2003.

44. Isaac Shapiro and Joel Friedman, "Administration's Use of 'Average' Tax Cut Figures Creates Misleading Impression about the Tax Cuts Most Households Would Receive," Center on Budget and Policy Priorities, January 15, 2003.

45. Thirty-eight percent of respondents expressed support for tax cuts to stimulate the economy. Gabe Martinez, "Republican Economic Pitch Gets Short Shrift in Wartime," *Congressional Quarterly Weekly,* April 5, 2003, 814–15.

46. Jack Kemp, "We Can Afford a Much Bigger Tax Cut."

47. Arthur B. Laffer and Stephen Moore, "A Tax Cut: The Perfect Wartime Boost," *Wall Street Journal,* April 7, 2003, A26.

48. David E. Rosenbaum, "G.O.P. Senators Oppose Size of Bush Tax Cut," *New York Times,* March 14, 2003, A24; Andrew Taylor, "Concessions to Moderates Imperil Early GOP Tax Cutting Accord," *Congressional Quarterly Weekly,* April 12, 2003, 866–68; Andrew Taylor, "Hang-Tough GOP Moderates Still Key to Budget Resolution," *Congressional Quarterly Weekly,* April 5, 2003.

49. Senator John McCain, "Forum: Restoring Fiscal Sanity—While We Still Can," remarks at the Forum on the Fiscal Crisis in the United States, May 18, 2004.

50. George W. Bush, "Remarks to Employees at the Timken Company in Canton, Ohio," April 24, 2003.

51. Richard W. Stevenson, "Bush to Use Ratings in War to Sell Proposed Tax Cut," *New York Times,* April 15, 2003, B10; Richard W. Stevenson, "To Save Tax Cut, Bush Banks on Political Capital," *New York Times,* April 21, 2003, A21; Alan K. Ota, "Deadlocked Tax Cut Proposals Expose Rift in GOP Ideology," *Congressional Quarterly Weekly,* May 3, 2003, 1032 (noting that the administration had "counted on the indirect effects of Bush's high approval ratings during the military action against Iraq").

52. Michael R. Gordon, "Allies to Retain Larger Iraq Force as Strife Persists," *New York Times,* May 29, 2003, A1.

53. "With Tax Bill Passed, Republicans Call for More," *New York Times,* May 24, 2003, A12.

54. *The Iraq Study Group Report* 59–60 (2006) (Recommendation 72).

55. "$78.5 Billion Supplemental Enacted," *Congressional Quarterly Almanac,* 2003, 2–27–30.

56. George W. Bush, "Address to the Nation on the War on Terror," September 7, 2003.

57. "Deficit May Pass Half a Trillion Mark," *Wall Street Journal,* September 9, 2003; David Kay Johnston, "Studies Say Tax Cuts Now Will Bring Bigger Bills Later," *New York Times,* September 23, 2003, C2 (estimating FY 2003 budget deficit at $480 billion).

58. Nicholas Kristof, "Holding Our Noses," *New York Times,* October 15, 2003, A19 (citing a *USA Today/*CNN/Gallup Poll); James Kuhnhenn, "Americans Questioning Bush Request for $87 Billion," Common Dreams News Center, September 25, 2003 (indicating that three out of five respondents opposed the Bush request).

59. As one contemporaneous report explained, "the loan-vs.-grant debate became a safe, symbolic way for lawmakers to raise their doubts about Bush's policies in Iraq." "Iraq Supplemental Breaks Records," *Congressional Quarterly Almanac,* 2003, 2–83.

60. David Firestone, "Democrats Demanding Answers from Bush on His Plans for Iraq," *New York Times,* September 10, 2003, A10; Paul Krugman, "Other People's Sacrifice," *New York Times,* September 9, 2003, A29; "Paying the Bills in Iraq," *New York Times,* September 10, 2003, A24; Robert B. Reich, "Tax Wealthy to Pay for Iraq War," *USA Today,* September 15, 2003.

61. Timothy Noah, "Repeal All Bush's Tax Cuts," *Slate,* September 11, 2003.

62. S. 1634, 108th Congress, 1st Session (2003). The bill was also introduced in the House by Rep. Tom Lantos. See H.R. 3150, 108th Congress, 1st Session (2003).

63. Senator John Kerry, Statement on the Senate Floor (October 2, 2003).

64. Brent Baker and Rich Noyes, "NBC Pumps Public Demand for Higher Taxes," *Media Research Center,* September 25, 2003.

65. *2003 Congressional Quarterly Almanac,* 2003, S-69.

66. Jennifer O'Sullivan, Hinda Chaikind, Sibyl Tilson, Jennifer Bouldanger, and Paulette Morgan, "Overview of the Medicare Prescription Drug, Improvement, and Modernization Act of 2003," *CRS Report for Congress,* April 21, 2004.

67. Ceci Connolly and Mike Allen, "Medicare Drug Benefit May Cost $1.2 Trillion," *Washington Post,* February 9, 2005, A1.

68. "Corporate Tax Breaks Enacted," *Congressional Quarterly Almanac* 13-3 (2004).

69. Kimberly A. Clausing, "The America Jobs Creation Act of 2004: Creating Jobs for Accountants and Lawyers," *Tax Policy Issues and Options Brief* no. 8 (Washington, DC: Urban-Brookings Tax Policy Center, 2004); "Congress Approves Corporate Tax Cuts—And Much More—in FSC/ETI Repeal Legislation," CCH Tax Briefing: America Jobs Creation Act of 2004, October 11, 2004.

70. George W. Bush, "Remarks at the Joint Armed Forces Officers' Wives Luncheon," October 25, 2005.

71. Peter Orszag, "Estimated Costs of U.S. Operations in Iraq and Afghanistan and of Other Activities Related to the War on Terrorism," Statement before the Committee on the Budget, U.S. House of Representatives, October 24, 2007. A subsequent report released by the Congressional Research Service, put the figure at $609 billion. Amy Belasco, *The Cost of Iraq, Afghanistan, and Other Global War on Terror Operations Since 9/11,* CRS Report for Congress (November 9, 2007).

72. It should be noted that, as serious as the short-term budget projections are, the more serious problem is the long-term budget outlook and increases in the fiscal gap due to a combination of factors, including not just the tax cuts and spending on defense and homeland security, but also expected increases in spending on entitlement programs such as Medicare, Medicaid and Social Security. For a discussion of the complexities involved in estimating the sources of the country's long-term fiscal outlook, see Alan J. Auerbach, William G. Gale, and Peter Orszag, "Sources of the Long-Term Fiscal Gap," *Tax Notes* May 24, 2004, 1049.

73. Richard Kogan and Matt Fiedler, "From Surplus to Deficit: Legislation Enacted Over the Last Six Years Has Raised the Debt by $2.3 Trillion," Center on Budget and Policy Priorities, December 13, 2006.

74. Mary Lu Carnevale, "Lieberman Suggests a War on Terrorism Tax," *Wall Street Journal,* February 6, 2007.

75. The full text of the Obey/Murtha/McGovern letter is set forth in the following article: Josephine Hearn, "Obey, Murtha Renew Calls for War Surtax," *Politico,* October 17, 2007 (available at http://www.politico.com). See also E. J. Dionne, Jr., "A Tax Test for the War," *Washington Post,* October 5, 2007, A21.

76. Deirdre Walsh, "Top Democrats Propose War Surtax," http://www.cnn.com, October 2, 2007; David M. Herszenhorn, "On War Funding, Democrats Have a Day of Disagreement," *New York Times,* October 3, 2007.

CONCLUSION

1. Claudia D. Goldin, "War," in *Encyclopedia of American Economic History* (New York: Charles Scribner's Sons, 1980), 935–57.

2. John B. Taylor, "Changes in American Economic Policy in the 1980s: Watershed or Pendulum Swing?" *Journal of Economic Literature* 33(1995): 777, 780–81 (describing changes in monetary policy during Volcker years).

3. Ron Suskind, *Price of Loyalty: George W. Bush, the White House, and the Education of Paul O'Neill* (New York: Simon and Schuster, 2004), 291.

4. Robert Hall, Martin Feldstein, Jeffrey Frankel, Robert Gordon, Christina Romer, David Romer, and Victor Zarnowitz, "The NBER's Recession Dating Procedure," (Cambridge, MA: National Bureau of Economic Research, 2003).

5. Nolan McCarty, Keith T. Poole, and Howard Rosenthal, *Polarized America: The Dance of Ideology and Unequal Riches* (Cambridge, MA: MIT Press, 2006), 30.

6. Andrew Taylor, "The Ideological Roots of Deficit Reduction Policy," *Review of Policy Research* 19, no. 11 (2002): 26 (observing that "moderates of both parties are the most vocal advocates of balanced budgets today").

7. Dana Milbank and Dan Balz, "GOP Eyes Tax Cuts as Annual Events," *Washington Post*, May 11, 2003, A1; Robert Kuttner, "What Killed off the GOP Deficit Hawks?" *Business Week*, December 27, 2004.

8. Congressional Record, 64th Congress, 2d Session, 2294 (May 14, 1917).

9. "Long Doubts Need for Tax Increase," *New York Times*, January 19, 1967, 18.

10. Charles Rangel, "Rangel Reintroduces Draft Bill" (February 16, 2006); Charles Babbington, "Amid Uproar over War, Rangel Renews Call for Draft," *Washington Post*, November 20, 2006, A4.

11. Jill Barshay, "For Bush, Tax Cut Package Is Next Must-Win Battle," *Congressional Quarterly Weekly*, April 26, 2003, 974–79.

12. For example, among the items included in the Democrats' "Six for '06" campaign pledge was a new deduction for college tuition. Charles Hurt, "Democrats to Offer Permanent Tax Cut," Washington Times, December 1, 2006. In addition, Democrats have indicated their intention to repeal the alternative minimum tax. (See Jeanne Sahadi, "Baucus, Grassley Introduce Bill to Repeal AMT," CNNMoney.com, January 5, 2007.)

About the Authors

Steven A. Bank is a professor of law and vice dean at the University of California, Los Angeles School of Law. His research frequently uses history and finance to explore the taxation of business entities in the United States and other countries. He is the author of two forthcoming books—*Corporate Income Taxation in Historical Perspective* (Oxford University Press) and *Anglo-American Corporate Taxation: Tracing the Common Roots of Divergent Approaches, 1799–Present* (Cambridge University Press)—and the coauthor of *Taxation of Business Enterprises* (West Publishers, 2006, with Peroni and Coven) and *Business Tax Stories* (Foundation Press, 2005, with Stark). His work has been selected for the Stanford/Yale Junior Faculty Forum, the John Minor Wisdom Award for Academic Excellence in Legal Scholarship, and the De Brauw Blackstone Westbroek Law Prize. Professor Bank has also been a Herbert Smith Visitor at the University of Cambridge and lectured at the United Kingdom's Inland Revenue on the development of the U.S. and British corporate income taxes.

Kirk J. Stark is a professor of law at the University of California, Los Angeles School of Law. He has published numerous articles on tax policy and public finance, with an emphasis on the history and structure of the American tax system. Much of his recent scholarship has examined the U.S. system of fiscal federalism and considers how best to allocate fiscal responsibilities among federal, state, and local governments. Professor

Stark is a coauthor of two leading casebooks in the field of taxation, *Federal Income Taxation* (Aspen Publishers, 2009, with Klein, Bankman, and Shaviro) and *State and Local Taxation* (West Publishers, 2009, with Hellerstein, Swain, and Youngman). Stark is a member of the board of directors of the National Tax Association, a nonpartisan organization founded in 1907 to promote the study of tax policy and public finance.

Joseph J. Thorndike is the director of the Tax History Project at Tax Analysts and a scholar in residence at the University of Virginia. He is the author of numerous publications on tax policy, both past and present, and is currently writing a history of tax fairness and social justice in the 20th century. His publications include articles for the *New York Times*, the *Washington Times*, the *American University Administrative Law Review*, *L'Economie Politique*, and various scholarly collections. He is the editor, with Dennis J. Ventry Jr., of *Tax Justice: The Ongoing Debate* (Urban Institute Press, 2002). He is also a columnist for *Tax Notes*, a leading journal of tax news and opinion.

Index

HJ
2381
.1335
2008